The Social Scientist's Bestiary

*A Guide to Fabled Threats to, and Defenses of,
Naturalistic Social Science*

Other Titles of Interest

PHILLIPS
Philosophy, Science and Social Inquiry

TANDERSON & BURNS
Research in Classrooms

Major Reference Works

DUNKIN
The International Encyclopedia of Teaching and Teacher Education

KEEVES
Educational Research, Methodology, and Measurement: An
International Handbook

THOMAS
The Encyclopedia of Human Development and Education: Theory,
Research and Studies

Journals of Related Interest

International Journal of Educational Development

International Journal of Educational Research

Learning and Instruction

Studies in Educational Evaluation

Teaching and Teacher Education

The Social Scientist's Bestiary

*A Guide to Fabled Threats to, and Defenses of,
Naturalistic Social Science*

by

D. C. PHILLIPS
Stanford University

PERGAMON PRESS
OXFORD · NEW YORK · SEOUL · TOKYO

UK   Pergamon Press Ltd, Headington Hill Hall,
            Oxford OX3 0BW, England
USA   Pergamon Press Inc, 660 White Plains Road, Tarrytown,
            New York 10591-5153, U.S.A.
KOREA   Pergamon Press Korea, KPO Box 315, Seoul 110-603,
            Korea
JAPAN   Pergamon Press Japan, Tsunashima Building Annex,
            3-20-12 Yushima, Bunkyo-ku, Tokyo 113, Japan

First edition 1992

Library of Congress Cataloging-in-Publication Data

Phillips, D. C. (Denis Charles), 1938-
The social scientist's bestiary: a guide to fabled threats to,
and defenses of, naturalistic social science/D. C. Phillips.
p. cm.
Includes bibliographical references.
1. Social sciences — Philosophy. I. Title.
H61.P542 1992 300'.1 — dc20 92-21654

ISBN 0 08 040254 2

British Library Cataloguing in Publication Data

A catalogue record for this book is available from the British
Library.

Printed in Great Britain by BPCC Wheatons Ltd, Exeter

BESTIARY: ... work in verse or prose describing with an allegorical moralizing commentary the appearance and habits of real and fabled animals.

—Webster's Dictionary

THE MICROBE

The microbe is so very small
You cannot make him out at all,
But many sanguine people hope
To see him through a microscope.
His jointed tongue that lies beneath
A hundred curious rows of teeth;
His seven tufted tails with lots
Of lovely pink and purple spots,
On each of which a pattern stands
Composed of forty separate bands;
His eyebrows of a tender green;
All these have never yet been seen—
But scientists, who ought to know,
Assure us that they must be so....
Oh! Let us never, never doubt
What nobody is sure about!

—HILAIRE BELLOC

Contents

Preface: On Good and
Bad Beasts

Not every change that takes place with the passing of the years can be regarded as an improvement. One case in point concerns the availability of literary genres: Folk in earlier ages had at their command genres that now have faded from use, or that linger on only to be sources of amusement. A prime example, of course, is the bestiary. The poet Hilaire Belloc is one of the few writers in the twentieth century to have used this medieval form in any extended manner, and his wonderful "cautionary verses" manage to preserve the moralizing tone of the genre; but the facts that he wrote in simple verse, and with humor, have given the impression to many that the bestiary is fit only for the entertainment of children.

But the truth is otherwise—there is still a great need for bestiaries addressed to adults, for late twentieth-century life is fraught with dangers. The political events of the first few years of the 1990s may have made the physical existence of the human species a little more secure (although this is not entirely clear), but the intellectual sphere is not unlike a swamp populated with a variety of exotic beasts—"isms" and "post-isms" abound; ideologies or paradigms are multiplying beyond necessity, and at the same time doctrinal fundamentalism is on the increase; too many people who should know better try to sway others by rhetoric or by appeals to crass self-interest rather than by reasoned argument; clarity and logical soundness of argument seem to be prized by diminishing numbers; and the intellectual ideals of the search for truth and of objective inquiry are held in some quarters to be outmoded inheritances from the past, or worse, they are seen as part of the technology of dominance of some groups, and some viewpoints, over others. The humanities are home to many of these beasts, but the social sciences also offer hospitable environmental niches.

Now, ecologists of the late twentieth century argue that all species of living things, whether beastly or not, have a right to exist; they ought not to face the threat of extinction. And it is probably a counsel of wisdom to adopt a similar policy in the intellectual realm. John Dewey (inspired in this, as in many other matters, by Hegel) would argue that if an intellectual position exists, there must be some problem-situation which inspired it and to which it proffers a solution; moreover, the fact that the position exists and has vocal adherents indicates that at least it has *some* "truth value". (See Dewey, 1956, for a simple discussion of the origin of "schools of thought".) It is hoped that the Deweyan spirit pervades the discussions in this present book; several positions are analyzed, and their beastly nature is exposed, but on the whole it has been remembered that beasts are complex and have both good and bad features. Very few of them are condemned outright, and some pains have been taken to indicate the genuine problems or influences that have served as stimuli to their evolution. It should be noted that while some chapters bear the name of an important beast in the title, others do not, and instead refer to some positive influence which the beast-hunter can use with profit. (Of course, beastliness resides to some degree in the eye of the beholder, so the chapters that do not—in the author's opinion—refer to beasts might be regarded as so doing by those readers with a different orientation. Added to which it must be said that not all beasts are *bad*; the elephant is nowadays highly regarded, although the Roman soldiers who first met the species when Hannibal used it against them in battle were not so positive in their evaluations.)

As in many bestiaries, the chapters of the present volume are—as far as possible—self-contained; they do not have to be read in any particular order. In this respect the book is like a mini-encyclopedia, for the beast of interest can be investigated without the effort, or drudgery, of reading a host of preliminary material. (Given this organizational feature, there is a small degree of overlap between the chapters; a nice quotation, for example, might be used in more than one chapter, rather than giving it once and then later referring to it—which would necessitate the interested reader flipping back through the perhaps unread pages to track it down. The chapters do, however, contain references to each other, so that the reader can readily locate related discussions.) Rather than imposing a uniform style upon all of the chapters, they have been allowed to undergo natural variation—the guiding belief has been that some stylistic devices are more suited to some topics than to others. As there seemed no better arrangement, the chapters appear in alphabetical order. It is hoped that these various features will make the book useful to the harried or task-oriented social scientist.

It is worth pointing to one other aspect of this volume. Again as in most classic bestiaries, beneath the diversity of subject-matter and expository styles there is an underlying philosophical orientation that should impose a degree of coherence upon the whole. The remainder of the Preface will be given over to highlighting this.

A good place to start is a story told (in a different context of course) by the philosopher and anthropologist Ernest Gellner:

> A quarter of a century or so ago there was a well-known eccentric in Edinburgh who used to accost passers-by on Prince's Street and ask them—are you sane? If any replied Yes, he would retort—ah, but can you *prove* it? And, as they could not, he proceeded triumphantly to show them that *he* at any rate could prove his sanity, by producing his own certificate of discharge from a mental hospital (Gellner, 1979, p. 41).

In much the same way, one can imagine a skeptical (and eccentric) intellectual accosting a social scientist and asking—is social science possible? Rising to the bait, the scientist would most likely reply by saying—Yes; and when asked for proof would point to the work that he or she is doing—Look, I am *doing* social science, *ergo* it *is* possible! To which the quick-witted eccentric would be liable to respond by pointing to the case of alchemy. For the point is, if we could travel back in time and ask the alchemist if he thought alchemy was possible, the reply would be the same: the alchemist would point to the fact that he was *doing* alchemy, hence it must be possible. But—armed with twentieth-century hindsight—we would not find this answer acceptable. We would argue that the alchemist was *deluded*. The alchemist genuinely believed his craft to be possible, but it was not, for it rested upon mistaken theories and erroneous philosophical foundations. And the twentieth-century skeptic would take a similar stance with respect to the answer given by the social scientist—the fact that social scientists *think* they are doing social science, clearly is not sufficient proof that the enterprise is not chimerical. There are numerous skeptics like this in the late nineteenth and twentieth centuries; to cite merely one example, the philosopher A. R. Louch (building to some extent on the work of Peter Winch in his *The Idea of a Social Science*) has written that "my main intent has been to show that the idea of a science of man or society is untenable" (Louch, quoted in Gellner, 1979, p. 66).

Is there no better answer available to the social scientist? What would satisfy the skeptic? The trouble here is that it is always difficult to argue that something *is* possible; but there is solace in the fact that it is even more difficult to establish that something is *im*possible. So, one strategy that is available—although clearly it is not quite as convincing as producing a direct proof—is to examine the arguments put forward by the skeptics, and to show that, although they are often motivated by genuine and important concerns, their own arguments do *not* establish what they think they do! In short, the attempt can be made to defuse the arguments that have led skeptics to the conclusion that the pursuit of social science is a delusion.

This, then, is the program that underlies this bestiary: In the contemporary world there are many who are skeptical about the possibility of producing a naturalistic social science, that is, a social science that is in important respects structurally or methodologically similar to the natural sciences. Some of these skeptical concerns run deeper than others, and some of the social sciences are more "at risk" from this attack than are others. It will be argued that these skeptical arguments—these beasts— fail to achieve their goal, although the social scientist would be wise to take seriously many of the issues that are raised. The bestiary, in short, is an indirect defense of the possibility of producing naturalistic social science.

It is clear that it is a matter of more than passing concern to clarify precisely in what sense of the term social science can or cannot aspire to be *naturalistic*. While it can be said, with some justice, that it is up to the skeptics to make clear what they have in mind and what it is to which they have objections (obligations which they often fail to fulfil satisfactorily), nevertheless the defender of naturalistic social science cannot rest entirely content with trying to pass the buck. Thus, the third chapter— "Naturalistic Ideals for Social Science"—is of some importance in at least giving a preliminary map of the territory; it could have served as the introductory chapter to the whole work.

Acknowledgments

The plan for this book was first conceived in the mid eighties, when I was asked by a social scientist colleague to address her research group. Members of the group had felt that theories in their field were deficient, especially in light of the data they had been collecting, and they hoped to produce something better. But they had started to argue about the *nature* of a theory, and, in their desperation, had turned to a philosopher for help. My talk to them was inadequate, but served to outline the relevant positions and controversies in philosophy of science, and the members of the group found it surprisingly helpful—they urged me to publish my remarks. And this led to the bestiary.

It is difficult for a busy member of the academic community to work single-mindedly on one project over an extended time period; for one thing, there is the expectation that one will make appearances at conferences and symposia. So it was not possible to avoid the temptation to deliver earlier versions of most of the chapters as talks at conferences and symposia at universities in the USA and Australia, and some of the chapters—in their earlier form—have found their way into print. In one case a paper that had been published much earlier was resuscitated on the grounds that its contents were very pertinent to the theme of the bestiary; but it was extensively rewritten and updated. Thus, thanks are due to the editors and publishers of the following journals or books for their co-operation in allowing reuse of material already published:

International Journal of Educational Research (Chapter 1).

Guba, E. (Ed.) (1990). *The Paradigm Dialog: Options for Inquiry in the Social Sciences*. Newbury Park, CA: Sage (Chapter 4).

Eisner, E. and Peshkin A. (Eds.) (1990). *Qualitative Inquiry in Education*. NY: Teachers College Press (Chapter 5).

Educational Theory (Chapter 6).

Education and Urban Society (Chapter 8).

Finally, friends and colleagues on several continents (and across the fields of philosophy and various of the social sciences) have provided critical input on one or more of the chapters; I am especially indebted to Debby Kerdeman, Ray McDermott, Nel Noddings, and Harvey Siegel. Valerie Phillips not only helped with the preparation of the manuscript, but loaned a critical eye when I wanted to submit particularly tricky draft passages to careful scrutiny. Finally, Michele Wheaton and Barbara Barrett of Pergamon Press have been sources of encouragement since the inception of the project.

References

Dewey, John (1956). The child and the curriculum. In J. Dewey, *The Child and the Curriculum; and, The School and Society*, Combined edition. Chicago: University of Chicago Press.

Gellner, Ernest (1979). *Spectacles and Predicaments: Essays in Social Theory*. Cambridge: Cambridge University Press.

Winch, Peter (1967). *The Idea of a Social Science*. London: Routledge and Kegan Paul.

1

Hermeneutics and Naturalistic Social Inquiry *

Introduction

Considering only the last three hundred years, from about the time of Vico onwards, a massive literature on hermeneutics has accumulated. But in the past two decades there has been a veritable avalanche of material—a poor academician can be driven to the edge of bankruptcy trying to keep pace with the new books.

Unfortunately this recent material is more a repository of enthusiasm than of enlightenment. There are differing accounts of the nature of the key issues, although what comes shining through is the fact that hermeneuticists manage to reach (via difficult and sometimes nearly impenetrable prose) some far-reaching and important conclusions about the nature of the social sciences. To the skeptical eye, the literature is full of *claims*, but the arguments are left sketchy or unclear (or both); and there is a dearth of concrete examples—Wolfgang Stegmuller (1988, p. 109) laments that "analysis of examples is totally absent". To add insult to injury, some writers (without much by way of supporting argumentation) extend the scope of hermeneutics—so that, like the Scarlet Pimpernel, hermeneutical issues are claimed to be everywhere.

The following discussion will attempt to bring some order to this complex domain. First, there will be a distillation of the hermeneuticist case, especially in the form in which it is advanced as a criticism of traditional empirical social science and related fields; then the discussion will focus upon the resulting claims that are made. In general, the center of interest will be the image held by hermeneuticists of both social science and research in applied fields such as education, and their epistemologies.

However, there is one more preliminary matter. Throughout the discussion the terms "hermeneutical" and "interpretive" will be used as synonyms; their use will be varied simply as a stylistic device to maintain the reader's interest. One word derives from Greek, the other from

1

Latin; but they mean the same and even, in their classical usages, refer to the same winged messenger of the gods (whose function was to communicate the wishes of the deities in a form that mere mortals could understand).

The Interpretivist Case

The interpretivist case runs as follows, although it must be stressed that what follows is a *general* account and of course individuals disagree about many of the details: According to interpretivists, physical scientists deal with objects by explaining their behavior either in terms of external forces or in terms of inner processes that result from their physico-chemical microstructure. Notions of force, energy, causation, and natural law are central; and the methods by which knowledge is built up are observational and experimental. The underlying epistemological premise is a form of empiricism. (Many interpretivists would say it is a form of logical positivism.) Until very recently, social science (especially in the USA) has proceeded by mimicing the physical science approach—behaviorism in psychology being one example among many, though also the most notorious.

On the other hand, hermeneuticists would argue, humans are not mere physical objects; people are impelled by ideas, knowledge, and hopes and desires. They harbor intentions. And these things depend upon the use of symbols, as in language; as Gadamer puts it (1977, p. 29), "language is not only an object in our hand, it is the reservoir of tradition and the medium in and through which we exist and perceive our world". Symbols and language, of course, are impossible without societies. Furthermore, many actions undertaken by individuals are actually *constituted* by public meanings, socially adopted rules, conventions, and the like; thus, to take a fairly trivial example, one cannot understand the game of tennis, let alone play it, unless one understands the rules and conventions that define the valid activities of the game (a serve that is "in", an acceptable placement of a return of the ball, etc.). But activities as diverse as participating in a dinner party, consulting a physician, writing a philosophical paper, and giving evidence in court, are no less constituted by socio-cultural rules and conventions. John Searle has put this point in an interesting way:

> ... there is a class of social facts having certain logical features that make them quite unlike the phenomena of physics and chemistry. In the case of phenomena such as marriage, money, divorce, elections, buying and selling ... the phenomena are—to speak vaguely at this stage—permeated with mental components; furthermore, the facts in question are self-referential ... because they can only be the facts they are if the people involved think that they are those facts (Searle, 1991, pp. 335-336).

Thus, Searle holds that the "modes of explanation" in the social sciences are "in certain respects" logically distinct from those in the natural sciences (Ibid., p. 334).

It seems to follow from all this that to explain the actions of a person (as opposed to the behavior of a physical object), an investigator must uncover the *understandings* of the actor—how the actor interprets the situation he or she is in, how the mores and beliefs of the society in which the actor is located are influential, what the actor sees as being the possible responses that are open (given the social beliefs the actor holds), and the symbolic meaning of the forms of behavior that are open to the actor in that particular setting. In Searle's language, subjective mental states function *causally* in the production of human behavior (Ibid., p. 334). Or, as the social scientist Zygmunt Bauman put it,

> Men and women do what they do on purpose. Social phenomena, since they are ultimately acts of men and women, demand to be understood in a different way than by mere explaining. Understanding them must contain an element missing from the explaining of natural phenomena: the retrieval of purpose, of intention, of the unique configuration of thoughts and feelings which preceded a social phenomenon and found its only manifestation, imperfect and incomplete, in the observable consequences of action. To understand a human act, therefore, was to grasp the meaning with which the actor's intention invested it; a task, as could easily be seen, essentially different from that of natural science (Bauman, 1978, p. 12).

This is the heart of the hermeneuticist or interpretivist position, and it is this that is being referred to by these labels in the subsequent discussion.

It should be noted in passing that a rift occurs at this point between several "schools" of interpretivists. Some believe that it is necessary—as a corollary of the points outlined above—to pursue the subjective understandings of actors; these can be labeled "phenomenologically oriented hermeneuticists". Others eschew this subjective approach and focus instead upon the *public* meanings together with the observable actions of, and interactions between, people in social settings. There is an accompanying disagreement, therefore, about the methods of inquiry that are appropriate. It is probably true to say that mainstream American social scientists tend to look askance at methods that smack of subjectivism; and philosophers in the English-speaking world have a similar attitude towards theories of meaning that focus upon the "pictures", ideas, or intentions internal to the individual. The dominant contemporary philosophical approach to meaning focuses instead on the public realm, on how people operate with language—a view that has clear implications for methodology. Although dominant in North America, this latter orientation is not confined to it (see, for example, Karl-Otto Apel, 1977, p. 301). However, it is not the purpose of the present chapter to pursue issues concerning the methodology of interpretive studies; the focus here is unabashedly the theoretical arguments and claims made on behalf of the importance of hermeneutics for the social sciences.

To return to the exposition of the interpretivist case: Human action, according to the very broad position being expounded here, is a type of text (albeit an unwritten one)—for a text is nothing more than a collection of symbols expressing meaning (or even layers of meaning), although this meaning itself may be expressed in terms of metaphors or complex cultural symbols. Hence it is possible to use the discipline that has developed over many centuries to interpret texts—the discipline of hermeneutics, with its central notion of the hermeneutic circle—to interpret and throw light upon human action. This extension of hermeneutics to cover the non-written realm began with the nineteenth-century figures Schleiermacher and Dilthey (see Palmer, 1969, part 11); but it reached its apogee with the work of Charles Taylor (Taylor, 1977) and Paul Ricoeur in the early 1970s. Thus, in his essay "The Model of the Text: Meaningful Action Considered as a Text", Ricoeur wrote:

> Now my hypothesis is this: if there are specific problems which are raised by the inter-pretation of texts because they are texts and not spoken language, and if these problems are the ones which constitute hermeneutics as such, then the human sciences may be said to be hermeneutical (1) inasmuch as their *object* displays some of the features constitutive of a text as text, and (2) inasmuch as their *methodology* develops the same kind of procedures as those of … text interpretation (Ricoeur, 1971, p. 316).

Many in the hermeneutics camp have gone on to point out that human societies are full of the "objectifications" of meaning (as Gadamer, Betti and others term it)—not only written texts, but social institutions, practices and rituals, and physical artifacts.

Hermeneuticists generally go further than this, however, and stress that interpreters who are attempting to grasp the meaning of an actor or to grasp meaning that has been objectified in some way have *their own* understandings shaped by the fact that they themselves are members of a particular culture at a particular historical moment. Interpretation, in other words, is not an act in which a "disembodied" investigator is trying to decipher the (pre-established) meaning of a culturally and historically situated actor or institution; rather, the interpreter, too, must become hermeneutically aware of his or her own historicity (or "preunderstand-ing", as some writers term it). As David Linge puts it, in his "Editor's Introduction" to a book of Gadamer's,

> This methodological alienation of the knower from his own historicity is precisely the focus of Gadamer's criticism. Is it the case, Gadamer asks, that the knower can leave his immediate situation in the present merely by adopting an (interpretive) attitude? An ideal of understanding that asks us to overcome our own present is intelligible only on the assumption that our own historicity is an accidental factor. But if it is an *ontological* rather than a merely accidental and subjective condition, then the knower's own present situation is already constitutively involved in the process of understanding (Linge, in Gadamer, 1977, p. xiv).

Interpretivists sometimes use examples such as the following: In the physical sciences, the behavior of objects is explained by bringing to bear physical laws—such as when the orbit of a planet is explained by deducing its behavior from Newton's or Kepler's laws (together with a statement of the initial conditions). On the other hand, the action of Julius Caesar in crossing the Rubicon is not explained by bringing it under a law—for there are no laws of nature pertinent to the voluntary actions of Roman generals standing on the banks of particular rivers like the Rubicon; rather, Julius's action is explained in terms of his intentions, and in terms of the symbolic importance of that particular river (which marked the border between divisions of the Roman empire). Julius Caesar's action was not the product of laws of nature (despite the fact that his body was a physical object), but it was voluntary—a result of his consciously reaching the decision to carry out a revolt (a revolt being, of course, a social phenomenon). Furthermore, our attempts to understand Caesar's action are mediated by the historical/cultural milieu in which we, as interpreters, are located; so, as hermeneuticists, we are struggling to understand ourselves at the very same time that we are struggling to understand Caesar.

Some Far-reaching Conclusions

Before the discussion proceeds it should be acknowledged that there is much in the interpretivist position, as just outlined, that is compelling. Humans are not mere physical objects; and to understand or explain why a person has acted in a particular manner, the meaning (or meanings) of the action have to be uncovered—and to do this the roles of language and of social symbolisms and values have to be taken into account. Many philosophers of social science in the English-speaking world have been acknowledging variants of this general position for decades (see, for example, Winch, 1958 and Simon, 1982). Furthermore, it seems uncontroversial that every society contains many "objectifications" of meaning—in rituals, symbolisms, institutions, and so forth. (These sentences are being written in the USA on July 4th amid the festivities, which serves to drive the point home.)

What shall be disputed are some of the very wide-ranging conclusions about research in education and the social sciences that are drawn by some, at least, of the hermeneuticists, conclusions that stray well past what is warranted by the preceding position. These debatable conclusions can be clustered into two major groups.

Epistemological Conclusions

The first set of wide-ranging conclusions can be introduced via reference to Charles Taylor. In his now classic essay "Interpretation and the Sciences of Man" (1971), Taylor reveals himself to be a powerful spokesman for the view that the epistemological foundations of empirical science are an unsatisfactory base on which to erect a "science of man". Taylor refers disparagingly to the ingredients that make up the "epistemological bias" of empirical social science, and he writes that

> ... many, including myself, would like to argue that these notions about the sciences of man are sterile, that we cannot come to understand important dimensions of human life within the bounds set by this epistemological orientation (Taylor, 1977, p. 106).

Along what seems to be similar lines, Graham Macdonald and Philip Pettit argue in their *Semantics and Social Science* that the epistemology of the social sciences is close to that of the humanities: "Social science, insofar as its concern is the explanation of human behavior, begins to look like a discipline which belongs with the humanities rather than the sciences" (Macdonald and Pettit, 1981, p. 104). This is a view which must come as something of a shock to empirical social scientists; and the shock is exacerbated by the fact that Macdonald and Pettit are not alone. Thus, somewhat less pithily, Rabinow and Sullivan assert, in their *Interpretive Social Science: A Reader*, that

> Interpretive social science has developed as the alternative to earlier logical empiricism as well as the later systems approaches, including structuralism, within the human sciences. It must continue to develop in opposition to and as a criticism of these tendencies. Here interpretive social science reveals itself as a response to the crisis of the human sciences that is constructive in the profound sense of establishing a connection between what is studied, the means of investigation, and the ends informing the investigators. But at the same time it initiates a process of recovery and reappropriation of the richness of meaning found in the symbolic contexts of all areas of culture (Rabinow and Sullivan, 1979, p. 13).

So, then, the first set of wide-ranging conclusions that are drawn are epistemological; and yet detailed and convincing *epistemological* arguments are in short supply in this literature—for example, it has not been shown in any detailed way how it is that hermeneuticists actually *know*, that is, how the products of their interpretive endeavors are warranted. (Once again Stegmuller's remark comes to mind; he states that philosophers of science customarily support their claims about the epistemology of science by detailed analyses of examples of scientific work, but hermeneuticists do not do the same in their own fields.) The issues here will be taken up again later.

A different but obviously closely related form in which the epistemological claims surface is in terms of the relation between the human sciences, the natural sciences, and the humanities. The issue can be phrased as a question: Is hermeneutical or interpretive social science really a science, or is it a branch of the humanities? As Connolly and

Keutner put it in the "Introduction" to their edited volume *Hermeneutics versus Science?* (1988, p. 1), "do the hermeneutical disciplines ... differ in some important way from the natural sciences, i.e., are those disciplines 'autonomous'?" And Alfred Schutz put it extremely clearly when he wrote (1962, p. 34):

> There will be hardly any issue among social scientists that the object of the social sciences is human behavior, its forms, its organization, and its products. There will be, however, different opinions about whether this behavior should be studied in the same manner in which the natural scientist studies his object or whether the goal of the social sciences is the explanation of the "social reality" as experienced by man living his everyday life within the social world.

A spatial analogy might help clarify this second form taken by the epistemological claims of the hermeneuticists. (This is meant only as a preliminary heuristic device; obviously it is hard to precisely locate specific theorists, for their thought is usually complex and defies simple accurate categorization.) The humanities, the social sciences, and the natural sciences can be visualized as arranged—in that order—along a continuum. With respect to this continuum, several schools of thought exist:

(i) Some scholars have wanted to drive a wedge between the humanities and the rest, by insisting upon the "autonomy" of the humanities; typically, this has been done by stressing the nature of the humanities as interpretive disciplines, in which hermeneutics (and especially the hermeneutic circle) has a central position (see Stegmuller, 1988).

(ii) Others have hammered at the same wedge, by insisting that the sciences are demarcated from the humanities by having a logical character accurately described by the logical positivists.

(iii) A number of scholars have wanted to remove the wedge entirely. One group has tried to do this by insisting that *all* inquiry, to be genuine inquiry aimed at producing warranted knowledge, must have the same underlying epistemology; usually, the epistemology of science is taken as the model. On some readings, John Dewey, and perhaps Karl Popper, belong to this group. (It should be stressed that in taking science as the paradigm case of knowledge, these thinkers are not necessarily advocating a narrow positivistic view of knowledge; in fact both Dewey and Popper have a fairly liberal view of the nature of science—a topic on which there shall be more discussion in later chapters of this book.)

(iv) A different group has wanted to remove the wedge entirely by stressing that all knowledge contains a strong interpretive element. Heidegger and Gadamer, according to some of their remarks, ought tentatively to be classified as members of this group. Thus Gadamer writes (1977, p. 38) that "Hermeneutical reflection fulfills the function that is accomplished in all bringing of something to conscious awareness.

Because it does, it can and must manifest itself in all our modern fields of knowledge, and especially science."

(v) Others, in particular writers like Taylor, Macdonald and Pettit, and Dilthey (1976) wish *at least* to drive a wedge into the continuum between the natural sciences and the social sciences, so that the social sciences end up being grouped with the humanities. Typically, as discussed earlier, the argument is that the social sciences, like the humanities, must give a central place to interpretive methods. It can be seen, therefore, that there is a degree of overlap between the views of those in groups (iv) and (v); but (iv) is a somewhat more radical position than (v).

Conclusions Concerning the Nature of Social Science

The interpretivist case as outlined earlier also embodies within it certain views about the nature and purpose of the various social and human sciences. Humans live in societies, and societies are saturated with objectifications of meaning; and it is with the elucidation of these that the social sciences are centrally concerned. As Dilthey put it,

> Here the concepts of the human studies is completed. Their range is identical with that of understanding and understanding consistently has the objectification of life as its subject-matter. Thus the range of the human studies is determined by the objectification of life in the external world. Mind can only understand what it has created.... Everything on which man has actively impressed his stamp forms the subject-matter of the human studies (Dilthey, 1976, p. 192).

But is it altogether clear that Dilthey is right? And even if the answer to this is in the affirmative, does it follow that the central methods of the "human studies" must be hermeneutical?

Skeptical Commentary

These two groups of far-reaching conclusions both require careful scrutiny. There is some overlap between them, of course, so the discussion of each cannot be kept absolutely water-tight. It will make sense to build up to the central issue concerning epistemology, so for want of a better arrangement the discussion will proceed in reverse order.

Commentary: The Nature of Social Science

In the view of the interpretivists, the social sciences or "human studies" are almost entirely concerned with meaningful human action together with the objectifications of meaning that are to be found in human societies. Dilthey (1976, pp. 163-167) did allow that a study of nature was also relevant, insofar as natural events are frequently the stimuli for human action, and form the focus of mankind's attempts to develop knowledge.) But the fact of the matter is that the social sciences are not so concerned with hermeneutical matters as has been supposed by supporters of the interpretivist position. To make this case, it need not be denied that *some* sort of interpretive activity is required in *some* of the social sciences; the point is that there is much else besides.

(i) In general, it may be true that the social sciences study phenomena that are *social*; and social phenomena, as the interpretivists claim, are constituted by the use of language and by other symbolic interaction—and thus cry out for hermeneutical analysis. But the "in general" marks an important caveat. The qualification is required because there are many social sciences and they do not constitute a "natural kind"; the category is human-made and is of necessity a somewhat vague one. The point is that there are some social sciences where hermeneutical activity does not appear to be central—witness various branches of psychology, and much of economics.

According to some accounts psychology is a member of the social (and certainly of the human) sciences; and it is clear that psychology includes within its domain the study of mechanisms, such as the cognitive and emotional ones, that underlie individual human performance. Mechanisms like these can be studied in a manner that is as little hermeneutical as is, say, biological research. Cases in point are the use, by cognitive psychologists, of nonsense syllable experiments, and designs that focus on performance on non-verbal tests such as Raven's Progressive Matrices.

And then there is economics, which is usually regarded as a clearcut member of the social sciences—yet much of it can hardly be claimed to be hermeneutical. Some branches of this "dismal science" certainly study the effects of social choices (as in market phenomena), but these choices are conceptualized as being the mathematical aggregate of individual choices. And it is crucial to note that, in general, the individual is treated in the manner of an "ideal type" in physics: the individual is presumed to be fully rational, fully knowledgeable, and to have a clear prioritization of needs and desires. Mathematical modeling plays an important role here, but not hermeneutics. (All that this adds up to is merely that economics is not, in essence, a descriptive discipline which aims to discover by historical and interpretive methods either why individuals make the economic choices that they do, or the "meanings" thereof.)

(ii) However, even in those social sciences that *do* focus upon social phenomena—cultural anthropology, political science, and sociology are typical cases—there is something more to study than human actions driven by motives, reasons, and socially-determined understandings and interactions. Human actions have *consequences* (both intended and unintended), and the study of these might not always require a hermeneutical stance. Theorists such as Popper place a great deal of emphasis on the unintended consequences of human behavior; indeed, these consequences are seen as a major driving force in history and are part of the reason that it is impossible to accurately predict the future. Popper writes, in italics no less, that "only a minority of social institutions are consciously designed while the vast majority have just 'grown', as the undesigned results of human actions" (1961, p. 65). A little later he stresses the "unavoidable unwanted consequences of any reform" (p. 67). Sometimes Popper uses a simple economic example to illustrate his point: A person who decides to buy a house does not want the market to suddenly go up, but it will be the unintended consequence of his or her entry into the housing market that prices indeed will rise. The study of the laws of economics, and of how much the price of a commodity will change as the number of individuals in the market changes, seems to be a non-hermeneutical scientific activity. (The broader implications of Popper's insight here will be discussed shortly.)

Consider a non-economic example: A political party in power in a country might adopt a foreign policy for a set of reasons that requires interpretive elucidation; but the unintended consequences of this policy might be that citizens resident overseas have to return, gasoline shortages might break out as a consequence of disruption of overseas supplies, and there could as a result be a rise in the unemployment rate, which in turn might differentially affect members of minority groups, leading to race riots and the eventual overthrow of the party in power! All of these things can be documented, correlated, and studied without venturing into hermeneutics. (This is not to deny, of course, that some of these issues *could* be studied, for other purposes, from a hermeneutical stance. The point is that they *also* can be studied, and are studied in the social sciences, from non-interpretive stances.)

At this point, if not earlier, an objection is likely to surface: The supporter of hermeneutics is likely to protest that, contrary to the claim that has just been made, of course all these research activities inescapably *do* require the adoption of an interpretive position! But it is hard to resist the conclusion that, in making this counter-claim, hermeneuticists have changed the meaning of the key term involved. Perhaps the point can be made in terms of a distinction between a weak (and almost trivial) sense of "hermeneutics" or "interpretation", and a strong sense. In the weak sense, all endeavors that use the medium of language involve interpretation—from following the directions in a recipe, to understanding an advanced lecture in an academic speciality, the language of the writer or speaker must be comprehended. In this weak sense, hermeneutics *is* like the Scarlet Pimpernel. Unfortunately, though, this point does not do much to advance the interpretivists' strong case; for it does *not* follow that because physicists or chemists or sociologists use (and must understand) language, the epistemology of their disciplines is somehow suspect or weaker than they thought it to be, or that they are humanists, or that without further evidence they must become adherents of a strong hermeneutical position. This strong program arises, not simply because of the universal human use of language, but because of special problems within this umbrella—the problem of understanding written records of human thought or action (or other objectifications of these things, such as monuments or social practices or ritual) from ages or cultures that are different from the interpreter's own; or from problems arising as a consequence of the fact that all people, even those from the investigator's own culture, react not to their environment but to what they understand or interpret their environment to be.

The issues here are central, and are worth pursuing in a little more detail. It is a truism that all scientific investigators must understand language and must engage in some degree of interpretive activity in order to communicate with each other and to be able to comprehend the textbooks and research literature of their field (this is what was labeled as the weak sense of hermeneutics). But only under special circumstances do investigators need to make the strong hermeneutical assumption that *the objects they are studying* have *their* behaviors influenced by meanings and understandings and interpretations. Thus, a physicist does not have to suppose that quarks or atoms have interpretations or preunderstandings that influence the ways they react. The crucial point is that while social scientists investigating *some* problems have to take into account their subjects' understandings and so on, there are numerous *other* problems in social science for which this strong hermeneutical program is not relevant.

(iii) To pick up the main thread of the argument: Even where the center of attention in a social science is an issue that clearly involves interpretation (in the strong sense), there are many related issues that are non-hermeneutical (in this sense). For example, members of a population might vote in a surprising way at an election, and their actions may require culturally-sensitive interpretation (in the strong sense) in order to be understood. (This is the sort of thing that is done, or that is attempted, by "TV experts" on election night.) But other issues arise in understanding elections—such things as the influence of the weather on the turnout of voters, what are the party preferences of younger versus older voters, and what is the turnout of members of various ethnic groups. To gather information on matters such as these, no strong hermeneutical activity has to be engaged in. Certainly on some matters, the voters might have to be asked for information (for example, in an exit poll of young voters to see which candidates they voted for), but what takes place here is quite unlike the strong hermeneutical activity carried out by literary experts interpreting the meaning of Hamlet's soliloquy, or by historians trying to understand some action of Julius Caesar's, or by a political scientist trying to understand why George Bush selected Dan Quayle as his running mate in the presidential campaign of 1988.

(iv) Finally, it should be noted that in many sciences different levels of phenomena are distinguished—as when physical scientists distinguish between the sub-atomic level, the atomic level, the molecular level, and so on. The relationship between such levels is a highly debated matter: Can phenomena at one level be "reduced to" (i.e., explained in terms of) phenomena and laws at a "lower" level? Although the issues here are exceedingly complex, it seems clear that explanatory principles used at one level do not always apply at higher or lower levels.

The same holds true in the social sciences and applied areas such as educational research; and it seems that supporters of the interpretivist position would be wise to consider the possibility that the use of hermeneutics might be appropriate at some levels but not at others—leaving at least some phenomena to be dealt with by non-hermeneutic social inquiry. It is worth noting here that the influential Chicago sociologist Herbert Blumer—a critic of quantitative sociology and a prominent proponent of the use of qualitative methods—argued that nevertheless statistical methods can be useful in studying "those areas of social life and formation that are not mediated by an interpretative process", and they may result in "unearthing stabilized patterns which are not likely to be detected through the direct study of the experience of people" (Blumer, cited in Hammersley, 1989, p. 117). Blumer's happy expression "mediated by an interpretative process" is pointing to precisely what was called earlier the "strong hermeneutical program"—a program that is required in order to make headway with some social investigations, but by no means all.

It has already been seen that economics is an example where the focus of attention is often (at least) on the group or aggregate level rather than on the level of the individual human actors—and at the aggregate level there seems to be a place for non-hermeneutical activity. Thomas Schelling (1978, ch. 1) gives a simple non-economic example that can be adapted here for illustrative purposes. (Artistic license has been exercised, and a different moral has been drawn from the one Schelling highlights—he is interested in the question of the fruitful coordination of the individual and group levels.) When audience members enter large lecture halls, they seat themselves according to their own individual preferences. That is, the choice of seating is an individual action, and the sitter's knowledge, beliefs, desires, and so forth may all play a role; and the choice of seating may also be a symbolic act, such as one of defiance. Furthermore, a person's choice is affected by the choices made by people who entered the hall earlier. To understand why an individual chose a particular seat, some sort of interpretive inquiry might be appropriate. And yet, if one leaves the individual level of analysis and moves to a "higher" level—the level where audiences in halls rather than individuals become the unit of analysis—then it might be apparent that there is a generalizable pattern to the filling of halls, the knowledge of which could be helpful to designers of lecture halls, safety experts, and so on. And to discover this pattern, no hermeneutical methods might have to be used; indeed, it can be put even more strongly—hermeneutical methods could hinder the discovery of the pattern rather than help. (Schelling argues, quite rightly, that the motives and understanding of individuals might have to be considered if any attempt is going to be made to change future seating patterns; but if the aim is not to change the pattern but to use knowledge of it in future planning, then understanding the "micromotives" is not necessary for the comprehension of the pattern in the "macrobehavior".)

Another way to phrase the point just made is that not all of the patterns that are found at the macro-level in society are "objectifications" of meanings and understandings. And reference to Popper can bolster the point: His argument that often what are most important in social affairs are the unintended consequences of action is, in effect, making the point that there are aspects of society that are *not* objectifications of meaning (for, by definition, unintended consequences do not embody *anyone's* intentions or meanings). Hermeneuticists who assume that all social phenomena *are* objectifications, have a distorted view of social phenomena—and at the very least they owe us an argument to justify their position. If they concede the point, they still owe us a discussion of the criteria that can be used to distinguish those phenomena that are objectifications of meaning from those that are not (a debt which, up to the present, they have seemed reluctant to discharge).

The conclusion that must be reached, then, is that although many social science inquiries need to be hermeneutical, because meanings and understandings are constitutive of the phenomena under investigation, many inquiries—perhaps very many—do not have to make this strong hermeneutical assumption. For it appears that the image of social science held by interpretivists is too narrow; it is a view that is colored and limited by their own enthusiasms. *This* conclusion is as far-reaching as those reached by the interpretivists, and it has important implications: it weakens the remaining set of conclusions of the interpretivists. Given that their view of social science is recognized as unduly narrow, it becomes more difficult to insert a wedge between social science (as it really is) and the natural sciences and thereby to group the social sciences with the humanities; and thus it becomes more difficult to sustain an epistemological onslaught. But it is to this remaining broad set of far-reaching epistemological conclusions of the interpretivists that the discussion now must turn.

Commentary: The Epistemological Conclusions

There are two elements that require discussion here. In the first place, hermeneuticists often attack the epistemology of traditional social science, which they regard as crudely empiricist, or worse, as a form of positivism. Second, there is the matter of the epistemology of hermeneutical social science itself—that is, what do interpretivists want to put in place of the present "inadequate" epistemology, and is their alternative itself adequate?

To deal with first things first.

(i) Clearly it is a travesty to regard all of mainstream social science, even just in the USA, as being neo-behaviorist in spirit. (What of the recent developments in cognitive science, social psychology, ethnomethodology and anthropology, linguistics, political science, organizational theory, and so on ?) In the closing years of the twentieth century it is abundantly clear that neither the natural nor the social sciences have to be viewed as being based on logical positivism; an image of science has emerged over the past few decades according to which it is a more open and more speculative endeavor than had previously been thought. (See the discussion of the work of Kuhn, Lakatos, Popper, Feyerabend and others in Phillips, 1987, Part A.) It is not stretching the truth to suggest that when hermeneuticists attack the epistemology of mainstream social science, what they have in mind is what Popper has called "misguided naturalism" (Popper, in Adorno *et al.*, 1976, pp. 90-91). In effect they are attacking what by now is recognized widely to be a straw man.

At least one alternative analysis of the epistemology of science has been offered by Popper himself; hermeneuticists like Taylor do not discuss it, for it seems immune from the sort of charges they offer of positivism. (This is not to say that Popper has all of the answers, or even some; his work remains a source of controversy—but in some respects it is clearly an advance over positivism.) Popper denies that human knowledge (including, of course, scientific knowledge) is certain by virtue of the fact that it is erected upon unshakeable foundations. His books develop the case for a *non-foundationalist* epistemology—see, for example, his *Logic of Scientific Discovery*, *Conjectures and Refutations*, and *Objective Knowledge*—although it should be stressed that Popper is not alone among twentieth-century epistemologists in regarding foundationalism as outdated. (For an example of a psychologist who holds this epistemology, see Weimer, 1979; see also the discussion in Chapter 4 of the present volume.) That is, Popper and many others do not approach the problem of knowledge in terms of seeking the "rock-bottom" and indubitable foundations upon which the certain knowledge of science (and of everyday life, so far as it has certain knowledge) is built by a process of induction. Instead, these luminaries stress that *no* knowledge is unshakeably certain, and that there are *no* absolutely sound foundations for knowledge. Human knowledge is speculative, it projects tentatively into the future; whatever reason we have to believe the things we do believe, it is not because they are based on absolutely sound foundations. Our beliefs, and the considerations that led us to hold them, are always open to the possibility of revision. (Popper has offered an account of the issues surrounding the "rationality of scientific belief" that arise here, but it is not clear that his resolution of all the problems is acceptable. See Newton-Smith, 1981.)

Acceptance of a non-foundationalist approach to epistemology, in which all knowledge is regarded as tentative, has an additional virtue: it allows a softening of the predicament highlighted by Gadamer (who did not see it as a predicament so much as a too-often neglected fact of life), namely, the fact that interpretations must inevitably emerge from the interpreter's own historically and culturally based vantage point. For the non-foundationalist will put interpretations on a par with the rest of human knowledge—they are tentative, hypothetical, and subject to revision with the passage of time. Acceptance of Popper's brand of non-foundationalism offers an even stronger response to Gadamer: Popper sees little virtue at all in worrying about the origins of our knowledge-claims. He would acknowledge that of course they emerge from the inquirer's own grounding in a particular time and place, but that is not relevant when considering their status as knowledge; what *is* relevant is how the interpretation (or knowledge-claim) is tested and criticized. For although no knowledge is certain, not all knowledge-claims are equal; some are better warranted than others in the sense that they have survived serious critique and strenuous attempts at overthrow. What is sauce for the scientific goose is also sauce for the hermeneutic gander.

(ii) Even in those areas of social science that must adopt the strong interpretive program, is there such a great epistemological contrast with science? What do hermeneuticists say about the epistemology of their own domain?

Essentially there are two camps here. One, labeled somewhat misleadingly as "subjectivist", holds that interpretations are always open or "undecidable"—there is no such thing as a "correct" interpretation. Whilst an interpreter has to be able to offer considerations in support of his or her interpretation, in the final analysis many (perhaps infinitely many) defensible readings of a text are possible:

> Texts exist only in being-read, and every interpretation gives the text a new reading within a framework constituted by the pre-judgements of the reader's time, epoch, or culture; thus there is no such thing as "the one text" capable of serving as the touchstone for the correctness of interpretations from different epochs. This position entails undecidability in principle (Connolly and Keutner, 1988, p. 26).

Stanley Fish is one prominent literary theorist who holds to this view; in an amusing essay "Is There a Text in This Class?" (1980) he denies there is one textbook in his class, even though all students purchase the same book! There is not one text, because the book becomes a different "text" for every reader.

It is an easy matter to come up with examples of undecidable interpretations from the humanities. And of course the hermeneuticists have a point—if in writing *Hamlet* Shakespeare depicted a believable person, then as greater understanding of humans accumulates over the ages, the Prince of Denmark can be revisited and new insights gleaned. Thus, interpreters in the twentieth century had new resources compared with their counterparts in the nineteenth (in the form of the work of Freud, Rogers, Jung, and so on) and discussion of the character and motivations of Hamlet were enriched. There is no foreseeable end to this process—it will continue so long as human knowledge continues to grow.

But is this really the issue about hermeneutics that concerns us when we consider the nature of the social sciences? The Italian hermeneuticist Emilio Betti, who is regarded as a member of the "objectivist" school, draws a distinction between meaning and significance that is helpful here. The question of the meaning of some historical text is one issue, and it concerns the meaning "objectified" by the "other" (the historical figure) and intended to be communicated by him or her; the question of the significance of the document is another matter, one that concerns the uses and the meanings that we can impose on the document from our own perspective in time and space—and this is open-ended (Betti, 1980, esp. pp. 68-69). The application of this distinction to literature leads to some controversies—Stanley Fish, for example, would deny that Shakespeare's intentions (the "meaning" of *Hamlet*) is important, for what is relevant in literature is what readers can impose or construct for themselves (the "significance", which of course Fish would prefer to label as "meaning"). However, even in the contentious realm of literary theory the distinction itself is useful and provides terminology that serves to highlight the issues at stake.

In those areas of the social sciences where the strong hermeneutical program seems appropriate, even greater light is shed by Betti's distinction. Consider a person in a social setting who performs some act that draws the attention of a social scientist. (The study of individual human action, it will be recalled from the preceding discussion, is one area where the strong hermeneutical program does seem appropriate in the social sciences.) Betti would have us, in effect, recognize at least two sets of issues: (a) what did the *actor* intend (that is, what was the meaning of the act for the actor), and (b) what can the social scientist or interpreter say about the act (that is, what is the significance of the act). This is not to say that on every occasion *both* of these matters are of interest, but both are *possible* concerns. Of course Betti is not alone in pointing to these two things; the philosopher Peter Winch (most notably in his well-known dispute with Ian Jarvie) also makes this point—and Winch argued that the issue having priority was the identification or description of the act, which by conceptual necessity involves the determination of the actor's intentions. Only *after* the act has been identified, Winch suggested, might the social scientist be able to go on and say something about it in terms of his or her own disciplinary perspective (assuming that this second phase is relevant to the particular inquiry) (Winch, 1970, pp. 249-259; see also Winch, 1958).

What can be said, then, about the epistemological underpinnings of this two-stage interpretive process? The second stage is less problematical, relatively speaking. After an act or document is interpreted as being an instance of X (for example, an expression of jealousy), then it is in principle relatively straightforward (though in practice it is not necessarily easy) to judge if it falls within the domain of some theory T. To be an acceptable theory, T would need to have a warrant that is appropriate— if T is a theory of literary criticism, then it would need whatever warrant is required for reputable status within that field, whereas if T is from sociology or economics, then different types of warrants would be appropriate. Within the social sciences, there is a degree of agreement— although it is far from universal—about such matters as whether a theory T is well-warranted (or if not, why not), and whether phenomenon X falls within the domain of T. (This sounds simple enough on the surface, but of course there are many complexities; these, however, are subject to lively debate and investigation within the traditional academic domains. Whether or not one judges the epistemological program sketched here to be reasonable depends upon whether one regards epistemology as a total field as viable, or as dead. If the reader judges it to be dead, there is not much more to be said, except that this discussion should have ceased being of relevance long ago!)

The epistemological difficulties of the second phase pale into insignificance, however, when compared to the problems faced by the first. How does an interpreter *know* that he or she has correctly identified the intentions of an actor (or has understood the meaning that has been objectified in some social institution)? Neither Winch, Betti, Gadamer, Dilthey, Taylor nor the rest of the hermeneutical horde has made much headway here, although many of them certainly espouse the *ideal* of settling on correct interpretations. Betti is an illuminating figure here, for he explicitly wants to establish an "objective" position; he writes (1980, p. 57) of "the demand for objectivity: the interpreter's reconstruction of the meaning contained in meaning-full forms has to correspond to their meaning-content as closely as possible", and this requires "honest subordination" (i.e., subordination of the interpreter to the "other" whose meaning is being deciphered). Betti criticizes Gadamer's book *Truth and Method* on the ground that (unintentionally) it undermines the quest for objectivity, which Gadamer also espouses. Yet the best that Betti can do himself is to argue that objectivity arises through the strenuous subjective efforts of the interpreter to intuitively or empathetically understand the meaning of the other! This hardly seems an adequate means to achieve the goal he set out in the form of a methodological canon which he labels, somewhat grandiosely, as "the canon of the hermeneutical autonomy of the subject":

> By this we mean that meaning-full forms have to be regarded as autonomous, and have to be understood in accordance with their own logic of development, their intended connections, and in their necessity, coherence and conclusiveness; they should be judged in relation to the standards immanent in the original intention: the intention, that is, which the created forms should correspond to from the point of view of the author ... (Betti, 1980, p. 58).

From the point of view of the present writer, this canon is fine, but the epistemological resources with which Betti wants to operationalize it are, to say the least, deficient.

A case can be made—although it can only be sketched here—that for the purposes of social science, meanings and intentions can be investigated using traditional scientific methods. That is, it can be argued that there is no epistemological difference in kind between gaining knowledge about the other objects of science and gaining knowledge about meanings and intentions. Many branches of science can provide cases where the objects of interest are not directly observable or measurable, but where their presence (and their nature) is inferred from what is observable. This process is hypothetical, and it is not guaranteed to be successful; but it is self-corrective—by a bootstrapping process involving testing and elimination of errors (which is itself a tentative business), the warrants for the claims that are made about such objects become stronger (though, many would argue, never so strong that matters become completely settled). Again, what is sauce for the scientific goose is sauce for the hermeneutic gander: intentions and meanings can be investigated in the same way. Tentative hypotheses can be checked, if somewhat indirectly; empirical evidence *can* have a bearing on hermeneutical issues; and hermeneuticists can—and do—use the hypothetico-deductive method that is common in the natural sciences (Follesdal, 1979; see also Hirsch, 1967, p. 264; and Popper, 1972, p. 185).

Conclusion

The net conclusion is that although there are some areas of social science and educational research where the strong hermeneutical program is important—where investigators must take account of the meanings and preunderstandings and so on of the social actors being studied—these areas neither exhaust the scope of the social sciences nor does their existence offer any serious grounds on which to hold that the social sciences and related applied fields are more closely allied with the humanities than with the natural sciences. Those who hold the contrary view, and claim that there is a similarity in kind with the humanities, or that empirical social science is completely misconceived, need to offer more detailed and stronger arguments and examples.

Nevertheless, the sometimes exaggerated claims of the hermeneuticists have served a very useful purpose: These claims have forced the adherents of traditional "pure" and "applied" social science to broaden their view of the nature of persons—instead of treating people on a par with inanimate objects they have been forced to regard persons as *actors* located within social and historical webs of meaning. And this constitutes a watershed.

* Reprinted with permission from the *International Journal of Educational Research*, 15(6). Phillips, D. C. "Hermeneutics: A Threat to Scientific Social Science?" © 1991, Pergamon Press Ltd.

References

Apel, K-O. (1977). The a priori of communication and the foundation of the humanities. In F. Dallmayr and T. McCarthy (Eds.), *Understanding and Social Inquiry*. Notre Dame, Indiana: Notre Dame Press.

Bauman, Z. (1978). *Hermeneutics and Social Science*. New York: Columbia University Press.

Betti, E. (1980). Hermeneutics as the general methodology of *Geisteswissenschaften*. In J. Bleicher (Ed.), *Contemporary Hermeneutics*. London: Routledge.

Connolly, J. and Keutner, T. (Eds.) (1988). *Hermeneutics Versus Science?* Notre Dame, Indiana: University of Notre Dame Press.

Dilthey, W. (1976). *Dilthey: Selected Writings*. Cambridge: Cambridge University Press.

Fish, S. (1980). *Is There a Text in This Class?* Cambridge, Mass.: Harvard University Press.

Follesdal, D. (1979). Hermeneutics and the hypothetico-deductive method. *Dialectica*, **33**, 319-336.

Gadamer, H-G. (1977). *Philosophical Hermeneutics*. Tr. D. Linge. Berkeley: University of California Press.

Hammersley, Martin (1989). *The Dilemma of Qualitative Method: Herbert Blumer and the Chicago Tradition*. London and NY: Routledge.

Hirsch, E. D., Jr. (1967). *Validity in Interpretation*. New Haven, CT: Yale University Press.

Macdonald, G. and Pettit, P. (1981). *Semantics and Social Science*. London: Routledge.

Newton-Smith, W. (1981). *The Rationality of Science*. London: Routledge.

Palmer, R. (1969). *Hermeneutics*. Evanston, Ill.: Northwestern University Press.

Philips, D. C. (1987). *Philosophy, Science, and Social Inquiry*. Oxford: Pergamon Press.

Popper, K. (1961). *The Poverty of Historicism*. London: Routledge.

Popper, K. (1972). *Objective Knowledge*. London: Oxford University Press.

Popper, K. (1976). The logic of the social sciences. In T. Adorno *et al.* (Eds.), *The Positivist Dispute in German Sociology*. London: Heinemann.

Rabinow, P. and Sullivan, W. (Eds.) (1979). *Interpretive Social Science: A Reader*. Berkeley: University of California Press.

Ricoeur, P. (1977). The model of the text. In F. Dallmayr and T. McCarthy (Eds.), *Understanding and Social Inquiry*. Notre Dame, Indiana: University of Notre Dame Press.

Schelling, T. (1978). *Micromotives and Macrobehavior*. New York: Norton.

Schutz, A. (1962). *The Problem of Social Reality: Collected Papers 1*. The Hague: Martinus Nijhoff.

Searle, John (1991). Intentionalistic explanations in the social sciences. *Philosophy of the Social Sciences*, **21**, 3, 332-344.

Simon, M. A. (1982). *Understanding Human Action*. Albany, NY: State University of New York Press.

Stegmuller, W. (1988). Walther von der Vogelweide's Lyric of Dream Love and Quasar 3C 273. In J. Connolly and T. Keutner (Eds.), *Hermeneutics Versus Science?* Notre Dame, Indiana: University of Notre Dame Press.

Taylor, C. (1977). Interpretation and the sciences of man. In F. Dallmayr and T. McCarthy (Eds.), *Understanding and Social Inquiry*. Notre Dame, Indiana: University of Notre Dame Press.

Weimer, W. (1979). *Notes on the Methodology of Scientific Research*. New Jersey: Lawrence Erlbaum.

Winch, P. (1958). *The Idea of a Social Science*. London: Routledge.

Winch, P. (1970). Comment. In R. Borger and F. Cioffi (Eds.), *Explanation in the Behavioral Sciences*. Cambridge: Cambridge University Press.

2

Holistic Tendencies in Social Science

ONE of the concerns that motivates those who are dubious about the possibility of producing successful naturalistic social science—social science that in some important respects resembles the natural sciences— centers upon the fact that social phenomena appear to be *holistic*. For a society is a whole or a system; its parts interact and mutually determine each other to such a degree that even to call them "parts" is to use a misnomer. Indeed, the parts seem to be *constituted* by the fact that they are parts of a social whole. In this respect a society is like an organism, which also has parts in dynamic interaction; social organicism has been alive and well in Western intellectual thought at least since the time of Hegel, if not for millennia before then (see Phillips, 1976).

Thus, for example, while it is true that a state cannot exist without citizens, it also is true that citizens cannot *be* citizens without the state, and of course it is the citizens who, in mutual interaction, actually seem to produce at least some of the features of the state. Nor can a legal system exist without judges, litigants and so on, but of course the judges and litigants are made what they are—*judges* and *litigants*—by their role *within* the state's legal system. (Arguably, judges and litigants are not "parts" of the legal system, they are made what they are *by* the legal system.) John Dewey and Arthur Bentley brought out very clearly the holistic nature of such cases; they wrote that, if the example of a loan of money is considered, it is a mistake to proceed as if there were certain discrete elements in terms of which the situation could be explicated—for there are no "primarily separate items" at all. What seem to be "parts" actually only exist within the framework of a larger "whole", and they called for "transactional" logic to deal with such cases:

> Borrower cannot borrow without lender to lend, nor lender lend without borrower to borrow, the loan being a transaction that is identifiable only in the wider transaction of the full legal-commercial system in which it is present as event (Dewey and Bentley, 1946, pp. 547).

Except for the fact that he antedated Dewey and Bentley's work by six

21

decades, William James might have been parodying this passage (and its underlying Hegelian or transactional logic) when he wrote these skeptical words:

> Husband makes, and is made by, wife, through marriage; one makes other by being itself other; everything self-created through its opposite—you go round like a squirrel in a cage.... *What, in fact, is the logic of these abstract systems? It is, as we said above: if any Member, then the Whole System; if not the Whole System, then Nothing* (James, 1884, pp. 282-283).

Now, the reason why all this is of concern is that—so it is sometimes argued—the traditional analytic or mechanistic methods of natural science are incapable of dealing with such holistic phenomena. Thus, according to researchers Lincoln and Guba,

> ontology suggests that realities are wholes that cannot be understood in isolation from their contexts, nor can they be fragmented for separate study of the parts (the whole is more than the sum of the parts) ... (Lincoln and Guba, 1985, p. 39)

But herein lies a complex tale.

It is clear that, lumped together here, we have a variety of rather tricky issues: (i) Ontological issues concerning what actually exists, such as the question—do social systems and so forth exist, or are individuals the only existents? And are social properties and phenomena merely "fictions", shorthand ways of referring to individuals and their properties and activities? Are individual people the "parts" of a "social whole"? (ii) Epistemological issues, such as—can we learn about, or explain, the properties of "social wholes" by focusing only upon their parts? (iii) Methodological issues, such as—is it true that analytic methods are incapable of dealing with relational properties? To muddy the waters further, at least one other classic problem seems also to be involved. (iv) The problem of reduction—can the phenomena at the higher levels always be explained in terms of (i.e., reduced to) laws and theories which focus upon the lower levels?

The following discussion will have the unenviable task of disentangling many of these matters; and given the degree of complexity here it will be easiest to proceed via a series of simple questions and less simple answers.

Question 1: Where in the social or human sciences can we find examples of this sort of holistic thinking?

Answer: We met some cases earlier: A whole society or culture, it has been argued, is a holistic system; the elements or "parts" are determined by the role they play within the whole, and because these elements are in "dynamic interrelationship" with each other, if one were to change then all others would change (and then, of course, the whole—the overall system—would also change, as William James so nicely pointed out).

Within societies, such things as organizations can be interpreted as being holistically structured. Some psychiatrists and clinical psychologists have held that the human psyche has a similar "organismic" nature (see Goldstein, 1963, for an influential early statement); Albert Bandura's widely discussed "cognitive learning theory" postulates that there is "reciprocal determinism" between a learner's behavior, environment, and inner "personal" factors—that is, these three form a system and mutually determine each other (Bandura, 1978; see also Phillips, 1987, ch. 7); social psychology lends itself to holistic treatment (Ford and Ford, 1987); an organism in relation to its physical environment seems from some perspectives to form a holistic system; and the recent *Handbook of Environmental Psychology* surveys many examples from this developing field (Stokols and Altman, 1987, ch. 1). And—as a last example—consider a recent paper on the methodology of educational research, where the author states that

> The analytic approach mainly assumes that discrete elements of complex educational phenomena can be isolated for study, leaving all else unchanged. The systemic approach mainly assumes that elements are interdependent, inseparable, and even define each other in a transactional manner so that a change in one changes everything else and thus requires the study of patterns, not of single variables (Salomon, 1991, p. 10).

In short, holism is at home whenever there is a situation where an "entity" is *constituted* by its relationship to other entities; an entire "science" even developed to explicate the principles involved in such cases—General Systems Theory (see Phillips, 1976, ch. 4; the *locus classicus* is Bertalanffy, 1969).

Question 2: In the preceding discussion the impression has been given that holism is a unified school of thought; but I am sophisticated enough to realize that matters are rarely so simple. Do all holists believe the same things—do they all accept the same principles?

Answer: Your intuitions are sound. Like many "isms", holism is far from being a simple position with one core notion. There are a variety of doctrines, and individuals differ over which ones they accept, and over how they prioritize them in importance.

In an earlier work (Phillips, 1976) I identified three groups of holistic themes, which I somewhat unimaginatively called holisms 1, 2, and 3. Although my evaluation of these positions has somewhat changed, the typography is still useful for descriptive purposes. *Holism 1*, or *organicism*, is a set of ideas as follows (Phillips, 1970; Phillips, 1976, ch. 1):

(a) The analytic approach as typified by the physico-chemical sciences proves inadequate when applied to certain cases—for example, to society, or even to reality as a whole.

(b)   The whole is more than the sum of its parts.
(c)   The whole determines the nature of its parts.
(d)   The parts cannot be understood if considered in isolation from the whole.
(e)   The parts are dynamically interrelated or interdependent.

What ties these together is the Hegelian principle of internal relations, or transactional logic, as we shall see in a moment.

Holism 2 is, in essence, an anti-reductionist position; it is the thesis that a whole or system, even after it has been extensively studied, cannot be explained in terms of its parts. And *holism 3* is the rather unexceptionable view that it is necessary for the advance of certain areas of science to have terminology that refers to wholes and their properties (Phillips, 1976, pp. 36-37 and *passim*).

The thesis advanced in my earlier work—to which I still subscribe—was that many holists jump from one to another of these sets of ideas as if they are synonymous (which they are not), and as if the arguments in support of one of these positions also automatically support the others. But I should note, before we pursue the issues here in more depth, that other writers give somewhat different accounts of holism. David-Hillel Ruben, for example, characterizes what he calls "metaphysical holism" (a general position that he supports) in terms of its opposition to "methodological individualism" (a reductionist position which holds that theories about social entities can be reduced to theories about individuals). He writes:

> Metaphysical individualism, then, can involve either of two distinct doctrines: (1) There are no irreducible social entities; (2) There are no irreducible social properties. In both (1) and (2), the word "irreducible" is important, because metaphysical individualists might not wish to deny that Strathclyde County Council existed, or that there was such a property as that of being an alderman. Rather, they might say that neither case involved the existence of some irreducible social entity or property (Ruben, 1985, p. 3).

Thus, to turn this account around, metaphysical holists believe that there are some irreducible social entities, or some irreducible social properties, or both. In my view this account narrows the focus too much to what I have called holism 2, and Ruben does not mention Hegel at all.

Question 3: This leads nicely to the next question. A number of times in the preceding discussion the point has been made that, according to your account, holists believe that if entities or "parts" are interrelated, then it follows that if one part changes, all the rest change. This was even labeled as "Hegelian or transactional logic". Could this be spelled out further? Why is Hegel so important?

Answer: The key concern of the holists, reflected in the theses of holism 1, is the nature of the relationships that are found in social wholes or systems (and, of course, in organic systems as well). I stated in the opening discussion that, in social wholes, the "parts"—which we are in danger of misconceiving when we label them this way—are constituted by their relationships to each other and to the whole in which they are located. Now, Hegel and his followers have discussed the underlying logic here in some detail. The problem, of course, is that Hegel is perhaps the most difficult, the most obscure, of all the major philosophers to read; but despite this—or because of it—he has been extremely influential. And, matters are not made easier by the fact that the topic of relations which concerns us here is far from simple.

Hegel and his followers regarded the whole of reality as forming a *system*, the parts of which were *organically* or *internally related*. Being a system, reality could not be studied successfully by dividing it into parts each of which was studied in isolation. For when a part was isolated from the whole system its nature changed—it was no longer a part of the whole, and it became an inaccurate guide to the nature of the whole. (To revert to an earlier example, a judge or a litigant, when removed from the context of the legal system, is no longer a *judge* or a *litigant*.) It therefore seemed apparent to the neo-Hegelians that the Hegelian theory of organic or internal relations was directly opposed to the analytic or mechanistic method of the leading natural sciences—a method which they characterized as depending upon isolating elements or units for investigation. (That this view has carried over into the late twentieth century is illustrated by the quotations earlier from Lincoln and Guba, and from Saloman—and, I would also argue, by Bandura's work.)

The theory of internal relations is based upon the supposition that entities (such as the parts of a system) are altered by the relationships into which they enter. If A, B and C are the interrelated "parts" of a system, then A gains properties x and y as a result of its interrelations with B and C, and these "parts" in turn gain relational properties as a result of their interactions within the system. But if A is removed for study, then its relational properties x and y will disappear, and we will no longer have A (because A is made what it is by its properties, and two of these have now been changed); concomitantly, B and C will also change, for they lose their relational properties with A. A similar argument can be developed if a new entity D is added to the whole or system; A, B and C will now gain new relational properties, and they will no longer *be* A, B and C but will have become instead E, F and G. This is the logic underlying all the theses of holism 1—the parts are dynamically interrelated; the whole system has properties that are greater than the properties of the parts (because outside the system the "sum" of the properties of the "parts" no longer includes the relational properties x, y and so on); and a change in one part changes the whole! In this spirit the twentieth-century human scientist Andras Angyal wrote in a discussion of the logic of systems (he uses the term "aggregate" to refer to a *collection*, a "heap" of entities that are not internally related):

> It should also be kept in mind that "part" means something different when applied to aggregates from what it means when applied to wholes. When the single objects a, b, c, d, are bound together in an aggregate they participate in the aggregation as object a, object b, object c, etc., that is, as lines, distances, color spots, or whatever they may be. When, however, a whole is constituted by the utilization of objects a, b, c, d, the parts of the resulting whole are *not* object a, object b, object c, etc., but α, β, γ, δ, ... (Angyal, 1969, p. 26).

Question 4: As you have just explained it, the principle of internal relations does seem to throw light upon what is taking place within systems. I might play a role within an organization, for example, and key features of this role will depend upon my interrelation to the roles of other individuals within the same system; and if any one person's role within the organization were to change dramatically, all the rest—including my own—would undergo concomitant alteration. Furthermore, I do not have that role when I leave the system! So I'm impressed, but yet I infer from the tone of your discussion that you are critical of Hegel's principle?

Answer: Yes—it seems to me that the principle goes too far in suggesting that if *one* relational property of an entity were to change, the entity's entire nature would change—A would change to α. In more technical philosophical language, the principle of internal relations requires that *every* relation into which an entity enters determines a *defining characteristic* of that entity. However, modern discussions of relations recognize that entities are not defined by a specific set of relational properties— some relations can change without us wanting to say that the entity has transformed into something entirely different. (That is, we do not accept that all relations determine a defining characteristic; for further discussion, see Phillips, 1976, ch. 1.)

A concrete example might be helpful here. Consider the nomination of Clarence Thomas to the US Supreme Court in 1991. It was clear from the outset that if Mr Thomas were to become a member of the Court, he would be adopting a new role within a new system, and thus he would gain new relational properties. But, as the public furor made clear, most people believed that he would take with him into this new role the characteristics that he already possessed—he would not become an entirely different person. These "old" characteristics would remain, and would influence his work as a member of the Court. Indeed, even more strongly, people on both sides of the controversy believed that much of his work in the Court could be predicted by the characteristics that he already possessed. Both supporters and detractors of Mr Thomas agreed about this; the issue was, what *were* the characteristics that he possessed—was he a good enough legal scholar, did he have an acceptable attitude towards civil rights and affirmative action, was he a political and social conservative, was he a decent person or was he sexist, and so on? His supporters, including President Bush, thought that he had admirable characteristics, which he would continue to possess and display upon his becoming Justice Thomas; while his critics thought he was not admirable, and would continue not to be admirable when he took on his new role. A strict Hegelian, however, would seem to be committed to opposing this commonsense view, and to hold instead that we could not predict, from Mr Thomas's characteristics before joining the Court, what his likely characteristics would be after taking his seat upon it—for the principle of internal relations holds that he would gain a new defining characteristic upon joining the Court, and so *all* his (interrelated) characteristics would change, and thus he would change from α to A (that is, Justice Thomas would be a different individual from Mr Thomas)!

Question 5: That was a helpful example, but I still have lingering concerns. Surely in order to understand an entity within a system, and to explain why that entity is the way that it is, we *have* to take into account the fact that the entity *is* part of, or is located within, a system that exerts an influence over all its parts or members?

Answer: Of course, but nobody has denied this—certainly I have never argued against the position you have just outlined. The point is, we can agree about this without having to subscribe to the principle of internal relations, or without having to accept the "through-and through" logic (as William James called it) of holism 1. To revert to our previous example, in order to understand what Clarence Thomas will be doing when he becomes Justice Thomas, it is uncontroversial (and indeed verges on being a truism) that we have to understand something about the US legal system and in particular about the Supreme Court and how its various members function. It is quite apparent that only in terms of this sort of understanding can we determine which of Mr Thomas's prior characteristics are relevant for predicting his behavior as Justice Thomas. (Of course, we might make mistakes here, but making predictions is *never* certain.) But there is nothing mysteriously holistic about any of this, just as there is nothing mysteriously holistic about the fact that to understand the way a chess-piece moves on the board, we have to understand the system of rules that constitute the game of chess!

Question 6: But why, then, do some people hold that the methods of natural science somehow run into serious problems when faced with systems whose parts are interrelated? Why are so-called "holistic phenomena" sometimes touted as blocking the way to developing naturalistic social science?

Answer: I'm not sure that I can give you a full answer. Part, at least, of the story is that holists have tended to give oversimplified accounts of what they are prone to call the mechanistic or analytic methods of naturalistic science.

There are two aspects of the methods of naturalistic science that need to be distinguished here (even though in some contexts these might overlap): the issue of what goes on in the process of investigation or discovery, and what goes on in the process of explanation. First, when scientists face a complex problem, they often will break it down into simpler sub-problems for study, and gradually and tentatively build up the whole complex picture again. Galileo is often credited as being the person who first clearly realized the need to make simplifying assumptions, or to analyze problems into parts—his investigation of pendulums, for instance, deliberately neglected air resistance, and friction at the pivot (although later investigators studied these and built upon Galileo's simple law of pendulum motion). But, despite the impulse to analyze problems into manageable parts, it simply is not true that scientists enamored of these analytic methods will neglect relations between parts—if the phenomenon under investigation seems to involve interrelations between entities, then the features of the whole system may well be looked at. For scientists realize that the point is not merely to cut the phenomenon up into small pieces for further study, but rather to divide it into *relevant* pieces that are likely to illuminate the phenomenon as a whole.

Second, a similar oversimplification of the "methods of science" occurs when holists describe the "logical" conditions that are necessary for the explanation of the behavior of any complex system, organic or inorganic. Thus, in the first place, holists have not emphasized that the laws or generalizations applicable to the system need to be known (this covers the Justice Thomas case); and second, they seem to ignore the requirement that the initial conditions of the system have to be described. To refer to the simple example of the behavior of gases in physics (this example is often used by social scientists—see Chapter 9): To be able to predict the future state of a sample of gas, or to explain the state after it occurs, the relevant gas laws and theories must be known (e.g., Boyle's and Charles's Laws and Kinetic Theory), and so must the initial conditions (the present values of key variables such as pressure, volume and temperature). Only then is it possible to proceed with precise predictions and explanations. Now, while scientists can state the relevant laws and initial conditions for many physico-chemical systems, it is much more difficult to do so in the biological and human sciences; and opponents of naturalistic methods take any failure in these cases not as a sign of the difficulties that are present, but rather as a sign that the analytic endeavor is *mistaken in principle*!

In other words, the critics conveniently forget the conditions that must be met for successful naturalistic explanation and prediction, and they go on to give an oversimplified and hence invalid account of the analytic method of the natural sciences, which they often label with such epithets as "the simpleminded epistemology of Galileo" (see Boudon, 1971, p. 13). A particularly clear example of this is to be found in Andras Angyal's classic book on personality theory:

> Since the basic idea of the holistic attitude is quite generally known, it will be sufficient here to indicate its meaning with but a single example. Let us draw on a surface a horizontal line A, and an oblique line B in such a manner that the two lines intersect. One can study and describe the properties of line A and those of line B. However, a knowledge of the whole resulting from these two lines, namely of the angle which the two lines form, does not emerge from such a study. The angle is something entirely new, and its properties cannot be derived from the properties of the lines which constitute it.... Just as complete information concerning the two lines which form an angle does not give us any knowledge about the angle itself, so knowledge of physiology, psychology, and sociology cannot result in a science of the total person (Angyal, 1941, pp. 2-4).

Thus, by *defining* the method of analysis as neglecting relations, Angyal can reach the conclusion that naturalistic science cannot deal with relations! But by what exercise of the imagination does he conclude that the direction of the two lines, or their spatial juxtaposition, is not to be included in "the complete information" about them? (By a similar feat, no doubt, he would be able to accuse non-holists of holding that complete information about Justice Thomas did not include the fact that he was a Justice of the US Supreme Court.) But, of course, mechanists or analysts (or atomists, as they are sometimes labeled) have always considered such relationships between the parts as vitally important—a point which holists choose to overlook. Edward H. Madden has argued this at length in connection with Gestalt psychologists (who seem to accept the principles of holism 1), and he has shown that in classical Newtonian dynamics (one of the high points of analytical naturalistic science) relational factors such as position and velocity (movement in a given direction) of the various elementary particles were considered to be vital pieces of information (Madden, 1962, ch. 1).

To sum up, then, the analytic methods of naturalistic science are not so simple-minded as they are made out to be. Now, I don't want to deny that understanding complex "organic" wholes or systems is a very complex matter, and sometimes our attempts to explain or to predict the functioning of the "parts" of such systems runs into trouble. But one of the strengths of science is that it is self-corrective; if our attempts to understand fail, we go back and do some more work, and then we try

again. To say that the methods of naturalistic science are *bound* to fail is
to severely underrate them!

Question 7: Perhaps it is time to turn our attention to holism 2. As I
recall, those who hold this position believe that properties or characteristics
of wholes or systems cannot be explained in terms of the properties of
their parts; you identified Ruben as a supporter of this holism, who
argues that there are at least some irreducible social entities. Could you
explain the anti-reductionism that is at the core of the issues here?

Answer: Reductionism is a doctrine concerning the explanatory relation
which holds between various branches of science. A contemporary
philosopher explains it as follows:

> For obvious reasons, issues concerning reduction loom large in all the non-physical
> sciences (biology, psychology and the social sciences). It is accepted on all sides that the
> ultimate constituents of the phenomena discussed by the various special sciences are
> physical in nature. Biological organisms, for example, are built up of cells, which in their
> turn are built up of complex molecules, which may be built up of simpler molecules, and
> so on, until we reach the level of phenomena that it is the aim of the physical sciences to
> explain. But ... does this mean that theories in the special sciences ultimately reduce to
> theories in physics? (Gasper, 1991, p. 546).

To which might be added—does this mean that theories in sociology
ultimately reduce to theories in psychology (for individual people are the
"constituents", it is often argued, of sociological phenomena); and do
the theories of psychology ultimately reduce to theories in biology (on
the grounds that people are biological organisms)? Or, to use an example
that has featured prominently in the literature over reduction in the
social sciences: Is it possible to frame an explanation in terms referring
only to individuals and their characteristics—i.e., without using terms
that refer to "social level" customs or institutions—of how it is that a
person can write out a check and have a bank clerk hand over money; in
other words, is it possible to reduce social concepts, like those of "a
check" or of "a banking system", without remainder into concepts that
refer only to individual persons? (See the papers reprinted in O'Neill,
1973; this example is discussed by Mandelbaum.)

Now, opponents of reductionism often treat it as an "all or nothing"
position: you are either a reductionist, or you are not. But of course this
is far too crude; for one can believe that chemistry, for instance, can be
reduced to physics, without holding that sociology or psychology can be
reduced to biology. The point is that whether or not reduction of one
science to another is feasible depends upon the state of knowledge in those
two branches of science. There was a time when the laws and theories of
chemistry could not have been explained in terms of the laws and theories
of physics; but with the growth of knowledge, the reduction in this

instance did become possible. At the moment it clearly is not possible to reduce the social sciences to psychology or biology, and there are considerations that suggest (but do not absolutely prove) that this may *never* be possible.

Ruben, for example, argues that individual people are not the *parts* of social wholes; individuals may be *members* of systems or wholes, but that is a different matter (Ruben, 1985, esp. ch. 2). If he is right about individuals not being parts, this would mean that we cannot be successful in attempting to explain the properties of social wholes in terms of the properties of individuals—that is, we cannot hope to reduce social science to psychology or biology. John Dupre also makes a point that strengthens this conclusion: In essence he shows that a science at one level will often produce theories in terms of certain entities or abstractions which are quite different from the entities or abstractions involved in the theories at the next "lower" level—in short, the two branches of science might "carve" reality up (or conceptualize it) quite differently. Hence it may not be possible to reduce the theories of the first science to the second (Dupre, 1983). Chemistry can be reduced to physics because the way they carve up their realities is similar; but the same is not true of the social sciences and psychology, or of much of psychology and biology, or of much of biology (for example, evolutionary biology) and physics and chemistry. (While I accept these arguments, I believe it is a fruitful policy to *try* for reduction, simply because we learn more the more we press our science; but realistically we cannot expect always to be successful.)

Clearly, then, reductionism involves many complex issues; and it should be apparent from the preceding discussion that one's views about it are logically independent of one's position with respect to holism 1— they are not merely two sides of the same coin. And there is one final point that needs to be stressed: wherever one comes down with respect to the controversies about holism 2 or reductionism makes no difference to the general issue that we are pursuing—the possibility of having a naturalistic social science. For, although in many branches of science a reductionist ideal is reasonable, in many other reputable branches of science it is more problematical. Thus, whether a science holds reductionist pretensions or not cannot be taken as an indication of its viability *as* a science. The fact that reduction does not (at present) seem a reasonable goal for the social sciences, does not indicate that they are any less *sciences*—just as the fact that evolutionary biology does not seem to be reducible, does not make it any the less a viable natural science!

Question 8: Holism 3 still remains to be discussed; earlier you seeemed to dismiss it rather quickly as being unproblematical. What is it, precisely?

Answer: As branches of science uncover new phenomena, suitable terminology—and often new concepts—have to be devised. When Röntgen discovered a new form of radiation in his laboratory, he called them "X rays"; and when particle physicists discovered new orders of particles with hitherto unknown properties, they coined names such as "quarks", "charm" and "color". Similarly, investigators studying systems of dynamically interrelated parts have argued that special terminology and special concepts are required here. Arthur Koestler, to cite one example, was particularly eloquent in arguing that systems are integrated hierarchies, in which the "parts" have a feature that hitherto had not been noticed— they are *holons*:

> The point first to be emphasized is that each member of this hierarchy, on whatever level, is a sub-whole or "*holon*" in its own right.... They are Janus-faced. The face turned upward, toward the higher levels, is that of a dependent part; the face turned downward, towards its own constituents, is that of a whole of remarkable self-sufficiency (Koestler, 1979, p. 27).

Now, whatever one makes of Koestler's interesting new concept of entities that are both parts and wholes, it surely seems uncontroversial that as sciences progress they *will* have to advance conceptually and terminologically. And many remarks of people who seem to be holists can be interpreted as nothing more than a very reasonable plea to recognize the new phenomena that the study of society as a system, or of systems *qua* systems, has turned up. But again there is nothing here that threatens the possibility of producing social science (or even a science of systems) that is naturalistic.

Question 9: I'm not sure whether this next question—which is my last—is a red herring or not. I have noticed that the words "holism" and "holistic" have been used in a variety of ways in the contemporary literature. One common usage, which clearly is different to—and less specialized than— the senses outlined in the foregoing discussion of holisms 1, 2 and 3, is in the health sciences where there are discussions of holistic medicine, holistic treatment, and the like. Here it is clearly the intention to refer to "the whole person", but there is no desire to conjure up troublesome Hegelian issues of relations of parts to wholes. But another common context is more confusing for me—indexes of contemporary works in philosophy of science frequently have entries on "semantic holism". Where does this fit into the picture you have given of the various types of holism?

Answer: Semantic holism pertains not to social or organic systems, but to symbolic or linguistic systems. Nevertheless it is of wider interest than this might imply—for example, a good case can be made that semantic holism is very relevant to discussions of the nature of theories in science—for scientific theories, of course, are symbolic systems. Thus, semantic holism is tied up with the assessment of Thomas Kuhn's notorious thesis of incommensurability between paradigms in science (Kuhn, 1962)—a thesis that has been particularly influential in the social sciences (Phillips, 1987, ch. 3). And it also is involved in discussions of whether or not we can understand different cultures (and translate their beliefs into our own terms). Furthermore, semantic holism certainly does raise many of the issues that were discussed earlier.

To start at the beginning: Dating back a long time in philosophy of science there has been a problem about the meaning of the terms that appear in scientific theories. For, as was realized by the logical positivists and others (see Chapters 7 and 9), these terms cannot be fully translated into observation language—for example, there is no simple set of observation statements that is equivalent to "there are electrons moving along this wire" or "the electron has a complex structure consisting of ...". One way out of the problem here is to deny that statements about theoretical entities such as electrons are literally meaningful (Skinner, to cite an example from the human sciences, sometimes gives the impression that this is his position about "inner psychological variables"); it is possible to argue that theoretical statements have the status of *instruments* which are useful shorthand and which can aid in calculations and making predictions, but which are not to be taken as giving an account of actual reality. Another stratagem is to hold that theoretical terms gain some degree of meaning because of the *role* that they play within a theory— they have "systematic import". In the writings of such diverse philosophers as Hempel and Quine (see Chapters 4, 7 and 9), scientific theories are seen as *webs* or *networks*, wherein each theoretical term is caught up in a number of complex relations to other terms, thereby (and insofar) gaining meaning. This, essentially, was the position adopted by many of the logical positivists, whose verifiability theory of meaning (see Chapter 7) raised the problem for them of the status of theoretical terms. And, in essence as well, this is semantic holism; for, as described by Fodor and Lepore, this is the

> doctrine that only whole languages or whole theories or whole belief systems *really* have meanings, so that the meanings of smaller units—words, sentences, hypotheses, predictions, discourses, dialogues, texts, thoughts, and the like—are merely derivative (Fodor and Lepore, 1992, p. x).

Now, semantic holism has the following interesting consequence, one that exactly parallels a central thesis held by all those enamored of holism 1: namely, that if one element of a linguistic or theoretical system undergoes change, or if a new element is added to the system, then all the other interrelated "parts" of the system will undergo change (for, everything in the systemic net will now be related to this new element, and hence the "systematic import" will have changed—it will be recalled that this is what James meant when he said "if any Member, then the Whole System"). In terms of a scientific theory, this means that if a theoretical term is changed, or deleted, or added, all the other terms in the theoretical system will undergo change in meaning. The philosopher Newton-Smith refers to this as the thesis of "radical meaning variance", and he shows how this leads to Kuhn's stance on the incommensurability of different paradigms:

> Consequently, both so-called theoretical terms and so-called observational terms are treated as being implicitly defined by the theory in which they occur. In this event Newton and Einstein cannot even communicate about the observational consequences of their theories ... (for) they mean something different by "mass" ... and so on.... Given this thesis that in theory change the meanings of all terms change ... all theories will be incommensurable and there will be no possibility of making rationally grounded theory choice (Newton-Smith, 1981, p. 12).

Several further points need to be made with reference to semantic holism. First, it is not recognized by most of those in the social sciences who have been greatly stimulated by Kuhn that they owe a great debt to the logical positivists and their theory about the meaning of theoretical terms; on the contrary, admirers of Kuhn usually think of themselves as dyed-in-the-wool opponents of positivists! Second, while of course it may raise our suspicions to be reminded of the affinity between semantic holism and the views of the logical positivists, it will hardly do as a "knock-down" criticism; but it would seem that a fair bit of (negative) weight ought to be given to the counter-intuitive consequence of this holism that two "rival" theories are supposed to be incomprehensible to each other's adherents. Furthermore, we are not forced to accept semantic holism for lack of alternatives, as there *are* other theories available concerning the meaning of theoretical terms. Newton-Smith, for example, supports the so-called "causal theory" of meaning that derives from the work of Hilary Putnam (see Newton-Smith, 1981, ch. VII). According to their theory, theoretical terms get introduced into science as a means of referring to causes of phenomena—"electron", for example, refers to whatever entity or mechanism it is that is causally responsible for certain observable phenomena such as wires getting hot when connected to batteries. When our theories about electricity change, the term "electron" does not change meaning—as Kuhn and the semantic holists suppose— for it still refers to the purported cause of the phenomena; what *does* change is the account we give of the properties or nature of this causal entity, the electron.

But, as a last word, I would stress that the various types of holism are logically independent. One might accept, or reject, holism 1 with respect to social phenomena, without being committed to a position with respect to semantic holism; and one's views on these matters does not entail a commitment to a particular stance about the possibility or impossibility of the reduction of the social sciences to some "lower level" science (holism 2). And—most important of all—the viability of pursuing a naturalistic program in the social sciences does not seem to be threatened by any of the things we have discussed.

References

Angyal, Andras (1941). *Foundations for a Science of Personality*. NY: The Commonwealth Fund.

Angyal, Andras (1969). Logic of systems. In Fred Emery (Ed.), *Systems Thinking*. Harmondsworth: Penguin.

Bandura, Albert (1978). The self system in reciprocal determinism. *American Psychologist*, **33**, 344-358.

Bertalanffy, Ludwig von (1969). *General System Theory*. NY: Brazilier.

Boudon, Raymond (1971). *The Uses of Structuralism*. London: Heinemann.

Dewey, John and Bentley, Arthur (1946). Transactions as known and named. *Journal of Philosophy*, **xliii**, 533-551.

Dupre, John (1983). The disunity of science. *Mind*, **xcii**, 321-346.

Fodor, Jerry and Lepore, Ernest (1992). *Holism: A Shopper's Guide*. Oxford: Blackwell.

Ford, Martin and Ford, Donald (Eds.) (1987). *Humans as Self-Constructing Living Systems*. Hillsdale, NJ: Erlbaum.

Gasper, Philip (1991). The philosophy of biology. In R. Boyd *et al.* (Eds.), *The Philosophy of Science*. Cambridge, Mass.: Bradford.

Goldstein, Kurt (1963). *The Organism*. Boston: Beacon.

James, William (1884). Absolutism and empiricism. *Mind*, ix.

Koestler, Arthur (1979). *Janus*. NY: Vintage.

Kuhn, Thomas (1962). *The Structure of Scientific Revolutions*. Chicago: University of Chicago Press.

Lincoln, Yvonna and Guba, Egon (1985). *Naturalistic Inquiry*. Beverly Hills, CA: Russell Sage.

Madden, Edward H. (1962). *Philosophical Problems of Psychology*. NY: Odyssey.

Newton-Smith, W. H. (1981). *The Rationality of Science*. London: Routledge.

O'Neill, John (Ed.) (1973). *Modes of Individualism and Collectivism*. London: Heinemann.

Phillips, D. C. (1970). Organicism in the late nineteenth and early twentieth centuries. *Journal of the History of Ideas*, **xxxi**, 413-432.

Phillips, D. C. (1976). *Holistic Thought in Social Science*. Stanford: Stanford University Press.

Phillips, D. C. (1987). *Philosophy, Science, and Social Inquiry*. Oxford: Pergamon Press.

Ruben, David-Hillel (1985). *The Metaphysics of the Social World*. London: Routledge.

Salomon, Gavriel (1991). Transcending the qualitative-quantitative debate: The analytic and systemic approaches to educational research. *Educational Researcher*, **20**, 10-18.

Stokols, Daniel and Altman, Irwin (Eds.) (1987). *Handbook of Environmental Psychology*. NY: John Wiley.

3

Naturalistic Ideals for
Social Science

It is a common human practice for us to label past ages in such a way that we can neatly but oversimply categorize their intellectual achievements (or lack of such)—the nineteenth century was "the age of ideology", the medieval period was "the age of faith", and so forth. (A series of widely read books of readings in the field of history of ideas was organized in this fashion; see Aiken, 1956, for one of these volumes.) Egoistically, perhaps, many of us do not regard *ourselves* as living in an "age"; it is as if each of us believed that intellectual history stopped (or reached fruition) on the day of our own birth. However, many of the contemporary theoretical and philosophical disputes about the nature of the social sciences become explicable if—by an out-of-the-body exercise of the imagination—we look at ourselves as living in an age when the naturalistic ideal has migrated from the physical and biological sciences into the social sciences, where it is not receiving a uniformly warm reception. (The existentialists and phenomenologists, for example—not to mention the hermeneuticists—can be seen as opposing any kind of naturalism which might have the effect of diminishing the distinction between humans and other parts of nature. See Husserl, 1970.)

The terms "naturalistic" and "naturalism" suffer from the fact that they have a range of meanings, covering a variety of things from the Romantic submission to nature or the collecting of butterflies to the practice of sunbathing on the beach clad only in one's birthday suit. In the social sciences, these terms are often as not used to refer to studies in which—in contrast to experimental work—the researcher does not interfere with the situation that is under scrutiny. The (philosophical) sense of these terms as used in the present discussion is somewhat different: In general, a naturalist is a scholar who attempts to explain phenomena that occur within the realm of the physical universe in terms of concepts and explanatory hypotheses that themselves refer to this same "natural" realm; in other words, the naturalist eschews explanations in terms of (literally) *super*-natural or *meta*-physical entities. Applied more specifically to the social sciences, the meaning is narrower still: A naturalist is a person who holds that, in some fashion that he or she is under an obligation to make precise, the social sciences are similar to the natural sciences (see Thomas, 1979). It will be noted that an important condition has been built into this account—each naturalist has to make clear the respect in which he or she believes the natural and social sciences are similar. Because different people give different accounts in this important area—they see the similarity in different terms—there is not *one* naturalistic ideal for the social sciences; rather, there are several. And thereby hangs our present tale.

The Spread of Naturalism: A Thumbnail Sketch

It is not entirely clear when the naturalistic ideal emerged in the physical sciences, but there is little doubt that it was well on the way to being established by the time Galileo's work was done. His observations through the telescope helped to remove the distinction between the (perfect) heavens and the (imperfect) Earth; for he displaced them both from places of special privilege and significance in the universe. But, probably more importantly, his investigations with the inclined plane demonstrated what could be accomplished with careful laboratory manipulation and measurement, and the use of mathematical analysis coupled with rigorous argumentation. (For a readable and relatively non-technical account of these contributions, given by a physicist, see Rogers, 1960.) Galileo died in 1642; in 1644 Descartes published the *Principles of Philosophy* in which he stated boldly that all he required in order to explain "all natural phenomena" were the concepts of matter and motion (Descartes, 1963, p. 221). In this work he also expressed his indebtedness to the idea of machines; and he stated that natural phenomena work on the same principles as man-made machines, except that the parts of natural phenomena are so small that "they utterly elude our senses" (Descartes, 1963, p. 236). By the end of Newton's lifetime, the picture of the universe (in its physical aspects) as a vast mechanism akin to clock-work was well on its way to general acceptance among the intelligentsia. The Creator was revealed to have been a mechanic and mathematician, who absented Himself from active participation after having set the cosmic machinery into motion. As the historian of science Herbert Butterfield put it,

> a subtle intellectual change was giving people an interest in the operation of pure mechanism; and some have even said that this came from the growing familiarity with clocks and machines, though it would be impossible to put one's finger on any authentic proof of this.... One thing is clear: not only was there in some intellectual leaders a great aspiration to demonstrate that the universe ran like a piece of clockwork, but this was itself initially a religious aspiration. It was felt that there would be something defective in Creation itself ...

unless the whole system of the universe could be shown to be interlocking, so that it carried the pattern of reasonableness and orderliness (Butterfield, 1957, p. 119).

The naturalization of the physical world view (or mechanization, as some have preferred to call it—see Dijksterhuis, 1961; also Randall, 1976, ch. X) has just about run its course in our own times. In the late 1980s the noted physicist Victor Weisskopf, a former president of the American Academy of Arts and Sciences, gave an address to the Academy on the topic "The Origin of the Universe". In masterly style he summarized the relevant recent work in the fields of astrophysics, cosmology and particle physics; and finally, arriving at the "Big Bang", he argued that this occurred as a consequence of the fact that the laws of quantum physics still operated when *nothing* existed:

> According to the fundamental tenets of this well-established theory, there is nothing in nature that remains quiet. Everything, including the true vacuum, is subject to fluctuations—in particular to energy fluctuations.... Thus, at one moment a small region somewhere in space may have fluctuated into a false vacuum. This would happen very rarely but cannot be excluded. That region almost instantly expands tremendously and creates a large space filled with energy according to the properties of a false vacuum (Weisskopf, 1989, pp. 36-37).

Perhaps to soften the impact of this news on any deists in his audience, Weisskopf arranged for the opening bars of Haydn's oratorio "The Creation" to be played as he concluded his lecture. Stephen Hawking, the contemporary occupant of Newton's Chair at Cambridge, holds what appears (to a relative layman) to be a similar position, but in his best-selling *A Brief History of Time* he goes a little further and asks whether this account leaves room for God to exert any influence at all—for even the Deity cannot transgress the laws of physics (Hawking, 1988). God has moved from being a mechanic, architect and mathematician, to being a passive spectator—a triumph for the process of naturalization. (For a philosophical critique of these recent ideas from physics, see Grunbaum, 1989.)

A similar process has been at work in the biological sciences. It is probably unnecessary to recount the spread of naturalism from Harvey on the role of the heart as a pump to Crick and Watson on the biochemical mechanisms underlying gene replication, although it should be made clear that the spread was not an easy accomplishment nor was it without setbacks. (To cite two examples: the spread of vitalism in the biology of the late nineteenth and early twentieth centuries seems in large part to have been a reaction as the complexities of living organisms became apparent—especially the complexities of cell-division—which no "natural" mechanism conceivable at the time could explain; and the Romantic movement of the late eighteenth and early nineteenth centuries was to a significant degree a reaction to what was taken to be the sterility, dehumanization, and lack of historical consciousness of the mechanical science of the Enlightenment.) The words of the intellectual historian John Herman Randall, Jr., are worth citing as a reminder of the critical role of Charles Darwin in widening the scope of naturalism to encompass humans:

> Of all the consequences that followed from the new evolutionary world of science, what seemed most momentous was the definite inclusion of man within the scope of the cosmic process. Not only was man an integral part of Nature, bound by her laws and subject to her forces ... after Darwin, however, there could be no further blinking of the fact that man was a product as well as a part of nature ... (Randall, 1976, p. 497).

(It also is worth noting here that we humans can be a part of nature, of course, without the scientific methods useful in studying the *other* parts necessarily being appropriate for studying *our* affairs! In other words, while the Darwinian placement of humans firmly into the natural order makes it easier to defend naturalism in the sense defined at the beginning of the chapter, it does not absolutely seal the case.)

Although again it is difficult to be precise, during the first half of the nineteenth century naturalistic ideals started to motivate some at least of those who wished to study human affairs in a more rigorous fashion—a phenomenon that was driven, in large part, by the success that naturalism was enjoying in other domains. (The hermeneutic school, as discussed elsewhere in the present volume, can be regarded as resisting this trend.) In the early decades of the century social statistics had been collected by the Belgian scholar Quetelet (Quetelet, 1968) in an attempt to find precise measurements of social forces; and also in the 1830s and 1840s Auguste Comte argued that what he called the "positive philosophy" would spread successfully into the new field of "social physics". (For further discussion see the entry on "positivism" in the present book.) At close to the same time, John Stuart Mill, in the Sixth Book of his *A System of Logic* (see Mill, 1988, ch. 3), offered the opinion that the difficulties standing in the way of developing a science of human affairs were analogous to the difficulties barring an accurate and fully predictive science of the tides (i.e., they were difficulties concerned with obtaining accurate initial data—in the case of tides about the precise slopes of beaches, wind strength, and so on—they were not what we might call difficulties in principle). Herbert Spencer, the influential essayist and proselytizer for scientific naturalism, produced a volume *The Principles of Psychology* in 1855; he had modestly (but, as it turns out, mistakenly) written to his father that this volume would "ultimately stand beside Newton's *Principia*" (Spencer, quoted in Kennedy, 1978, p. 47). Around this time, too, Karl Marx believed that he had produced a scientific and materialistic account of the dynamics of history; and Darwin, who had declined the invitation to write the "Introduction" for the former's *Capital*, reluctantly turned his attention explicitly to humans in both his *Expression of the Emotions* and *The Descent of Man* (1871). (Darwin's *Origin of Species*, in 1859, only implicitly dealt with humans, but nevertheless his readers jumped to the conclusion discussed earlier—humans are animals, and thus part of the natural order.)

Experimental psychology also originated in this era; one of its first achievements was Fechner's "psychophysical law" which purported to show the mathematical relationship between (objective) "outer" stimuli and (subjective) "inner" sensations—in other words, the law seemed to mathematically relate matter with mind, a neat trick if only valid (see contributions by Fechner and others in Dennis, 1948). What now is acknowledged to be the first great textbook of modern scientific psychology, William James's *The Principles of Psychology*, was published in 1890.

In the last few decades of the nineteenth century there was another significant development: statistical analysis started to blossom as a research tool in science (its origins go back further, of course; see Hacking, 1990), and began its rapid development to become the cornerstone of much twentieth-century social science. While some statistical techniques were imported into the social sciences from agriculture and even brewing ("Student", as the inventor of the notorious "t test" chose to identify himself, was an employee of the Guinness brewery), some were developed by researchers specifically interested in human affairs. Early work on what is now called the curve of normal distribution talked about "the curve of errors"—nature was conceived as making mistakes as it aimed to produce individuals with all the same measure of the same characteristic (height of adult males in a population, for example). Darwin's cousin, Francis Galton, used various human and social examples to illustrate this notion together with the idea of correlation (which he originated); and in what must have been to some extent a mischievous tongue-in-cheek example (Galton, 1872), he even used his nascent statistical techniques to investigate "the efficacy of prayer". (Briefly, Galton argued that the British national anthem—"God Save the Queen"—was a prayer for the longevity of the monarch; so he took the ages at death of British monarchs, and statistically compared them to a sample of other non-related members of the nobility. There *was* a "significant" difference, but in a distasteful direction—prayer seemed to be killing off the royal family prematurely! Although this example was—presumably—mainly intended as an engaging illustration of the possibilities of the new statistical tools there may well have been some intent to attack the clergy (see Forrest, 1974, ch. 8), and as might be expected there was a public controversy. Galton's knighthood did not come until the new century!)

During the early decades of the present century the naturalistic program became firmly entrenched in the human and social sciences, especially in North America. B. F. Skinner was the leading spokesperson for one particular (and, it must be said, narrow) version of the naturalistic program; one crucial chapter of his book *Science and Human Behavior* (Skinner, 1953) displays its author's naturalism even in the title (which may have been a Freudian slip)—"Why Organisms Behave". For the point is, of course, that the organism of chief interest to Skinner was *Homo sapiens*, but clearly as a convinced naturalist he was planning to make no distinctions within the animal kingdom! He wrote:

> We undertake to predict and control the behavior of the individual organism. This is our "dependent variable"—the effect for which we are to find the cause. Our "independent variables"—the causes of behavior—are the external conditions of which behavior is a function. Relations between the two—the "cause and effect relationships" in behavior—are the laws of a science. A synthesis of these laws expressed in quantitative terms yields a comprehensive picture of the organism as a behaving system. This must be done within the grounds of a natural science. We cannot assume that behavior has any peculiar properties which require unique methods of special kinds of knowledge (Ibid., pp. 35-36).

This passage is saturated with notions that would have seemed fantastic one and a half centuries ago (if they don't seem far-fetched enough now): Human and animal behavior are of a kind, behavior can be predicted, the laws of behavior can be determined, behavior is best conceptualized as a dependent variable, behavior does not differ in kind from physical phenomena.... These are the elements of Western naturalism that Skinner wove into his own particular program of research. But Skinner's is not the only naturalistic game in town.

Naturalistic Strategies

As indicated earlier, there are several general strategies open to naturalists, for there are a number of ways in which the social sciences can be held to be similar to the natural sciences. This is an important point, which often escapes those who are inclined to be opposed to naturalism—the easiest path for opponents to take is to set up a straw man by focusing on a narrow, outmoded or very limited view of the nature of natural science, whereupon it is an easy matter to show that the social sciences are not like *that*. (The point is, of course, that the natural sciences are not like that either!) Popper put the point well when he wrote that when critics

> denounce a view like mine as "positivistic" or "scientistic", then I may perhaps answer that they themselves seem to accept, *implicitly and uncritically*, that positivism or scientism is *the only philosophy appropriate to the natural sciences* (Popper, 1972, p. 185).

Another example is provided by the work of the philosopher and political theorist Charles Taylor, whose classic paper "Interpretation and the Sciences of Man" (1971) became an important document for the development of the hermeneutical or interpretive approach to the social sciences on the North American continent (as discussed in an earlier chapter of the present volume). It is clear from the examples used that in 1971 Taylor considered behavioristic social science to be *the* form of naturalism that needed to be combatted. Now, whilst behaviorism was still common and relatively prominent at the time Taylor was originally writing— although even then it was in clear decline—it is not apparent that in his later essays he abandoned or updated his views about its fitness to serve as the sole representative of naturalism. Worse still, many of those who have been influenced by Taylor over the intervening decades, and who should know better the state of play across the full range of the social sciences, make a similar mistake. For the fact is that, considered as an overarching approach to the study of human affairs, behaviorism is almost universally recognized as flawed and is relatively easy to dismiss. (This is not to deny that in some areas behaviorism has led to impressive results, for example in the treatment of some severe behavioral symptoms in disordered patients.)

What, then, are the general possibilities open to a supporter of naturalistic social science? In what general ways can the social sciences be held to parallel the natural sciences? In the following discussion four of the strategies that have been tried in the past century and a half will be discussed, but it should be stressed at the outset that it is not being claimed that these are fully independent—clearly they are not mutually exclusive, as some of the illustrative examples should make clear.

(a) The use of certain favored concepts and findings from the natural sciences. It is not uncommon for human inquirers, when faced with a puzzling phenomenon in some new area, to try to impose intellectual order by bringing to bear ideas that worked well in other fields. This, of course, is related to the use of those powerful intellectual tools, metaphor and analogy—and some might want to argue that it is related to the phenomenon common throughout the animal kingdom of using well-established behavioral patterns in new domains. But the transfer of ideas from one intellectual domain to another is not a matter of mere reflex; it is a process that often requires great ingenuity and intellectual persistence.

Thus, with the great success of certain core notions in the physical sciences, it comes as no great surprise to find that from time to time they have been taken and applied in the domain of the social sciences, with the expectation that this would be the key (or at least one key) to making a scientific breakthrough in the new domain. Two examples should suffice. Herbert Spencer, to whom passing reference was made earlier, spent the greater part of his adult life developing his "synthetic philosophy", and attempting to unify the known branches of science, including the social sciences. He produced a volume on psychology at the early date of 1855, and this was followed by a series of very influential volumes on the infant (if not embryonic) field of sociology—*The Principles of Sociology*, which were published between 1876 and 1896. But he also wrote on biology, education, anthropology, and a host of other topics. The key to Spencer's unification of these disparate domains was the law of progress, which he believed was the same in all fields—physical, biological, and human. In turn, this universal progress was underwritten by a physical mechanism, namely, the fact that every force produces more than one effect (Spencer, 1949, especially pp. 176-177). To the modern reader Spencer's train of argument seems bizarre, but his contemporaries found him stimulating (at least for a time). Thus, at one time or another, he could number among his admirers John Stuart Mill, Thomas Henry Huxley, William James, Ivan Pavlov, the multi-millionaire Andrew Carnegie, and a generation or two of American social scientists and political theorists who were adherents of what we would now call "Social Darwinism" (Hofstadter, 1955).

The second example of the first naturalistic strategy is probably better known. Sigmund Freud was trained in medicine at a time when the "mechanistic" ideas of Helmholtz and his followers were dominant; German medical research at the time was committed to finding naturalistic explanations, and furthermore, to finding explanations that would preserve Helmholtz's law of conservation of energy. Reflecting these influences, Freud approached the human psyche in terms of the conservation of "psychic" energy—this is why he believed that treating only the symptoms of mental disorder was a strategy doomed to failure, for energy denied one outlet would merely seek another and would thus display itself in some new set of symptoms. (This use of Helmholtz's law is particularly apparent in the lectures Freud gave in the United States in 1910; see Freud, 1989, especially Lectures 1 and 3.)

It is difficult to avoid the feeling that this first naturalistic strategy can be pushed to extremes. Certainly one can never tell, beforehand, whether a borrowed idea will prove to be fruitful in a new domain, but it is also the case that each domain probably is going to require concepts that are faithful to the new and unique phenomena that it contains. Furthermore, and more seriously, the application of ideas taken from the physical and biological sciences—no matter how inventive or fruitful—does not seem sufficient to cement the naturalist's case. For it is apparent that the use of such borrowed ideas only makes intellectual sense if the borrower is *already* committed to the view that there is no relevant difference between the natural and social or human sciences. Freud and Spencer were able to apply ideas from the physical and biological domains because they already had a commitment to universal naturalism. (The same case can be made about others who adopt this first strategy, such as the behaviorists Watson and Skinner.)

(b) The use of the "deeper" presuppositions of natural science. The four figures already mentioned—Spencer, Freud, Watson and Skinner—all made use of this second strategy in their extension of naturalism. They shared a strong belief that the human phenomena that were of concern to them were marked by causation as strictly deterministic as it was in physical mechanical systems. They also shared the belief that nature was regular—natural laws were to be found in the human or social domain as well as in the physical. The differences between them were due to the way they played out these fundamental metaphysical commitments in practice—they were interested in somewhat different phenomena, and the mechanisms that they saw at work in nature and which they generalized were different in their four cases: Spencer latched onto the fact that forces produced more than one effect, Freud focused on conservation of ("psychic") energy, Watson adopted the Pavlovian mechanism of classic conditioning, and Skinner took over the idea of operant conditioning which had made an appearance in E. L. Thorndike's work with imprisoned cats. (For more details on some of these examples, see Cleverley and Phillips, 1986.)

To cut what could be a long story short, then, it seems incontrovertible that at least some branches of the modern social sciences have taken over the metaphysical underpinnings of the natural sciences (or what has commonly been thought to be those underpinnings): nature is regular, in the sense that there are lawlike generalizations waiting to be discovered (or, more accurately, invented); causal language is appropriate in the social sciences (although often this is disguised, as when researchers talk of dependent and independent variables, or when they use locutions such as "this event happened as a result of ..."); and even in social affairs there is a "fact of the matter", a "social reality", which is independent of what the researcher happens to believe. The fact that these days there is no shortage of writers who attack these assumptions as being out of place in the social sciences only goes to prove the point that they *are* present. (For merely one example, see the exchange between Phillips and Guba in Eisner and Peshkin, 1990.)

Are these assumptions reasonable? Are there good reasons for following this second strategy? Clearly the issues here are very complex. Some writers would say that all inquiry necessarily must have a soft under-belly of assumptions—Kuhn, for example, would hold that in natural science there always will be paradigmatic assumptions (although, to throw a spanner in the works, Kuhn doubted that there were any paradigms in the social sciences); for Lakatos there is a set of "hard core" assumptions at the heart of every research program (Phillips, 1987, Part A). From the vantage point of one of these perspectives, then, it would come as no surprise that some naturalists take over into the social sciences the hard core assumptions they believe to be present in the physical or biological sciences; the only alternative to borrowing would be to devise a new set and start *ab initio*. There is, of course, no way of *establishing* the soundness or otherwise of metaphysical assumptions; but on the other hand, as people like Popper have insisted, such items can be discussed and criticized, and it certainly is possible for us to reach the conclusion that some assumptions are—given the considerations that have been advanced— more reasonable than others (see Popper, 1985, ch. 16).

But it also remains possible for a person to be a naturalist, and to believe that in some respects the social sciences resemble the natural sciences (or vice versa), *without* subscribing to the view that the metaphysical underpinnings of natural science must be replicated in the social sciences. (What becomes really crucial here is precisely *what* these metaphysical foundations are taken to be.) Thus, for example, it would seem possible to hold that the physical notions of law and of causation are out of place when human society is the object of inquiry—humans act for reasons, not as a result of impressed forces (hermeneuticists, as discussed in an earlier chapter, develop this position in some detail). But it still could be held that human-oriented inquiry can be subjected to naturalistic study—the point being that some *other* naturalistic strategy would thereby be favored, rather than the second one that has been the subject of attention here. (Some members, but by no means all, of the hermeneutical school also believe that their program, with its rival conception of the nature of the human person as meaning-maker, can be investigated in a disciplined and even "scientific" manner.)

(c) The adoption of "structural" features of natural science. The mature natural sciences have developed an impressive structure consisting of empirical laws related through the medium of theories. Thus (as discussed more fully in the chapter on theory), the laws of gas behavior that bear the names of Boyle and Charles are subsumed under the kinetic theory of gases, from which they can be shown to follow deductively (given certain reasonable linking assumptions). But the theory also was able to generate predictions that could be tested, and which led to the discovery of phenomena that were completely unexpected on the basis of knowledge of only Boyle's Law and Charles' Law. Carl Hempel paints the situation in the following manner:

> Theories are usually introduced when previous study of a class of phenomena has revealed a system of uniformities that can be expressed in the form of empirical laws. Theories then seek to explain those regularities and, generally, to afford a deeper and more accurate understanding of the phenomena in question. To this end, a theory construes those phenomena as manifestations of entities and processes that lie behind or beneath them, as it were. These are assumed to be governed by characteristic theoretical laws, or theoretical principles, by means of which the theory then explains the empirical uniformities that have been previously discovered, and usually also predicts "new" regularities of similar kinds (Hempel, 1966, p. 70).

The logical structure of theories is currently a matter of intense debate among philosophers of science (see the chapter on theory), but Hempel's account is a classic formulation of what the literature calls the "received view" (Suppe, 1974).

Whatever the outcome of the debates over the "structure" of natural science, there has been no shortage of social scientists who are impressed by one or other of the accounts of this structure, and who have lusted after a social science that would be similar. The field of economics, to cite the most notorious example, is packed with theories that resemble the structure of the kinetic theory of gases (and which go so far as to treat individuals rather like molecules, even to the length of endowing them with properties as unrealistic—or, more charitably as idealized—as are the properties possessed by the molecules of classic kinetic theory). Organization theory, too, is a field marked by the development of theories on the model of the physical sciences.

The work of the sociologist Robert Merton deserves special mention here. In his celebrated discussion of "sociological theories of the middle range" he writes, in a passage that closely resembles the work of Hempel:

> ... the term *sociological theory* refers to logically interconnected sets of propositions from which empirical uniformities can be derived. Throughout we focus on what I have called *theories of the middle range*: theories that lie between the minor but necessary working hypotheses that evolve in abundance during day-to-day research and the all-inclusive systematic efforts to develop a unified theory that will explain all observed uniformities of social behavior, social organization, and social change (Merton, 1967, p. 39).

Merton continues with these significant words: "One speaks of a theory of reference groups, of social mobility, of role-conflict and of the formation of social norms just as one speaks of a theory of prices, a germ theory of disease, or a kinetic theory of gases" (Ibid., pp. 39-40). Here, then, it is clear that the third naturalistic strategy is at work; indeed, it sits so comfortably with Merton that he does not even consider justifying his assumption that it is *possible* to produce sociological theories that are logically parallel to kinetic theory.

In advocating the quest for middle-range theories, Merton was concerned to combat the work of "grand theorists" such as Talcott Parsons—the physical science analog of grand theory being, perhaps, Einstein's unified theory or contemporary particle physicists' "theory of everything" (neither of which has been successfully produced). Merton's discussion of why the production of grand theory is a mistaken enterprise highlights further how well entrenched the naturalistic ideal had become by the 1950s and 1960s. In an argument that unabashedly draws on the physical sciences, Merton suggests that "the attempt to create total systems of sociology" rests on three mistakes about science: first, that systems of thought (i.e., grand theories) can be erected before a great mass of "basic observations has been accumulated" (Ibid., p. 46); second, that all branches of inquiry existing at the same time have the same level of maturity (Ibid., p. 47)—that is, for example, that contemporary social science is in the same state of development as contemporary physics; and third, that physical science has, indeed, produced grand theory that can serve as the inspirational model for social scientists (Ibid.). The point here is not, of course, whether Merton's analysis is right or wrong, but rather the way in which he assumes *without argument* that what is sauce for the physical science goose is also sauce for the social science gander. (And again, the point is not so much to challenge this assumption, but merely to highlight that it is there—the third naturalistic strategy has become, as it were, internalized.)

(d) Cementing the hegemony of scientific method. This fourth naturalistic strategy is, perhaps, the most widespread of all—the methods of science, which of course must be given credit for the great success of the natural sciences, can be used fruitfully in the social sciences. The naturalist who takes this route must, of course, follow through and put on the table an analysis of precisely what the scientific method *is* (a task that is simpler in the describing than in the doing).

This position is so familiar that it is probably unnecessary to swamp the reader with examples. Two will suffice. In 1910 John Dewey published *How We Think*, which he revised in 1933; the volume opens with the statement that some ways of thinking "are better than others", and the reasons why they are better "can be set forth". He calls the better way "reflective thinking" rather than scientific thinking (Dewey, 1971, p. 3), but a rose by any other name still smells as sweet. He was less circumspect in 1916, when he wrote of science as "authorized conviction", and he stated that "without initiation into the scientific spirit one is not in possession of the best tools which humanity has so far devised for effectively directed reflection" (Dewey, 1966, p. 189). (It is worth noting that Dewey was a contributor to the *International Encyclopedia of Unified Science*, which produced nineteen monographs before its demise; the title of the series—sometimes called *The Foundations of the Unity of Science*—is self-explanatory.)

Another example of the fourth line that can be taken by naturalists is provided by the work of Auguste Comte. He believed the key method of science was, indeed, the only intellectual method that could produce *real* knowledge:

> All competent thinkers agree with Bacon that there can be no real knowledge except that which rests upon observed facts. This fundamental maxim is so evidently indisputable if it is applied, as it ought to be, to the mature state of our intelligence (Comte, 1970, p. 4).

Again this is not the place to undertake a detailed assessment of such arguments; but it can be suggested, without undue prejudice, that this fourth strategy involving the generalization of scientific method is probably (to mix the metaphor) an easier row to hoe than the previous three. Certainly it is not particularly restrictive or threatening—various social science fields can maintain their individuality, and researchers in these fields are not severely handicapped, if a Deweyan (or for that matter a Popperian) "scientific" intellectual methodology is adopted. Indeed, as Follesdal (1979) and Hirsch (1978, pp. 151-152) have both argued, the hypothetico-deductive method of science can readily be found in the humanities.

There is no need for a grand concluding statement. The purpose of the foregoing discussion was simply to establish two points, namely, that the push for naturalistic social science is part of a major trend in Western intellectual thought over the past few centuries, and that naturalism is not a simple position—there are a variety of naturalistic strategies. Thus, those who see themselves as opponents of the quest to develop naturalistic social science are under an obligation to avoid being simplistic: it does not suffice to refute naturalism (if refutation of such a broad spectrum of positions is the appropriate thing to aim for), to refute or severely criticize merely *one form* of naturalism.

References

Aiken, Henry D. (1956). *The Age of Ideology*. NY: Mentor.

Butterfield, Henry (1957). *The Origins of Modern Science*, New edition. London: G. Bell and Sons.

Cleverley, John, and Phillips, D. C. (1986). *Visions of Childhood*. NY: Teachers College Press.

Comte, Auguste (1970). *Introduction to Positive Philosophy*. Indianapolis: Bobbs-Merrill.

Dennis, Wayne (1948). *Readings in the History of Psychology*. NY: Appleton-Century-Crofts.

Descartes, Rene (1963). In Elizabeth Anscombe and Peter Geach (Eds.), *Philosophical Writings*. Edinburgh: Thomas Nelson and Sons.

Dewey, John (1966). *Democracy and Education*. NY: Free Press.

Dewey, John (1971). *How We Think*. Chicago: Henry Regnery.

Dijksterhuis, E. J. (1961). *The Mechanization of the World Picture*. Tr. C. Dikshoorn. Oxford: Clarendon Press.

Eisner, Elliot and Peshkin, Alan (Eds.) (1990). *Qualitative Inquiry in Education*. NY: Teachers College Press.

Follesdal, Dagfinn (1979). Hermeneutics and the hypothetico-deductive method. *Dialectica*, 33, 3-4.

Forrest, D. W. (1974). *Francis Galton: The Life and Work of a Victorian Genius*. NY: Taplinger.

Freud, Sigmund (1989). *Five Lectures on Psychoanalysis*. NY: Norton.

Galton, Francis (1872). Statistical inquiries into the efficacy of prayer. *Fortnightly Review*, 68, 125-135.

Grunbaum, Adolf (1989). The pseudo-problem of creation in physical cosmology. *Philosophy of Science*, 56, 3, 373-394.

Hacking, Ian (1990). *The Taming of Chance*. Cambridge: Cambridge University Press.

Hawking, Stephen (1988). *A Brief History of Time*. NY: Bantam.

Hempel, Carl (1966). *Philosophy of Natural Science*. Englewood Cliffs, NJ: Prentice-Hall.

Hirsch, E. D., Jr. (1978). *The Aims of Interpretation*. Chicago: University of Chicago Press.

Hofstadter, Richard (1955). *Social Darwinism in American Thought*. Boston: Beacon Press.

Husserl, Edmund (1970). *The Crisis of European Sciences and Transcendental Phenomenology.* Evanston, Illinois: Northwestern University Press.

Kennedy, J. G. (1978). *Herbert Spencer.* Boston: Twayne.

Merton, Robert (1967). *On Theoretical Sociology.* NY: Free Press.

Mill, John Stuart (1988). *The Logic of the Moral Sciences.* LaSalle, Illinois: Open Court.

Phillips, D. C. (1987). *Philosophy, Science, and Social Inquiry.* Oxford: Pergamon Press.

Popper, Karl (1972). *Objective Knowledge.* Oxford: Clarendon Press.

Popper, Karl (1985). In David Miller (Ed.), *Popper Selections.* Princeton, NJ: Princeton University Press.

Quetelet, M. A. (1968). *A Treatise on Man.* NY: Franklin.

Randall, John Herman, Jr. (1976). *The Making of the Modern Mind.* NY: Columbia University Press.

Rogers, Eric (1960). *Physics for the Inquiring Mind.* Princeton, NJ: Princeton University Press.

Skinner, B. F. (1953). *Science and Human Behavior.* NY: Free Press.

Spencer, Herbert (1949). *Essays on Education etc.* London: Dent/Everyman.

Suppe, Frederick (1974). *The Structure of Scientific Theories.* Urbana, IL: University of Illinois Press.

Taylor, Charles (1977). Interpretation and the sciences of man. Reprinted in F. Dallmayr and T. McCarthy (Eds.), *Understanding and Social Inquiry.* Notre Dame, IN: University of Notre Dame Press.

Thomas, David (1979). *Naturalism and Social Science.* Cambridge: Cambridge University Press.

Weisskopf, Victor (1989). The origin of the universe. *Bulletin of the American Academy of Arts and Sciences*, **xlii**, 4, 22-39.

4

New Philosophy of Science *

IT is arguable that recent advances in the philosophical understanding of science have vindicated many of John Dewey's views on the matter. Scientific reason is not marked off from other forms of human intellectual endeavor as a sort of model of perfection which these lesser activities must always strive (unsuccessfully) to mimic. Rather, science embodies exactly the same types of fallible reasoning as is found elsewhere—it is just that scientists do, a little more self-consciously and in a more controlled way, what all effective thinkers do. As Dewey pointed out more than half a century ago, he believed that intellectual inquiry,

> in spite of the diverse subjects to which it applies, and the consequent diversity of its special techniques has a common structure or pattern: that this common structure is applied both in common sense and science ... (Dewey, 1966, p. 101).

Thus it is no surprise that Dewey contributed to the "unified science" movement of the early to mid decades of the twentieth century (a matter commented upon further in the previous chapter). Recent work has shown that scientists, like workers in other areas, are in the business of providing reasonable justifications for their assertions, but nothing they do can make these assertions absolutely safe from criticism and potential overthrow. (There are no absolute justifications, hence the somewhat misleading name sometimes given to recent epistemology—"non-justificationist". This is misleading because it suggests that if there are no *absolute* justifications, there are no justifications at all.) It is salutary to remember that Dewey preferred not to use the term "truth", but rather "warranted assertibility", and he recognized that different types of assertions required different warrants. Furthermore, this change of language highlighted the fact that a warrant is not forever; today's warrant can be rescinded tomorrow, following further inquiry. Karl Popper, too, expressed a similar view; and in impassioned prose he pointed out that "the question of the sources of our knowledge, like so many authoritarian questions, is a *genetic* one. It asks for the origin of our knowledge, in the belief that knowledge may legitimize itself by its pedigree" (Popper, 1985, p. 52). A little later he added:

So my answer to the questions "How do you know? What is the source or basis of your assertion? What observations have led you to it?" would be: "I do *not* know: my assertion was merely a guess. Never mind the source, or the sources, from which it may spring.... But if you are interested in the problem which I tried to solve by my tentative assertion, you may help me by criticising it as severely as you can" (Popper, 1985, p. 53).

Criticism, for Popper, includes the offering of disconfirming (refuting) experimental data. (For further discussion of Dewey and Popper, see Chapter 6.)

It should be clear, therefore, that none of this means that science is *unbelievable*, or that "anything goes" or "anything may be accepted", or that "there is no justification at all for scientific claims", or that "there are no standards by which the truth or adequacy (or both) of a piece of science can be judged". It simply means that it no longer can be claimed that there are any *absolutely authoritative foundations* upon which scientific knowledge is based. Hence the other title often given to contemporary epistemology—"non-foundationalist".

This account of science fits comfortably with the view that many scientists themselves hold—especially, perhaps, action researchers in the applied social sciences and evaluators of social programs; these latter are *par excellence* fields of "the believable", of building the "good case", but where even the best of cases can be challenged or reanalyzed or reinterpreted. Nothing is more suspicious in the field of program evaluation, for example, than a report which is presented with the implication that it has the status of "Holy Writ". Researchers in the "pure" sciences, and in the more laboratory-oriented of the social and human sciences, now have to accept that good science is a blood brother if not a sibling to what transpires in these messier and more open-ended fields of endeavor.

What happened in philosophy of science to build this new and modest view? Or, alternatively, what destroyed the older view?

An Outline of Recent Developments

The new view of science could not get off the ground until the foundations of the dominant older view, positivism, had been shown to be untenable. The role that had been ascribed to observation—being the rock-bottom foundation of science and at the same time being the final arbiter of what could be believed—was reevaluated; and the relation between scientific theories and evidence was shown to be more complex than had been thought. The related view that science grows by steady accumulation of findings and theories was challenged by the work of Thomas Kuhn and subsequent scholars such as Lakatos and Feyerabend. Obviously these matters are too complex to discuss in encyclopedic detail, but a few of the crucial issues can be highlighted.

1. It is clear (to all except some mystics) that if the aim of science is to establish bodies of knowledge about the world, then somewhere in the process of doing science the world must be allowed to constrain or discipline our theories. But it has been recognized for many decades that the positivistic and operationalistic view that all theoretical terms of science must be reducible to (i.e., definable in terms of) observational language is Quixotic. The status of operationalism in the behavioral sciences was a hot issue in the decade immediately following the Second World War, and there were international symposia on the matter. A consensus was reached (except, of course, for a few diehards—an old story). The point was driven home that the theoretical concepts of science have meanings that transcend definition in observational terms; if this was not the case, science would have trouble in growing, and extending into new areas. And it was realized that if the positivist/ operationist view was accepted, it would have a chilling effect on theorizing about unobservable mechanisms such as the subatomic events that have won Nobel prizes for so many physicists. (See the discussion of positivism elsewhere in the present book.) Even some logical positivists and fellow-travelers softened their views to make room for meaningful theoretical terms; thus, Carl Hempel, a somewhat "lapsed" logical positivist, drew the following enticing picture which makes absurd the strict operationalist notion that concepts can each be reduced to a set of observation statements:

> Scientific systematization requires the establishment of diverse connections, by laws or theoretical principles, between different aspects of the empirical world, which are characterized by scientific concepts. Thus, the concepts of science are the knots in a network of systematic interrelationships in which laws and theoretical principles form the threads.... The more threads that converge upon, or issue from, a conceptual knot, the stronger will be its systematizing role, or its systematic import (Hempel, 1966, p. 94).

(It should be noted that there is another—perhaps even more attractive— account of theoretical terms, an account which realistics can embrace but which positivists have to avoid. See Newton-Smith, 1981, especially ch. 2. See also Chapter 2 in the present volume.)

Now there is another issue about the role of observation. It has often been held that it is the "neutral court" which adjudicates between rival scientific claims; together with this has usually gone the belief that science is actually built upon the foundation of indubitable observation. (The operationalist thesis discussed before concerned the *status* of theoretical concepts, not their *origin*.) The crucial critical work here is that of N. R. Hanson, whose *Patterns of Discovery* (1958) has taken on the status of a classic. Hanson was not the first to have said the things that he said; Wittgenstein used the key illustration that Hanson used, and even Dewey made much the same point. But it was Hanson's work that for some reason fired imaginations.

Hanson's thesis may be stated in one sentence: "The theory, hypothesis, or background knowledge held by an observer can influence in a major way what is observed." Or as he put it in a nice aphorism, "There is more to seeing than meets the eyeball" (Hanson, 1958, p. 7). Thus, in a famous psychological experiment, slides were made from cards selected from a normal deck, and these were projected for very short periods onto a screen in front of observers. All were correctly identified, except for a trick slide that had the color altered (for example, it might have been a black four of diamonds). Most commonly this slide was *seen* as a blur, or as a black suit (spades or clubs). A Hansonian interpretation is that there is an interaction between the visual stimulus and the observers' background knowledge ("diamonds are red"), so the final result is that a blur is observed.

Subsequent writers have drawn a variety of conclusions from Hanson's thesis of theory-laden perception (although it should be noted in passing that some special cases where it does not hold—such as optical illusions— have been discussed in the recent literature; see Fodor, 1984). For instance, there have been many who have taken it as supporting relativism—"there is no such thing as objective truth, for what observers take to be true depends upon the framework of knowledge and assumptions they bring with them". Sometimes an example is given that comes from Hanson himself: He imagined the astronomers Tycho Brahe and Johannes Kepler watching the dawn together; because they had different frameworks, one would see the sun moving above the horizon, while the other would see the earth rotating away to reveal the sun. However, a closer reading of Hanson provides no succor for such an extravagant relativism, for he explicitly acknowledged that *both* astronomers would agree that what they actually *observed* during the dawn was the sun increasing its relative distance above the Earth's eastern horizon (Ibid., p. 23). This acknowledgment is evidence that Hanson realized people with different frameworks have some views in common, views that can serve as the basis for further discussion and clarification of their respective positions— something a dedicated relativist has to deny.

A less extreme interpretation of Hanson, then, is that while we must be aware of the role played by our preconceptions, and while we have to abandon the view that observation is "neutral" and theory free, there is nothing to force us to the conclusion that we cannot decide between rival claims and, therefore, cannot arrive at consensus about which viewpoint (or which observations) seem to be most trustworthy under the prevailing circumstances. Israel Scheffler put it well:

> There is no evidence for a general incapacity to learn from contrary observations, no proof of a pre-established harmony between what we believe and what we see.... Our categorizations and expectations guide by orienting us selectively toward the future; they set us, in particular, to perceive in certain ways and not in others. Yet they do not blind us

to the unforeseen. They allow us to recognize what fails to match anticipation ... (Scheffler, 1967, p. 44).

2. Over the last few decades it has become increasingly clear that scientific theories are "underdetermined" by nature; that is, whatever evidence is available about nature, it is never sufficient to rule authoritatively between the merits of rival theories. Or to put it in yet another way, a variety of rival theories or hypotheses can always be constructed that are equally compatible with whatever finite body of evidence is currently available. (An implication of this, of course, is that we can never be certain that the particular theory we have accepted to account for the evidence is the correct one.) Recently, however, Laudan has pointed out that it must not be assumed that all the rival or alternative theories that are *logically possible* will be equally plausible—in other words, he cautions that the argument from underdetermination might be overblown (Laudan, 1990).

There are several issues here that are worthy of further comment (these are discussed at greater length in Phillips, 1987):

(a) The first point is illustrated by Nelson Goodman's notorious example of "grue and bleen" (Goodman, 1973). A large amount of observational evidence has accumulated over the age concerning the color of emeralds; all that have been studied thus far have been found to be green. It might be supposed, then, that this amounts to irrefutable evidence for the hypothesis "all emeralds are green". But the *very same* evidence also supports the hypothesis that "all emeralds are grue" (where "grue" is the name of a property such that an object is green up to a certain date, for instance the year 2000, and blue thereafter). The fanciful nature of this example is beside the point; it nicely illustrates the underdetermination of theory by available evidence, for it shows that a general theory ("emeralds are green—i.e., always have been, and always will be") necessarily goes beyond the finite evidence that is available ("the finite number of emeralds observed to date have been green"), thus leaving open the possibility that some ingenious scientist will come up with an alternative explanation for the very same finite set of data.

(b) A related issue here is that when new evidence turns up which necessitates that *some* accommodatory change has to be made in whatever theory is currently the favored one, there is *no one specific change that is necessitated*. Different scientists may change different portions of the theory—they are free to use their professional judgment and their creativity. It would be a mistake to interpret this as indicating that scientific theories are a matter of mere whim or individual taste; to stress that judgment is required is not to throw away all standards, it is just to stress that decisions cannot be made using some mechanical or algorithmic procedure. It is appropriate to point out here that John Stuart Mill had inklings of this point as long ago as the mid-nineteenth century; for, according to Hilary Putnam, Mill said

> that one cannot do science by slavishly following the rules of Mill's *Logic*. (There is no general method, Mill remarked, that will not give bad results "if conjoined with universal idiocy".) (Putnam, 1987, p. 73).

This general point is often made in terms of the "Duhem-Quine" thesis. Scientific theories, indeed vast areas of science, are interrelated; the image of science as a huge fishnet is a predominant one in much recent writing. It is this network as a whole, rather than little portions of it, that has to withstand the test of dealing with whatever evidence is gathered. Thus, it might appear that a piece of recalcitrant data offers a serious challenge to one particular section of the net, but the threat cannot be localized in this way; one scientist may react to the data by altering the "obvious" portion of the net, but others might want to preserve this piece and so might advocate changing some other portion of the net so as to accommodate the new information.

(c) It might even be the case that when some counter-evidence turns up, scientists might decide to make no accommodatory changes at all—a course of action (or rather, a course of inaction) that receives the blessing of the new philosophy of science. For one thing, it might well be the case that one of the auxiliary assumptions that have to be made in any piece of scientific work is faulty, and scientists can blame one or other of these rather than accept the counter-evidence at face value and be forced to change their net. In doing laboratory work, for example, it is often assumed that the chemical samples that are being used are pure, or that there were no temperature fluctuations, or that the testing equipment was reliable, or that an observer was unbiased, or ... (See Popper, 1985, ch. 10, for an early discussion of auxiliary hypotheses.)

On the other hand, scientists might ignore the counter-evidence in the hope that "something eventually will turn up that will explain it". It was a traditional tenet of methodology that a scientist must abandon a theory, no matter how attractive it might appear, once some counter-evidence became available. It now appears, however, that there are good reasons to suppose that it can be quite rational to adhere to the theory even under these adverse conditions. Paul Feyerabend has been the most forceful writer on this and related issues:

> The idea of a method that contains firm, unchanging, and absolutely binding principles for conducting the business of science gets into considerable difficulty when confronted with the results of historical research. We find, then, that there is not a single rule, however plausible, and however firmly grounded in epistemology, that is not violated at some time or other. It becomes evident that such violations are not accidental events.... On the contrary, we see they are necessary for progress (Feyerabend, 1970, pp. 21-22).

Even Popper, the arch-proponent of falsification, has stressed that negative or refuting evidence is never absolutely binding; the scientist has to make a methodological decision to *accept* the evidence as valid—and sometimes it is reasonable not to take this action. But, of course, Popper recommends that we adopt the rule that, in general, refuting evidence *be* accepted (see Popper, 1985, ch. 10). Imre Lakatos devised his "methodology of scientific research programs" in an alternative attempt to gauge when changes made in an ongoing research tradition were progressive or degenerative (Lakatos, 1972).

3. Perhaps the most famous feature of the new philosophy of science, however, has been its focus upon the dynamics of science. The process of scientific change has come under increasing investigation since Kuhn's work on scientific revolutions popularized the notion of "paradigm clashes". Science is not static; theories come and theories go, and new data accumulates and old findings are interpreted in new ways. As Newton-Smith put it, "viewed *sub specie eternitatis* scientists (even physical scientists) are a fickle lot. The history of science is a tale of multifarious shiftings of allegiance from theory to theory" (Newton-Smith, 1981, p. 3). And involved in all this is the question of the *rationality* of change—what justifies scientists in throwing out old ideas and accepting new ones? There has been much debate here, but little con-census—witness, for example, the work of Kuhn, Popper, Lakatos, Feyerabend, Toulmin, Laudan, and Newton-Smith (see previous citations, plus Laudan, 1977; and Newton-Smith, 1981). It will suffice to quote a brief passage from Popper to illustrate this major theme in the new post-positivist philosophy:

> I assert that continued growth is essential to the rational and empirical character of scientific knowledge; that if science ceases to grow it must lose that character. It is the way of its growth which makes science rational and empirical; the way, that is, in which scientists discriminate between available theories and choose the better one ... (Popper, 1968, p. 215).

Questions and Answers

There are some who have drawn a dangerous moral from the develop-ments just outlined. Science has fallen from its pedestal; and if no knowledge can be justified totally and unchallengeably, then none can be disbarred. The rocky road to relativism is embarked upon. But it is possible to retain a hopeful outlook, and even to relish the challenge that this new picture of science presents. It is here that we can obtain succor from the fields of program evaluation and action research in the applied social sciences. Investigators here do not lose heart, yet they are faced with a reality which (we now realize) closely parallels that of "pure" scientists;

and some even thrive on the uncertainties of their field. The ideal that is embraced seems to be this: Seekers after enlightenment in any field do the best that they can; they honestly seek evidence, they critically scrutinize it, they are (relatively) open to alternative viewpoints, they take criticism (fairly) seriously and try to profit from it, they play their hunches, they stick to their guns, but they also have a sense of when it is time to quit. It may be a dirty and hard and uncertain game, but with no fixed algorithms to determine progress, it is the only game in town.

Although to the present author this seems a modest, non-doctrinaire, unsurprising, and eminently reasonable position, there are many who feel uneasy and who continue to raise questions about it. So it might be fruitful to grapple with some of these directly.

Question 1: In what sense is the new position that has been outlined above "post-positivistic"? Isn't it merely a weaker form of positivism in disguise? It may have come *after* positivism, and that is the only reason for calling it "post"-positivism.

Answer: In no sense is the new philosophy of science—broad and ill-defined though it is—closely akin to positivism (or, more especially, to the most notorious form of positivism, logical positivism). Logical positivism became discredited in the years immediately following the end of the Second World War; few if any philosophers these days subscribe to its core tenet, the "verifiability criterion of meaning", according to which a statement is meaningful only if it is verifiable in terms of sense experience (excepting logico-mathematical propositions). (For more discussion of this topic, see Chapters 2 and 7.) As was pointed out earlier, one of the serious problems associated with the use of this principle in science was that it made theoretical terms meaningless, for the fact is that many theoretical entities cannot be verified in terms of sense experience; but there are few today who would want to argue that the discourse of sub-atomic particle physicists or of black-hole theorists is meaningless! The fact of the matter is that the logical positivists were, by and large, anti-realists who held—or came close to holding—some form of instrumentalism.

Question 2: Aren't contemporary post-positivists clinging to an old and outmoded realist paradigm?

Answer: This question embodies a serious confusion. The old positivist view was anti-realist; as explained in the previous answer, the logical positivists (on the whole) denied the reality of theoretical entities, and indeed claimed that talk of such entities was literally meaningless (some took refuge in a position about theories similar to the one cited earlier from Hempel). Modern realism is a recent, post-positivistic development. Furthermore, there is little consensus within the philosophical community; whether or not realism is viable is a hotly-debated topic—there are many contemporary philosophers for it, but there are many against it. (A leading post-positivistic anti-realist is Bas van Fraassen, 1980; but his *grounds* for anti-realism are not those of the logical positivists.) There is even controversy about the precise definition of realism: Arthur Fine has written:

> Given the diverse array of philosophical positions that have sought the "realist" label, it is probably not possible to give a sketch of realism that will encompass them all. Indeed, it may be hopeless to try, even, to capture the essential features of realism (Fine, 1987, p. 359).

There is a nice passage in Hilary Putnam's "Paul Carus Lectures" that highlights these complexities:

> Thus, it is clear that the name "Realism" can be claimed by or given to at least two very different philosophical attitudes (and, in fact, to many). The philosopher who claims that only scientific objects "really exist" and that much, if not all, of the commonsense world is mere "projection" claims to be a realist, but so does the philosopher who insists that there *really are* chairs and ice cubes ... and these two attitudes, these two images of the world can lead to and have led to many different programs for philosophy (Putnam, 1987, p. 4).

Question 3: Well, old or new, many influential post-positivists are realists. Aren't they overlooking the fact that multiple realities exist, and aren't they overlooking the well-known fact that each society *constructs* its own reality? If you accept these two points, you cannot be a realist! Consider merely one example; Egon Guba has written that social scientists are studying phenomena that are

> *social* in nature. There is no need to posit a natural state-of-affairs and a natural set of laws for phenomena that are socially invented—I shall say socially constructed—in people's minds. I suggest ... an ontology that is relativist in nature. It begins with the premise that all social realities are constructed and shared through well-understood socialization processes. It is this socialized sharing that gives these constructions their apparent reality ... (Guba, 1990, p. 89).

Answer: There are several important issues here, some of which were touched upon in the earlier discussion. (See also the discussion in Bunge, 1992, section 9.)

(i) In the first place, this question seems inspired by an extreme reading of Kuhn—the view that all of us are trapped within some particular paradigm, and that we cannot converse rationally with those in other paradigms because our beliefs are incommensurable. Even the later Kuhn—the Kuhn of *The Essential Tension*—did not accept this extreme relativism. (Furthermore, such relativism seems contradicted by everyday experience within science. Freudians do understand—but of course disagree with—Skinnerians, and neo-Marxist social scientists understand colleagues of more conservative bent, and vice versa.)

(ii) Second, there are a number of things that get run together illicitly in discussions about "reality". First, there is a simple confusion here between, on the one hand, the fact that different people and different societies have different views about what is real (a fact that seems undeniable), and on the other hand the issue of whether or not we can know which of these views is the correct one (or, indeed, whether there is a correct one at all). From the fact that we might not be able to reach agreement (an epistemological matter), it does not follow that there is more than one "reality" (an ontological matter). Second, it is clear that on some issues what is *regarded or judged* to be "real" depends upon the conceptual apparatus that is available—one group, for example, may only have concepts or classificatory schemes that recognize three types of snow, whilst a different group might make distinctions between ten types, and the result will be that the two groups differ with respect to the question "How many types of snow exist?"

Now, the relativist seems to be committed to the view that *all* such differing views are correct—i.e., there *really are* three types of snow and ten types of snow; whereas the realist is only committed to the minimal (and more informative) view that something, "snow", really exists although different groups conceptualize it differently. The realist (*qua realist*) is not forced to say which of these conceptualizations is "correct", indeed it is a viable position for the realist to say that it is a silly question to ask which conceptualization is correct, for different conceptualizations do different work in different communities.

There is, however, another type of situation where the realist will want to take a stronger stand. This is the (perhaps rare) situation where different groups or different individuals are using terms in the same sense. To make this a little more precise: Suppose that one social group believes that "X is the case", and another group believes—in the very same sense of X—that "not-X is the case". The realist holds that both of these views cannot be correct, although of course some people *believe* one or the other of these to be true; either it is the case that X, or not-X, but not both. (The realist does not have to believe that we can always settle which of these views, X or not-X, is true; the issue is whether both or at best only one *can* be true.) The relativist has to hold that, in this situation too, there are multiple realities—that reality is both X and not-X—for if the relativist does not hold this, then his or her position dissolves into the realist position. Stated thus boldly, it can be seen that the relativist case here hinges on obscuring the distinction between "what people believe to be true" and "what really is true, whether or not we can determine this truth at the moment". (There are many other problems with relativism; see Siegel, 1987.)

(iii) Third, it is important to note that this issue dividing realists from relativists is not the same as the issue (discussed earlier) that separates realists from anti-realists; the second of these is the issue (broadly speaking) of the reality or otherwise of theoretical entities (that is, the status of the entities referred to in such theories as those found in the field of particle physics). There is, as might be expected in so complex a field, a tendency for the neophyte to run these two sets of issues together! (See, for the second of the two issues mentioned, Leplin, 1984.)

(iv) Finally, this third question raises the very important matter of the social construction of reality, touched upon briefly earlier. Certainly there is nothing in post-positivism, *per se*, that requires denying that societies determine many of the things that are to count as real for their members; what things are *taken* to be real depends upon the concepts and classifications available within those societies. Thus, a "primitive" society may define certain spirits as being real, and the members of that society might accept them as real and act accordingly. A similar thing certainly happens in our own society, and not just with spirits. All a post-positivist would want to insist upon is that these matters can be open to research: We can inquire into the beliefs of a society, how they came about, what are their effects, and what is the status of the evidence that is offered in support of the truth of the beliefs. And we can get these matters right or wrong— we can get our descriptions of these beliefs right or wrong, or we can be right or make mistakes about their origins or their effects. It simply does not follow from the fact of the social construction of reality that scientific inquiry becomes impossible, or that we have to become relativists. And certainly, it does not follow from the fact that a tribe of headhunters socially determines its own reality, that we thereby have to *accept* that reality as *true*. What is true—if we have done our research properly—is that the members of that tribe actually do *believe* in their own realities. But that is a different issue, one that raises no great problem of principle for post-positivists. Thus, Popper, one of the major post-positivists (and the man who claimed to have been the person who killed positivism), stressed that his philosophy "assumes a physical world in which we act", although he added that we may not know very much about it. But, he wrote, it was also necessary to "assume a social world, populated by other people, about whose goals we know something (often not very much), and, furthermore, social institutions. These social institutions determine the peculiarly social character of our social environment" (Popper, 1976, p. 103). Popper includes laws and customs among "institutions".

Question 4: Given the acceptance by post-positivists of Hanson's thesis concerning the theory-ladenness of perception, and given the general non-foundationalist tenor that nothing can be considered as absolutely certain, and so forth, does it not follow that post-positivists have to abandon the notion of objectivity? Hasn't it been stripped of any meaning that it might have had?

Answer: Certainly not! The notion of objectivity, like the notion of truth, is a regulative ideal that underlies all inquiry. (For further discussion of this issue, see Chapter 5.) If we abandon such notions, it is not sensible to make inquiries at all. For if a sloppy inquiry is as acceptable as a careful one, and if any inquiry that is careless about evidence is as acceptable as an inquiry that has taken pains to be precise and unbiased, then there is no need to inquire—we might as well accept, without further fuss, any old view that tickles our fancy.

Now, it is true that the fact that an inquiry is objective does not guarantee its truth—it was shown earlier that *nothing* can guarantee that we have reached the truth. Perhaps an analogy will help to clarify matters: Consider two firms who manufacture radios; one is proud of its workmanship and backs its products with a strong guarantee; while the other firm is after a quick profit, practises shoddy workmanship, and does not offer any warranty to the buyer. A consumer would be unwise to purchase the latter's product, but nevertheless it is clearly understood that the first firm's guarantee does not absolutely mean that the radio will not break down. The fact that this situation exists is not taken by consumers as invalidating the notion of a warranty, nor is it seen as making each purchase equally wise. And the very same situation exists in science.

The Popperian account of objectivity is widely, though not universally, accepted by post-positivists. The following sentences capture the essence of his approach:

> What may be described as scientific objectivity is based solely upon a critical tradition which, despite resistance, often makes it possible to criticize a dominant dogma. To put it another way, the objectivity of science is not a matter of the individual scientists but rather the social result of their mutual criticism, of the friendly-hostile division of labour among scientists, of their co-operation and also of their competition. For this reason, it depends, in part, upon a number of social and political circumstances which make criticism possible (Popper, p. 95).

Conclusions

It can be seen from the foregoing that post-positivism is a broad, complex, and dynamic approach to understanding the nature of science. There is little unanimity on important issues among its "adherents" (if people can be said to adhere to so amorphous a position)—but this is a healthy feature, and not a weakness. Paul Feyerabend wrote, more than a quarter-century ago, that unanimity of opinion may be fitting for some church, or for the followers of a tyrant, but it is most unfitting for science (Feyerabend, 1970, p. 33).

The danger to post-positivism comes not from internal dissension, but from outside—from those who draw false, and often over-simple, conclusions from some of the very same developments that have produced post-positivism itself.

* Reprinted by permission of Sage Publications Inc. from Guba, E. (ed.), *The Paradigm Dialog*, "Postpositivistic Science." by D. C. Phillips. © 1990, Sage Publications Inc.

References

Bunge, Mario (1992). A critical examination of the new sociology of science: Part 2. *Philosophy of the Social Sciences*, **22**, 1, 46-76.

Dewey, John (1966). *Logic: the Theory of Inquiry*. NY: Holt, Rinehart & Winston.

Feyerabend, P. (1970). Against method. In M. Radner and S. Winokur, (Eds.), *Analyses of Theories and Methods of Physics and Psychology*. Minneapolis: University of Minnesota Press.

Fine, A. (1987). And not anti-realism either. Reprinted in J. Kourany, (Ed.), *Scientific Knowledge*. Belmont, CA: Wadsworth.

Fodor, J. (1984). Observation reconsidered. *Philosophy of Science*, **51**, 1, 23-44.

Goodman, N. (1973). *Fact, Fiction and Forecast*. Indianapolis: Bobbs-Merrill.

Goodman, N. and Elgin, C. Z. (1988). *Reconceptions in Philosophy*. Indianapolis: Hackett.

Guba, Egon (1990). Subjectivity and objectivity. In E. Eisner and A. Peshkin (Eds.), *Qualitative Inquiry in Education*. NY: Teachers College Press.

Hanson, N. R. (1958). *Patterns of Discovery*. Cambridge: Cambridge University Press.

Hempel, C. (1966). *Philosophy of Natural Science*. Englewood Cliffs, NJ: Prentice Hall.

Lakatos, I. (1972). In I. Lakatos and A. Musgrave (Eds.), *Criticism and the Growth of Knowledge*. Cambridge: Cambridge University Press.

Laudan, L. (1977). *Progress and Its Problems*. Berkeley: University of California Press.

Laudan, L. (1990). Demystifying underdetermination. In C. Wade Savage (Ed.), *Scientific Theories*. Minnesota Studies in Philosophy of Science, XIV. Minneapolis, MN: University of Minnesota Press.

Leplin, J. (Ed.) (1984). *Scientific Realism*. Berkeley, University of California Press.

Newton-Smith, W. (1981). *The Rationality of Science*. London and Boston: Routledge.

Phillips, D. C. (1987). *Philosophy, Science, and Social Inquiry*. Oxford and NY: Pergamon Press.

Popper, K. (1968). *Conjectures and Refutations*. NY: Harper.

Popper, K. (1976). The logic of the social sciences. In T. Adorno *et al.*, *The Positivist Dispute in German Sociology*. NY: Harper Torchbooks.

Popper, K. (1985). In D. Miller (Ed.), *Popper Selections*. Princeton, NJ: Princeton University Press.

Putnam, H. (1987). *The Many Faces of Realism*. La Salle, IL: Open Court.

Scheffler, I. (1967). *Science and Subjectivity*. NY: Bobbs-Merrill.

Siegel, H. (1987). *Relativism Refuted*. Dordrecht, The Netherlands: Reidel.

van Fraassen, B. (1980). *The Scientific Image*. Oxford: Oxford University Press.

5

Objectivity and Subjectivity *

A PERSON does not have to read very widely in the contemporary methodological or theoretical literature pertaining to research in the "pure" and "applied" social sciences, in order to discover that objectivity is dead. When the term happens to be used, it is likely to be set in scare-marks— "objectivity"—to bring out the point that a dodo-like entity is being discussed. Or, "there is no such thing", authors confidently state, unmindful of the fact that if they are right, then the reader does not have to break into a sweat—because if there is no such thing as objectivity, then the view that there is no such thing is itself not objective. But, then, if this view is the subjective judgment of a particular author, readers are entitled to prefer their own subjective viewpoint—which, of course, might be that objectivity is *not* dead!

A couple of illustrations should suffice to set the stage; the first is from Gunnar Myrdal:

> The ethos of social science is the search for "objective" truth. The faith of the student is his conviction that truth is wholesome and that illusions are damaging, especially opportunistic ones. He seeks "realism", a term which in one of its meanings denotes an "objective" view of reality.... How can a biased view be avoided? (Myrdal, 1969, p. 3).

After an interesting discussion of the deep-seated sources of bias and opportunism in belief, Myrdal suggests that some techniques exist to help achieve at least a degree of objectivity.

A second example comes from the sociologist Robert Nisbet writing in 1970; even then objectivity was under severe attack, a phenomenon that Nisbet regarded as "unbelievable" and potentially fatal to the social sciences. He pointed out that many were arguing "that objectivity of inquiry is not even a proper end of the social sciences" (Nisbet, 1974, p. 16), and that these people also argued that an

> objective understanding of social behavior is impossible; such understanding will always be limited by the political, or ethnic, or social and economic position one occupies in the social order. Its embedded values must become the values of the investigator and, hence, the bias of his conclusions. There is nothing that can be done about this (Ibid., p. 17).

These views did not die out during the seventies. Thus, to cite merely one example, in 1986 on the occasion of receiving an honorary doctorate overseas, the prominent American educational researcher, Elliot Eisner, stated that

> What I have even more quarrel with is the view that a scientifically acceptable research method is "objective" or value-free, that it harbors no particular point of view. All methods and forms of representation are partial ... (Eisner, 1986, p. 15).

It is not intended that the present chapter will develop into a paradoxical discussion of the self-referential puzzles generated by such attacks on objectivity. But it is the intent, at the outset of the inquiry, to point out the oddity of trying to write an essay for an academic volume—a paradigm case of an exercise in the marshaling of objective considerations—if, indeed, there is no escape from subjectivity. It would be too Quixotic; and it would be better to take the bull by the horns and proceed by using rhetoric (much as is being done now), or special pleading, or appeals to the readers' baser motives.

Believing the task *not* to be Quixotic, the present author is inspired to inquire into the intellectual reasons for objectivity sinking into such disrepute, and to investigate whether—as an ideal—it deserves the fate that has befallen it. (Nisbet focused his discussion on the *political*, and not the *intellectual*, grounds of the attack on objectivity.) The issues, then, are these: Why is it doubted that research can be objective, and are these doubts reasonable? What notion of objectivity is involved here? Are critics correct in suggesting that it is naive to hold objectivity as a goal for social inquiry? If all views are subjective, are they all on a par, or are some more subjective than others? (The closely related issue of the precise role of value judgments in the social sciences is pursued in Chapter 10.)

One further point remains to be made in this prelude. It is clear that—despite the attacks—in normal parlance the term "objective" is commendatory, whilst "subjective" carries negative connotations. After all, the "person in the street" does not think it is a good thing for a judge, a physicist, an anthropologist, or a professor, to be subjective. It is even worse to be biased—this latter term being sometimes used to mark the contrast with objectivity. Myrdal seems to use "bias" in this way throughout his book (Myrdal, 1969). (Such negative evaluations are likely to change over time, of course, if it turns out that objectivity is dead, and that there is no option but to be subjective.) In what follows, the discussion will attempt to avoid using the terms in a judgmental way—at least until it has been established, objectively, that either term can justifiably be so used.

The Intellectual Roots of the Attack on Objectivity

The fields of philosophy of science and epistemology have undergone something of a revolution in recent decades. The traditional foundationalist or justificationist approach to epistemology has largely been abandoned in favor of a non-foundationalist approach; in philosophy of science, the work of Popper, closely followed by that of Kuhn, Hanson, Feyerabend and Lakatos, has been the center of much debate (see the discussion of these matters in Chapter 4). Acting under these influences, some individuals have moved in the direction of relativism (although this is not what had been intended by most of the individuals just mentioned). But the very same forces—supplemented by one or two others—have also given rise to the strong attack on objectivity. It will be as well to discuss the major influences in turn.

(a) Non-foundationalist Epistemology

Traditional epistemologies, whether of rationalist or empiricist persuasion, were foundationalist or justificationist in the sense that they regarded knowledge as being built upon (or justified in terms of) some solid and unchallengeable foundation. It was the presence of this solid foundation that served as the justification for the knowledge claims that were made. Where the traditional schools of epistemology fell out with each other was over the issue of what, precisely, constituted this foundation. Empiricists (like Locke, Berkeley and Hume) saw the foundation as being human experience—sense impressions or some such item. Rationalists (like Descartes) claimed it was human reason; the starting place for the construction of knowledge (Descartes termed it the "Archimedian point") was to be those beliefs that appeared indubitable after scrutiny in the light of reason.

In the twentieth century there has been a steady erosion of foundationalism of both varieties. It is now recognized that there is no absolutely secure starting point for knowledge; nothing is known with such certainty that all possibility of future revision is removed. All knowledge is tentative. Karl Popper is probably the best known advocate of this newer perspective, but he is not, by far, a solitary figure. In his words:

> The question about the sources of our knowledge ... has always been asked in the spirit of: "What are the best sources of our knowledge—the most reliable ones, those which will not lead us into error, and those to which we can and must turn, in case of doubt, as the last court of appeal?" I propose to assume, instead, that no such ideal sources exist—no more than ideal rules—and that *all* "sources" are liable to lead us into error at times. And I propose to replace, therefore, the question of the sources of our knowledge by the entirely different question: *"How can we hope to detect and eliminate error?"* (Popper, 1968, p. 25).

It is important to note that abandonment of the notion that knowledge is built on an unshakeable foundation does not mean that the traditional notion of truth has been abandoned. Popper constantly reminds his readers that truth is an essential "regulative ideal". He offers this nice image:

> The status of truth in the objective sense, as correspondence to the facts, and its role as a regulative principle, may be compared to that of a mountain peak which is permanently, or almost permanently, wrapped in clouds. The climber may not merely have difficulties in getting there—he may not know when he gets there, because he may be unable to distinguish, in the clouds, between the main summit and some subsidiary peak. Yet this does not affect the objective existence of the summit.... The very idea of error, or of doubt ... implies the idea of an objective truth which we may fail to reach (Ibid., p. 226).

It makes little sense to search for a summit if you do not believe that a summit exists; and it makes little sense to try to understand some situation if you believe that *any* story about that situation is as good as any other. In this latter case, to inquire is to waste one's energy—one might as well have just invented any old story. But if some stories are regarded as being better than others, then this belief, upon unpacking, will be found to presuppose the notion of truth as a regulative ideal.

The crucial point for the present discussion is that it does not follow from any of these recent developments in epistemology that the notion of objectivity has been undermined. This "unbelievable consequence" would only follow if objectivity were equated with certainty. This is to say that the following argument is a *non sequitur*, at least until some further premise is added to link the antecedent to the consequent: "If no knowledge is certain, then there is no possibility for any viewpoint to be objective." (It might be objected here that Popper himself referred to the real existence of his cloud-covered mountain top, and he said it might never be possible to know that one had reached it—showing that attainment of "objective truth" might not be possible. But it is crucial to note that here he was not discussing "objectivity", he was discussing "truth"; certainly, Popper was speaking for most of us when he stressed that we may never know when—and if—we have stumbled across the truth. When we abandon foundationalism, we abandon the assurance that we can know when we have reached the truth; but, as Popper's story also illustrates, we do not have to abandon the *notion* of truth or the quest for it, and we do not abandon the view that some types of inquiries are better than others.)

Leaving aside the notion of truth, and returning to the issue of the objectivity of inquiries: There is good reason to hold that certainty and objectivity should not be linked. For if they were, all human knowledge would thereby become subjective (for no knowledge is certain), and this would have the effect of washing out the following vital distinction: Consider two researchers in a classroom in which a science teacher has been conducting a lesson on a difficult topic. One researcher claims to have noticed that the students did not understand the material, but the only evidence she gives is that "I did not understand the material myself"; the other social scientist also claims that the students did not learn, but offers by way of evidence the test scores of the students, a videotape of the classroom showing the puzzled demeanor of the students, and interview protocols which a panel of readers agree show that a random sample of the students were rather confused about the topic. The new epistemology would have us recognize that neither of these two views is absolutely certain; but it is not the consequence of the new non-foundationalist epistemology that we would have to judge both views as being equally "subjective". For it is evident that one of the researchers was greatly influenced by her own personal reactions to the lesson, and this unduly affected how she perceived the classroom ("unduly" signifying here that this researcher's personal biases or inclinations were not, in this situation, epistemically relevant—for the issue under study was: what was happening in the *classroom*). In contrast, the other social scientist had taken pains to marshal epistemically relevant evidence (even if that evidence was not absolutely incorrigible). In a straightforward and non-troublesome sense, the second researcher's opinion would be regarded by all normal users of the English language as being more objective (even if the opinion later turned out to be wrong).

This example suggests the following hypothesis: "Objective" seems to be a label that we apply to inquiries that meet certain procedural standards, but objectivity does not *guarantee* that the results of inquiries have any certainty. (It implies that the inquiries so labeled are free of gross defects, and this should be of some comfort—just as a consumer prefers to buy an item that has met rigorous inspection standards, although this does not absolutely insure that it will not break down.) The other side of the coin is that a biased, bigoted person who jumps to some subjective conclusion about, say, a political candidate who happens to be of different ethnicity, may not always be wrong. His or her biased judgment may turn out to be true. Thus the narrow-minded black Democrat who had no time for Richard Nixon, and who claimed he would be a dishonest President, nevertheless turned out to be right. (Just as a consumer who purchases a shoddy piece of merchandise occasionally "lucks out" and never has any trouble with it.) Or, to use a less loaded example but one that is historically accurate, in its heyday Newtonian physics was supported by a wealth of objective evidence, that is, evidence that was free from personal "contamination" and which was, in large part, accepted by an international community the members of which had subjected it to critical scrutiny and cross-check. Nevertheless, in our day, evidence has accumulated that makes it difficult to maintain the view that the Newtonian framework is anything but a reasonably good approximation to the truth (but not as good, for example, as the Einsteinian framework, which itself is probably not absolutely true). Thus, those scientists of earlier times who rejected Newton for their own personal (subjective) reasons turned out to have been right in doing so, although we can say that they were not *rationally justified* in so doing.

To put the point pithily, neither subjectivity nor objectivity has an exclusive stranglehold on truth. But why, then, should objectivity be preferred if it is not guaranteed to lead to the truth? The answer is implied in the discussion above: At any one time, the viewpoint that is the most objective is the one that currently is the most *warranted* or *rational*— to deny this is to deny that there is any significant difference between the warrants for the views of the two classroom researchers in the earlier example. If we give up this distinction, if we hold that a biased or personally loaded viewpoint is as good as a viewpoint supported by carefully gathered evidence, we are undermining the very point of human inquiry. (This is why Nisbet, for example, was so concerned.) If a shoddy inquiry is to be trusted as much as a careful one, then it is pointless to inquire carefully. The philosopher Ernest Nagel put it well:

> ... those attacks on the notion that scientific inquiry can be objective are tantamount to an endorsement of the view that the grounds on which conclusions in the sciences are accepted are at bottom no better than are the grounds on which superstitious beliefs are adopted. Those attacks may therefore ... justify any doctrine, no matter how unwarranted it may be ... (Nagel, 1979, p. 85).

In the light of these remarks, it would seem that the educational researcher Elliot Eisner (used as an example earlier) was both right and wrong when he stated that "To hold that our conceptions of reality are true or objective to the extent that they are isomorphic with reality is to embrace a hopeless correspondence theory of truth ..." (Eisner, 1979, p. 214). He was right to criticize the identification of objectivity with "isomorphic with reality"; however, he was wrong to treat "objective" and "true" as synonyms, and he was wrong to suggest that non-foundationalism leads to the rejection of the correspondence theory of truth. It is worth commenting here, to forestall a philosophical misunderstanding, that the correspondence theory of truth is firmly entrenched in contemporary philosophy, and it is supported by weighty—but not by absolutely conclusive—considerations. Eisner runs together two issues that philosophers keep separate for good reasons: The first of these issues is concerned with what account best clarifies the *meaning* of the term "truth", and it is here that the correspondence theory is alive and well, as Popper's story of the cloudy mountain illustrates; the second issue is what *test* or *criterion* we can rely upon in order to judge if a theory actually *is* isomorphic with reality. On this second matter, non-foundationalists would answer that there is *no* such test or criterion, as once again Popper's allegory illustrates. Eisner and others have reasoned backwards, invalidly, from the negative response to the second issue, to a negative judgment about the first. (A similar confusion bedevilled critics of William James's work. See D. C. Phillips, 1984.)

(b) Hansonism

It is now widely accepted that observation is always theory-laden. Due largely to the work of N. R. Hanson (although Wittgenstein and Popper could claim priority), researchers are aware that when they make observations they cannot argue that these are objective in the sense of being "pure", free from the influence of background theories or hypotheses or personal hopes and desires. (Hanson's work, and its general impact—and the ways in which it has been misinterpreted—is discussed in Phillips, 1987; see also Chapter 4.) Qualitative researcher John Ratcliffe was reflecting this view when he wrote "most research methodologists are now aware that *all* data are theory-, method-, and measurement- dependent" (Ratcliffe, 1983, p. 148). And he went on to turn this point into a thinly-veiled attack on objectivity: "That is, 'facts' are determined by the theories and methods that generate their collection; indeed, theories and methods *create* the facts" (Ibid.). If the observer's prior theoretical commitments do, indeed, determine what he or she sees as being the facts of a situation, and if there can be no criticism of one observer's results by others holding different theoretical backgrounds, then subjectivity or at least some form of relativism would seem to reign supreme.

It is here that the distinction between low-level and higher-level observation becomes relevant. The distinction is similar to the one that research psychologists have in mind when they speak of "high inference" and "low inference" variables. While observation is never theory-free, it does not follow that many (or most) observations are such that people from a wide variety of quite different theoretical frames will be in total disagreement about the facts of the case. There are many situations where all frameworks are likely to lead to the same results—they overlap, as it were. This is particularly so in cases of low level observations, such as "there is a patch of red", or "the object on the left is heavier". Even people who do not share the same language can agree on such matters, for the only problem they face is the relatively trivial one of translation. Thus, my Korean students might not understand when I speak of "a patch of red", but with the help of a bilingual dictionary they can quickly come to comprehend, and to agree with me. Or, to take an example from the philosopher Hilary Putnam, it may well be the case that there are different logical systems that may lead to different answers being given to the question: How many objects are here? Putnam shows that, in the cases he considers, one group might answer three, and another group answer seven. It does not make sense, Putnam argues, to ask how many objects there *really* are. And, of course, he is right—the answer you give depends upon how you count, and what you regard as objects; in other words, it depends upon the rules of counting and classification that you use. But the point is, there is no *pernicious* subjectivity here, a conclusion Putnam apparently endorses; *everyone* can agree that, if you use one system there are—objectively—three objects, and if you use the other convention, the answer is seven. (See Putnam, 1987, pp. 18-20.)

To put it in a nutshell, relatively speaking low-level observation is high in objectivity, in the sense that the reports of my observations transcend the merely personal or subjective. My observations are open for cross-check, testing, and criticism by other inquirers, even if I use a different set of conventions from these colleagues. Furthermore, it is important to stress that there is nothing in Hanson to suggest that people with beliefs that differ from my own are *bound* to disagree with me about such observations. Contrary to what some radical Hansonists claim, there is no evidence that people with markedly different theoretical frames—for example, Freudians and behaviorists—actually see different things at the basic or low inference level being discussed here. They might notice—or fail to notice—different things, but when these are brought to their attention they agree about what they have seen. Of course, they might still disagree about the significance of what they have observed, but this is not a point under contention in the present context.

Even Hanson's famous claim that the astronomers Tycho Brahe and Johannes Kepler would see different things while watching the dawn, is a claim that can be recast to support the point being made here (Hanson, 1965, ch. 1, *passim*; but see particularly the concession made at the bottom of p. 23). Both scientists would agree that the sun was moving higher in the sky relative to the horizon—a point Hanson acknowledges; but of course Tycho would interpret this as the sun moving, while Kepler would regard it as a case of the earth rotating away from the sun. Their disagreement is spectacular, and Hansonists get good mileage from it, but what gets obscured is the agreement of the two men at the "low inference" level. Ernest Nagel has made a similar point, using a different example:

> ... it is simply not true that every theory has its own observation terms, none of which is also an observation term belonging to any other theory. For example, at least some of the terms employed in recording the observations that may be made to test Newton's corpuscular theory of light (such terms as "prism", "color", and "shadow"), underwent no recognizable changes in meaning when they came to be used to describe observations made in testing Fresnel's wave theory of light. But if this is so, the observation statements used to test a theory are not necessarily biased antecedently in favor of or against a theory; and in consequence, a decision between two competing theories need not express only our "subjective wishes", but may be made in the light of the available evidence (Nagel, 1979, p. 93).

If, however, the results of observation are couched in abstract theoretical terms—in "high inference" terms—then there might well be disagreement or misunderstanding. Consider the following example: Most people, whether Freudians or behaviorists, Republicans or Democrats, Americans or Australians or Koreans, deists or atheists, astrologers or astronomers, would agree upon a visit to a classroom that they saw a teacher working with a particular number of pupils. They also probably would agree with the low inference observation that at a certain stage in the lesson the teacher asked one pupil a series of questions. They might not all agree, however, with the higher inference observation that at this point the teacher was forcing the pupil to do some high-order cognitive task involving Piagetian abstract reasoning. (Here it is clear that the distinction between observation and inference or conclusion is becoming blurred.) To get all the observers to agree with *this* observation—and more to the point, to get them to be able to critically evaluate (which is the heart of objectivity)—more than mere translation into a native tongue would be required. To be able to discuss, to criticize, to evaluate warrants, the observers would all have to share—at least for purposes of discussion and communication—the same theoretical framework (this is what Hanson seemed to have in mind when he wrote of "theory-laden perception"). And it is worth noting, in passing, that even if they all did have the same framework, it is not certain that they would necessarily agree—for some might judge that the Piagetian categorization of the pupil's task was erroneous. (Similarity of framework is a guarantee—at best—of communication, but not of much else.)

The moral of the example is this: Just because, on some accounts, the more abstract description is "less objective" in the sense that it is less "pure" and is more "contaminated" by theory, it does not follow that there is no hope for observers to enter into mutual and fruitful discussion, criticism, and evaluation. For at a lower level of abstraction there might well be full overlap of categories and terminology (and thus there is the possibility of a higher degree of objectivity), and this more objective low inference observation would serve both as a constraint on the nature of the abstract accounts that could be put forward, and as a springboard for critical evaluation. And there is always the possibility that the observers can share, even if only on a temporary basis, each other's frameworks— as in the "three versus seven objects" example from Putnam.

Israel Scheffler seems to have had something like this in mind when he stated that though none of the statements we assert

can be *guaranteed* to be an absolutely reliable link to reality does not mean that we are free to assert any statements at will, provided only that they cohere. That the statement "There's a horse" cannot be rendered theoretically certain does not permit me to call anything a horse....

Scheffler points out that language offers constraints on what is to count as a horse (just as, in the earlier examples, it provided constraints on what is to count as a patch of red and what is to count as a pupil answering a question), and "such constraints generate credibility claims which enter my reckoning critically as I survey my system of beliefs" (Scheffler, 1967, p. 119). In short, then, Hanson has pointed to a problem that ought to be in the forefront of the minds of observers, but in pointing out the theory-laden nature of high inference observations he has not offered grounds for abandonment of the notion of objectivity.

There is a further consideration that strengthens this optimistic conclusion. In the earlier discussion the point was made that the term "objective" is used more or less as a seal of approval, marking the fact that an inquiry or conclusion meets certain quality standards. There are poor inquiries, infected with personal biases, and there are more worthy inquiries where the warrants that are offered are pertinent and have been subjected to critical scrutiny. The same situation exists with respect to observations. There are certain well-documented factors that influence observers, and which can make their work less credible. (In social science terminology, they can be spoken of as "threats to the validity" of observational or qualitative work.) For example, it is known that observers are prone to misjudge frequencies of occurrence of events they are watching, unless they use some quantitative scoring; and they are prone to be over-influenced by positive instances, and under-influenced by negative instances. (The significance of these factors is discussed in Phillips, 1987; see also Chapter 8.) Thus, the conclusions reached by a shoddy observer who has not taken account of these factors, would be properly judged by the research community as being less objective than the conclusions reached by a more careful person. Once again, objectivity is seen to be a vital notion, and its abandonment would be fatal—as Nisbet realized— for the integrity of the research endeavor.

(c) The Myth of "the More the Merrier"

In an influential essay (Ernest House, for example, discusses it admiringly and in some depth; see House, 1980, pp. 86ff), Michael Scriven points out that sometimes objectivity is thought about in terms of the number of inquirers or observers: Data that only one person has been able to collect is regarded as subjective and dubious, but there is usually a more favorable judgment when a number of people have been involved (Scriven, 1972). Scriven argues, however, that quality and numbers of investigators do not always go together. Thus he distinguishes between qualitative objectivity, where the data are of high quality (no matter how many observers or inquirers were involved), and quantitative objectivity where more than one person has replicated the findings (which does not guarantee veracity). Scriven writes of the two types of objectivity:

> Now it would certainly be delightful if these two senses coincided, so that all reports of personal experience, for example, were less reliable than all reports of events witnessed by a large number of people. But as one thinks of the reliability of reports about felt pain or perceived size, on the one hand, and reports about the achievements of stage magicians and mentalists on the other, one would not find this coincidence impressive (Ibid., pp. 95-96).

Scriven's points are crucial; he has shown that it is untenable to give an account of objectivity solely in terms of group consensus—qualitative objectivity is not reducible to quantitative. Thus the audience consensus that a magician has made a woman levitate freely in the air, and the group consensus that the world is flat, are objective views in the quantitative sense only, that is, those things are what the groups concerned are agreed upon. But the consensus is *only* that; and the agreement does not mean that the views concerned are correct, or warranted, or that they have been reached in a way that has avoided sources of bias and distortion. And yet the numbers of observers remains a crucial factor in many influential accounts of objectivity. Fred Kerlinger, for example, in his widely used textbook on behavioral research, refers to an "objective procedure" as "one in which agreement among observers is at a maximum" (Kerlinger, 1973, p. 491). Kerlinger neglected to point out that what is crucial is *how* the agreement was brought about!

Something more is needed to account for the qualitative sense of "objectivity"; some account has to be given of what makes a viewpoint objective in the sense of having a respectable warrant and being free from bias. Alternatively, one could follow the lead of Elliot Eisner and many others; in effect they deny that there is any such thing as qualitative objectivity, and thus there is *only* group consensus or quantitative objectivity. The problem here—apart from the issue of whether they are right about the null status of qualitative objectivity—is that quantitative objectivity is not worth very much. Indeed, it is not worthy of the label "objectivity" at all; a more appropriate term is simply "consensus". And the problem, of course, is that consensus about an incorrect or untrustworthy or substandard position is hardly worth writing home about. Eisner's view has the same defect as Kerlinger's:

> What so-called objectivity means is that we believe in what we believe and that others share our beliefs as well. This process is called consensual validation (Eisner, 1979, p. 214).

It is important to realize, along with Scriven, that "consensual" and "validation" are uncomfortable bedfellows. Scriven makes it clear that "validity" is a term that belongs with "qualitative objectivity", not with "quantitative" or "consensus". Nevertheless, the concern of Kerlinger,

Eisner and others with the role of the community of believers is not entirely misplaced, as will soon be seen.

The missing ingredient, the element that is required to produce object-ivity in the qualitative sense, is nothing mysterious—but it has nothing to do with consensus. Gunnar Myrdal, Karl Popper, and Israel Scheffler have put their fingers on it: it is acceptance of the *critical tradition*. A view that is objective is one that has been opened up to scrutiny, to vigorous examination, to challenge. It is a view that has been teased out, analyzed, criticized, debated—in general, it is a view that has been forced to face the demands of reason and of evidence. When this has happened, we have some assurance (though never absolute assurance) that the view does not reflect the whim or bias of some individual or group; it is a view that has respectable warrant. Myrdal states:

> The method of detecting biases is simple although somewhat laborious. When the unstated value premises of research are kept hidden and for the most part vague, the results presented contain logical flaws. When inferences are confronted with premises, there is found to be a *non sequitur* concealed, leaving the reasoning open to invasion by uncontrolled influences.... This element of inconclusiveness can be established by critical analysis (Myrdal, 1969, pp. 53-54).

Popper expresses a similar point in a manner that makes even clearer that a community of inquirers can only hope to be qualitatively objective when conditions allow them to subscribe to—and actually apply in practice—the critical spirit:

> What may be described as scientific objectivity is based solely upon a critical tradition which, despite resistance, often makes it possible to criticize a dominant dogma. To put it another way, the objectivity of science is not a matter of the individual scientists but rather the social result of their mutual criticism, of the friendly-hostile division of labour among scientists, of their co-operation and also of their competition. For this reason, it depends, in part, upon a number of social and political circumstances which make criticism possible (Popper, 1976, p. 95).

Thus, Kerlinger and the others need to do two things to strengthen their accounts. In the first place, they have to stress that the community of inquirers must be a critical community, where dissent and reasoned disputation (and sustained efforts to overthrow even the most favored of viewpoints) are welcomed as being central to the process of inquiry. Second, they must abandon their references to agreement or consensus. A critical community might never reach agreement over (say) two viable alternative views, but if both of these views have been subjected to critical scrutiny, then both would have to be regarded as objective. (Once again, the term "objective" does not mean "true".) And even if agreement is reached, it can still happen that the objective view reached within such a community will turn out to be wrong—for those of us living in the new non-foundationalist age, this is the cross that we have to learn to bear!

(d) Kuhnism

Thomas S. Kuhn popularized the notion that inquirers always work within the context of a paradigm—a framework that determines the concepts that are used, but which also contains exemplars or model inquiries, and which directs attention to some problems as being key and directs attention away from other problems or issues which (from that perspective) are regarded as somewhat trivial. Many scholars have interpreted Kuhn as supporting a relativistic position whereby it does not make sense to ask which one of various competing paradigms is the correct one; such judgments can only be made from within a paradigm, so inquirers are not able to step outside to examine their paradigms "etically". In a sense, then, all inquirers are trapped within their own paradigms, and they will judge certain things as being true for them, that other inquirers in other paradigms will judge as being false (for them). To those who have taken such Kuhnian relativism seriously, in the Kuhnian universe there has seemed to be little place for objectivity. (See also the discussion of multiple realities in Chapter 4.)

Thus, sometimes when the possibility of achieving objectivity is being questioned, the focus of attention is the framework within which inquiry is being pursued. For example, Freudians use a particular theoretical frame—they are guided by distinctive concepts and hypotheses—and of course, for a dedicated worker in this psychoanalytic tradition, the possibility of using some quite different framework does not arise as a practicable alternative. The same situation exists, it has been argued, even if the inquirer does not subscribe to some well-known paradigm; for even here, the inquirer must be working with *some* concepts and hypotheses that serve as bedrock for the endeavor. Thus:

> ... most research methodologists are now aware that *all* data are theory-, method-, and measurement-dependent. That is, "facts" are determined by the theories and methods that generate their collection; indeed, theories and methods *create* the facts. And theories, in turn, are grounded in and derived from the basic philosophical assumptions their formulators hold regarding the nature of and functional relationship between the individual, society, and science (Ratcliffe, op. cit., p. 148).

Gunnar Myrdal, Elliot Eisner, Hilary Putnam, and the "anarchist" philosopher of science Paul Feyerabend (Feyerabend, 1978) are among those who frequently make similar points.

It is a somewhat controversial point whether or not choice of a framework or paradigm can be made objectively; but it is clear that the tide of philosophical debate has been running steadily against Kuhn (and relativism) and hence in favor of the view that it is possible to judge as better or worse the considerations that are advanced in support of any particular paradigm (Newton-Smith, 1981 and Siegel, 1987). More to the point, the following is also very clear: *Within* any particular framework inquirers can go about their work with more or less facility. Not all Freudians are equally adept; some are bunglers, some are misogynists or suffer from homophobia, and some may even be anti-Republican or anti-Democrat in orientation, and their work as Freudians might be indelibly stamped by these predilections. So sometimes when objectivity is being discussed, the focus of interest is whether or not it is possible to escape from bias while working or making judgments inside one's framework. Myrdal seems to have had this focus when he wrote:

> Biases are thus not confined to the practical and political conclusions drawn from research. They are much more deeply seated than that. They are the unfortunate results of concealed valuations that insinuate themselves into research at all stages, from its planning to its final presentation. As a result of their concealment, they are not properly sorted out and thus can be kept undefined and vague (Myrdal, 1969, p. 52).

The point, of course, is that the two foci—choice between paradigms, and choices and work within a particular paradigm—must not be confused. An argument that establishes that at one of these levels objectivity is impossible to achieve (accepting, for the sake of discussion, that such an argument could be mounted), does not address the issue of whether the other type of objectivity lies out of reach. There are, however, grounds for believing that this confusion does exist. Eisner, for example, argues strongly that it is naive to believe in framework objectivity, but his published advice on methodology of qualitative research does not stress the dangers of bias in judgment within frameworks, and he does not discuss in any detail the steps that can be taken to avoid it (see the discussion in Chapter 8). As was seen earlier, with one broad stroke he does away with objectivity in all its senses, and he replaces it with consensual validation.

Can objectivity of judgment within a framework or paradigm be achieved? It seems clear that the answer is in the affirmative. Consider a group of qualitative researchers who are working on similar problems, using the same intellectual framework to shape their approaches. What property must their judgments have in order to be regarded as objective? As was shown earlier, it will not suffice for these inquirers merely to *agree* in their judgments. Instead, they would have to show that their own personal biases and valuations had been exposed to critical examination, and the role that these predilections played in their investigations would need to have been rigorously examined. Furthermore, as already mentioned, qualitative research (no less than quantitative research) is subject to a variety of threats to its validity—qualitative researchers are liable to misjudge the frequency-rate of certain behaviors that are of interest, they are likely to be unduly influenced by positive instances and not so sensitive to the significance of negative instances, they are likely to be unduly influenced or "anchored" by experiences undergone early in the research, and so on (Royce Sadler, 1982). To achieve objectivity within a paradigm, then, the researcher has to ensure that his or her work is free from these problems, and again the presence of a critical tradition is the best safeguard. When work is sent to blind peer-review, when researchers are forced to answer their critics, when researchers are supposed to be acquainted with the methodological and substantive literature (and when others can point out when they are not), and when researchers try honestly to refute their own dearly-held beliefs, then bias and the other obvious shortcomings are likely to be eliminated, and the judgment (or judgments) reached by the community of scholars should be objective in the relevant sense.

(e) The Conflation of the Contexts of Discovery and Justification

The philosopher of science Hans Reichenbach drew what is now a well-known distinction between the context of discovery in science, and the context of justification. In recent years it has been argued by some that the distinction between these is blurred at best, and a few seminal writers seem to have ignored the distinction altogether—though with arguably disastrous results. (See, for example, the mischief this causes in some of Piaget's work; this is discussed in Phillips, 1982.) Nevertheless, for heuristic purposes Reichenbach's distinction turns out to be a very fruitful one.

The relevant point in the present context is this: Processes involved in—and even central to—the *making* of discoveries during the pursuit of a research program may not be involved—and might be counterproductive if allowed to intrude—when the discoveries are *checked* and *tested* and *critically evaluated*. Both Israel Scheffler and Karl Popper see this distinction as crucial for understanding objectivity in research. Thus Popper, having in mind the context of discovery, writes that

> ... we cannot rob the scientist of his partisanship without also robbing him of his humanity, and we cannot suppress or destroy his value judgments without destroying him as a human being *and as a scientist*. Our motives and even our purely scientific ideals ... are deeply anchored in extra-scientific and, in part, in religious valuations. Thus the "objective" or the "value-free" scientist is hardly the ideal scientist (Popper, op. cit., p. 97).

Objectivity in research is not, for Popper, a property of the individual researcher—"It is a mistake to assume that the objectivity of a science depends upon the objectivity of the scientist" (Ibid., p. 96). Objectivity, in this view, is a property of the context of justification, and as we have seen in the earlier discussion it is in a sense a social matter (for it depends upon communal acceptance of the critical spirit).

Conclusions

Before bringing this discussion to a close, a penultimate point must be made. It may have been noted that, throughout, nothing very much has been made of the distinction between quantitative and qualitative inquiry. For many authors, of course, the distinction is crucial, and qualitative inquiry can only be objective in so far as it approximates to quantitative inquiry. Fred Kerlinger seems to be representative:

> Objective methods of observation are those in which anyone following the prescribed rules will assign the same numerals to objects and sets of objects as anyone else. An objective procedure is one in which agreement among observers is at a maximum. In variance terms, observer variance is at a minimum. This means that judgmental variance, the variance due to differences in judges assignment of numerals to objects, is zero (Kerlinger, 1973, p. 491).

He acknowledges that all methods of observation are inferential, but the procedures that assign numbers are "more objective".

From the point of view of the new non-foundationalist philosophy of science, there is little difference between qualitative and quantitative inquiry. Bad work of either kind is equally to be deplored; and good work of either kind is still—at best—only tentative. But the good work in both cases will be objective, in the sense that it has been opened up to criticism, and the reasons and evidence offered in both cases will have withstood serious scrutiny. The works will have faced potential refutation, and in so far as they have survived, they will be regarded as worthy of further investigation.

Another way of putting this is that in all types of inquiry, in so far as they want to reach credible conclusions, there is an underlying epistemological similarity. Even in hermeneutics—a mode of qualitative inquiry that at first sight seems far from the "objective" science of physics—there is appeal to evidence, there is testing and criticism of hypotheses (Follesdal, 1979; see also Chapter 1).

It turns out, then, that what is crucial for the objectivity of any inquiry—whether it is qualitative or quantitative—is the critical spirit in which it has been carried out. And of course this suggests that there can be *degrees*; for the pursuit of criticism and refutation obviously can be carried out more or less seriously. "Objectivity" is the term—the "stamp of approval"—that is used to label inquiries that are at one end of the continuum; they are inquiries that are prized because of the great care and responsiveness to criticism with which they have been carried out. At the other end of the continuum are inquiries that are stamped as being "subjective"; these are inquiries that have not been sufficiently opened to the light of reason and criticism. Most human inquiries are probably located somewhere near the middle, but the aim should be to move in the direction that will earn a full stamp of approval.

References

Eisner, Elliot (1979). *The Educational Imagination*.NY: Macmillan.

Eisner, Elliot (1986). The primacy of experience and the politics of method. A lecture delivered at the University of Oslo, Norway, September 1986.

Feyerabend, Paul (1978). *Against Method*. London: Verso.

Follesdal, Dagfin (1979). Hermeneutics and the hypothetico-deductive method. *Dialectics*, **33**, 3-4.

Hanson, N. R. (1965). *Patterns of Discovery*. Cambridge: Cambridge University Press.

House, Ernest (1980). *Evaluating with Validity*. Beverly Hills: Sage.

Kerlinger, Fred (1973). *Foundations of Behavioral Research*. NY: Rinehart and Winston.

Myrdal, Gunnar (1969). *Objectivity in Social Research*. NY: Pantheon Books.

Nagel, Ernest (1979). *Teleology Revised*. NY: Columbia University Press.

Newton-Smith, W. (1981). *The Rationality of Science*. London: Routledge.

Nisbet, Robert (1974). Subjective Si! Objective No! In G. Riley (Ed.), *Values, Objectivity, and the Social Sciences*. Reading, MA: Addison-Wesley.

Phillips, D. C. (1982). Perspectives on Piaget as philosopher. In S. and C. Modgil (Eds.), *Jean Piaget: Consensus and Controversy*. London: Holt.

Phillips, D. C. (1984). Was William James telling the truth after all? *The Monist*, **67**, July.

Phillips, D. C. (1987). *Philosophy, Science, and Social Inquiry*. Oxford and NY: Pergamon Press.

Popper, Karl (1968). *Conjectures and Refutations*. NY: Harper Torchbooks.

Popper, Karl (1976). The logic of the social sciences. In T. Adorno *et al.* (Eds.), *Positivist Dispute in German Sociology*. NY: Harper Torchbooks.

Putnam, Hilary (1987). *The Many Faces of Realism*. Open Court, La Salle, Indiana.

Ratcliffe, John W. (1983). Notions of validity in qualitative research methodology. *Knowledge Creation, Diffusion, Utilization*. **5**, 2, December.

Royce Sadler, D. (1982). Intuitive data processing as a potential source of bias in naturalistic evaluations. In E. House *et al.* (Eds.), *Evaluation Studies Review Annual*, **7**. Beverly Hills: Sage.

Scheffler, Israel (1967). *Science and Subjectivity*. Indianapolis: Bobbs-Merrill.

Scriven, Michael (1972). Objectivity and subjectivity in educational research. In L. Thomas (Ed.), *Philosophical Redirection of Educational Research*. (Seventy-first Yearbook of the NSSE). Chicago: NSSE.

Siegel, Harvey (1987). *Relativism Refuted*. Dordrecht, The Netherlands: Reidel.

6

Popper, Dewey and the Nature of Inquiry *§

Interviewer: We are privileged to be able to interview two of the twentieth century's leading philosophers, who have made important contributions to our understanding of the nature of human inquiry. Both have been impressed with science as the domain which, *par excellence*, shows what human intelligence is capable of achieving. Without being *scientistic*, both men take the epistemology of the natural sciences as the model for the growth of human knowledge in general; in other words, they provide us with a basis for saying that inquiry can be naturalistic in the sense that the intellectual methods of the successful natural sciences can be the basis for methods of inquiry in other domains such as the social sciences. (See also the discussion in Chapter 3.)

One of our guests was born in Austria, taught in New Zealand, and reached the peak of his career in philosophy of science at the London School of Economics; I refer of course to Sir Karl Popper. The other is a prolific American, who has been away from the philosophical arena since 1952; some years ago he was named as one of the three great philosophers of the twentieth century (see Rorty, 1979). He is, however, still occasionally vilified as the person responsible for trends in modern education that have led to loss of standards; and a learned society bears his name. Let me introduce Professor John Dewey. Now, Sir Karl, to begin with you: Several of your books have titles that indicate their relevance for our discussion today, but could you tell us a little about the theme of *Objective Knowledge*, which sounds as if it is right on target?

Popper: Well, the theme of the essays in the book is brought out by the sub-title, for I believe that important light can be thrown on human inquiry if we take "An Evolutionary Approach". This was a fairly new

---

* The words spoken by Popper and Dewey here are, to a large degree, quotations from (or very close paraphrases of) their actual writings; transitional passages have been added, as have occasional references to each other—the two men, of course, never met. The now awkward use of "man" instead of "person" has been allowed to stand throughout.

line for me in 1972; previously I was rather rude about evolutionary theory, and I even endorsed Canon Raven's remark that the furor following the publication of Darwin's *Origin of Species* in 1859 was a "storm in a Victorian tea-cup" (Popper, 1972, p. 241).

Dewey: That was an unfortunate remark and one I personally found distressing. After all, it has been said that there is deep significance in the fact that I was born in 1859. Darwin's theory was perhaps the main influence on my thought, and one of my early books was called *The Influence of Darwin on Philosophy*. I regard the struggle to establish an evolutionary perspective not as a minor storm but as a major revolutionary movement that has not even yet been successful. But I note with interest Sir Karl's conversion.

Inter: Yes, point well taken. Sir Karl, could you outline the chief lines your evolutionary train of thought has followed, with particular reference to the relevance of this for our understanding of the nature of scientific inquiry?

Popper: Maybe, then, I should start with my theory of knowledge as I disagree over it with almost everybody, except perhaps Charles Darwin and Albert Einstein. The main point at issue is the relation between observation and theory, which of course are two key ingredients of scientific inquiry. I believe that theory—at least some rudimentary theory or expectation—always comes first; that it always precedes observation; and that the fundamental role of observations and experimental tests is to show that some of our theories are false. Accordingly I assert that we do not start our inquiries from observations, but always from *problems*—either from practical problems or from a theory which has run into difficulties (Popper, 1972, pp. 257-258). And so I also do not agree with Descartes, Locke, Berkeley, and even the "skeptic" Hume, and their many successors, especially Russell and Moore, that what is crucial is the finding of some particularly secure, stable starting point or foundation for human knowledge (such as subjective experience) (Popper, 1972, p. 36).

Inter: Ah, yes—you attack what is now called foundationalism in epistemology, and you support non-foundationalism. (See also Chapter 5.) It was, of course, quite revolutionary for you to reject the view that our knowledge is built up by inductive reasoning from some secure foundation. This non-foundationalism is probably nowadays the mainstream view. We must leave time later to discuss the issue of how we can be sure we know anything (for instance, in social science) if in fact our knowledge is *not* firmly based! But I wanted to clarify, Sir Karl, in what sense this view of yours is "evolutionary".

Dewey: As another non-foundationalist and evolutionist, can I attempt an answer on Sir Karl's behalf? I have read his book with a great deal of interest a number of times since it was first published, and it appears to me that he does not differ from quite so many philosophers as he imagines. My own view, and the views of my colleagues who are often called pragmatists, at least run parallel to Sir Karl's. In 1917 I stated that a belief in organic evolution which does not extend unreservedly to the way in which the subject of experience is thought of, and which does not strive to bring the entire theory of experience and knowing into line with biological and social facts, is hardly more than Pickwickian (Dewey, 1917, p. 35). Sir Karl has indeed tried to take such an evolutionary view of the knower. The crux of his position, it seems to me, is that knowledge grows by the evolutionary process of error-elimination. Just as worthless variants within a species of animals may be eliminated by their failure to survive in the struggle for existence, so it is with worthless or errant hypotheses in the realm of human knowledge.

Inter: Is this an accurate account, Sir Karl? And if so, isn't error-elimination in human knowledge *analogous* to evolutionary selection rather than being an actual case of evolution?

Popper: What Professor Dewey said was fair. Certainly I see the evolution of life as a process of trial and error-elimination; and it allows us to understand rationally, though far from fully, the emergence of bio-logical novelty and the growth of human knowledge and human freedom (Popper, 1972, p. 255). It is *not* figurative to regard error-elimination as an evolutionary process, but to appreciate my point you must come to regard evolving species as prospective answers to problems. Take an example. Although of course it does not realize it, the life-style of an amoeba raises certain problems when considered in relation to the available environment (the problems are identified by us, as it were, with the benefit of hindsight). If the amoeba's adaptations do not solve the problems then it will succumb. In my book I argued that the main difference between Einstein and the amoeba was that Einstein consciously tried his best, whenever a new solution occurred to him, to fault it and detect an error in it: he approached his own solutions critically. I pointed out that it is different with primitive man and with the amoeba. Here there is no critical attitude, and so it happens more often than not that natural selection eliminates a mistaken hypothesis or expectation by eliminating those organisms which hold it, or believe in it (Popper, 1972, pp. 247-248; see also p. 261).

Inter: I am not happy with this notion of a "problem" that seems to be an objective, existing thing that can be identified at some later time. Obviously people are needed to identify problems.

Dewey: I put forward a view similar to Popper's, and it, too, was often misunderstood. I was even accused of holding an anthropomorphic philosophy (Cohen, 1940), which is the charge you are really bringing against Sir Karl now.

Popper: I suspected I might be misunderstood, so I added a page or two of further discussion to bolster the point in my book. We *can* speak of problems in an objective or nonpsychological sense. In practice the situation is often as follows: a man may be working on a problem but he cannot say clearly what his problem is (unless he has found a solution); and even if he can explain his problem he may mistake it. Even a scientist may think he has solved problem A when later developments show that he really solved problem B (Popper, 1972, p. 246).

Inter: This would seem to tie-in with your metaphysical theory—which has a lot in common with Plato's—that knowledge is objective and forms a "third world" that is distinct from the world of physical objects or physical states, and also from the world of states of consciousness or mental states (Popper, 1972, pp. 73-74; also p. 106).

Popper: Of course there is a connection, but rather than going off on that controversial track could I ask Professor Dewey for more details about his claim that he, too, has expounded a theory of objective problems?

Dewey: It is rather hard to explain my theory off the cuff as it were. In fact, since we were talking of hindsight, I must say that in looking back I have decided I have written too much—it is hard to get a clear perspective on forty or so books and about eight hundred journal articles. But in my *Logic: The Theory of Inquiry* (1938) I think I gave the matter the best treatment. I viewed inquiry and questioning as taking place within an *indeterminate situation* (a "situation" being my term for man interacting with his environment). Situations that are disturbed and troubled, confused or obscure, cannot be straightened out, cleaned up and put in order, by manipulation of our personal states of mind. The habit of disposing of the doubtful as if it belonged only to us rather than to the existential situation in which we are caught and implicated is an inheritance from subjectivist psychology (Dewey, 1966, p. 106). And I noted with some satisfaction, Sir Karl, that in *Objective Knowledge* you also attacked subjectivism and you supported my diagnosis of much philosophical sickness as being due to the quixotic quest for certainty—in fact you kindly referred to my book of the same name (Popper, 1972, p. 63).

Inter: I have an uneasy feeling, from what you have said about the situation itself being problematical rather than the doubt being just a property of the person who is in the situation, that you are about to claim there is another similarity between your work and Sir Karl's.

Dewey: You are a woman with insight. As the situation is problematical—really problematical, and not just troublesome in a subjective sense—then a solution can only be found by operations which actually modify existing conditions (Dewey, 1966, p. 106). In 1916 I put it rather nicely by stressing that although reflection or thought may of course be involved in reaching the solution, overt action is demanded if the worth or validity of the reflective considerations is to be determined. Otherwise, we have, at most, only an hypothesis that the conditions of the difficulty are such and such, and that the way to go at them so as to get over or through them is thus and so. This way must be applied, physically, in the situation. By finding out what then happens, we test our intellectual findings. That all knowledge, as issuing from reflection, is experimental (in the literal physical sense of experimental) is then a constituent proposition of this doctrine. Upon this view, thinking, or knowledge-getting, is far from being the armchair thing it is often supposed to be. The reason it is not an armchair thing is that it is not an event going on exclusively within the cortex or cortex and vocal organs. Hands and feet, apparatus and appliances of all kinds are as much a part of it as are changes within the brain (Dewey, 1953, pp. 13-14).

Popper: I concede that this is similar to my own view, especially if the differences in style are taken into account. After all, you did say you formulated this position in 1916. I do hold that knowledge—which constitutes the objective third world that was mentioned earlier—originates as a product of human activity (Popper, 1972, p. 159). Like you, Professor Dewey, I conceive of hypotheses facing tests in the physical world—Einstein's hypotheses were tested by experiments of Eddington and others, and the hypotheses embodied in the amoeba face the test of natural selection (Popper, 1972, pp. 247-248). I have called this the *critical method*; it is a method of trial and elimination of errors, of proposing theories and submitting them to the severest tests we can design (Popper, 1972, p. 16).

The process can be described by the following somewhat oversimplified schema:

$$P_1 \longrightarrow TT \longrightarrow EE \longrightarrow P_2$$

That is, we start from some problem P_1, proceed to a tentative solution or tentative theory TT, which may be (partly or wholly) mistaken; in any case it will be subject to error-elimination, EE, which may consist of critical discussion or experimental tests; at any rate, new problems P_2 arise from our own creative activity; and these new problems are not in general intentionally created by us; they emerge autonomously from the field of new relationships which we cannot help bringing into existence with every action, however little we intend to do so (Popper, 1972, p. 119).

While I have the floor I must stress that I have always recognized that a scientist can avoid refutation—can avoid EE—by claiming it is not his tentative theory that is wrong but that some auxiliary hypothesis is faulty. (See Chapter 4.) I called such devices "conventionalist stratagems" (Popper, 1959, ch. IV). Thus I am what Lakatos called a sophisticated rather than a naive falsificationist (Lakatos, 1970). But although scientists *can* avoid refutation, I have always urged them to take a "methodological decision" not to do so (Popper, 1959, *passim*).

Inter: So, once again, we meet the revolutionary idea that knowledge does not grow by induction from some absolutely certain premises; rather, it grows by the creation of bold conjectures or hypotheses intended to solve problems, followed by "sophisticated" refutation and rejection of those conjectures that do not stand up to test! What is your reaction to this, Professor Dewey?

Dewey: Once again Sir Karl and I seem very close. In 1910, in a book called *How We Think*, I argued that human inquiry (that is, the activity by which we obtain knowledge) reveals—whether it be in science, in matters of morality, or common situations in everyday life—more or less clearly, five *logically distinct* steps: (i) a felt difficulty; (ii) its location and definition; (iii) suggestion of possible solution; (iv) development by reasoning of the bearings of the suggestion; (v) further observation and experiment leading to its acceptance or rejection (Dewey, 1910, p. 72). And I stressed, in this book and also in *Logic: The Theory of Inquiry*, that one inquiry leads on to others (Dewey, 1966, part 2). Thus my views on the nature of inquiry and those of Sir Karl are almost identical. The only differences between us, Sir Karl, are that I have taken the analysis of the process of inquiry a little further than you have, and you have given more attention than I have to the stage of testing or error-elimination, and of course I acknowledge the value of your discussions in the *Logic of Scientific Discovery* and elsewhere. (By the way, the fact that our respective books on "logic" have similar titles suggesting active quest or discovery of knowledge is interesting, don't you think?)

Inter: If I may cut in here, Professor Dewey, I agree that you have pointed to some interesting similarities. I am struck, among other things, by the fact that both you and Sir Karl stress that knowledge emanates from the inquiring organism feeling the force of a "problem" or "a felt difficulty"; knowledge, in other words, does not start with the accumulation of data, observations, and the like. But surely similarities like these are no more than mere similarities? The positions of Sir Karl and yourself are quite different, but nevertheless happen to overlap in a few places.

Dewey: On the contrary. You should realize that the agreements between us that I have already highlighted are agreements on points that are central to both our philosophical positions. It may well be that this convergence stems from our mutual admiration of evolutionary theory and non-foundationalist epistemology.

Popper: Surely you are not intimating that I am a pragmatist?

Inter: He couldn't be suggesting *that*. Pragmatism has long been refuted—its theory of truth and so on.

Dewey: Nonsense! Have you recently looked at Bertrand Russell's attempts to refute pragmatism? Or at G. E. Moore's "classic" paper that was supposed to be a devastating critique? (See Russell, 1946, chs. 29 and 30 for one sample of his views; and Moore, 1960.) At best they tackle straw men. But this is a digression. The fact of the matter is that Sir Karl is a pragmatist. And you must remember that pragmatism is not an "ism" consisting of a watertight set of beliefs that all its adherents accept. It is a methodology; I recall one cynic saying that pragmatism is not so much a philosophy as a way of doing without one, and like many cynical remarks it has an element of truth.

Popper: How would you characterize pragmatism, then?

Dewey: It can be seen in at least two ways, but in both cases, Sir Karl, you are a pragmatist. I think this matter is worth pursuing, for it does throw light on the topic under consideration—the nature of inquiry. In the first place, pragmatism can be viewed in terms of a theory of truth and a criterion of meaning. William James popularized this—he regarded pragmatism as based on C. S. Peirce's criterion of meaning (which antedated by some fifty years the verifiability criterion of meaning of the logical positivists), and he stated that pragmatism was "primarily a method of settling metaphysical disputes that otherwise might be interminable" (James, 1960, p. 42). It must be remembered when discussing the origins of pragmatism, that Peirce was both a scientist and a philosophical student of scientific methodology. He devised his criterion of meaning, in what he took to be the spirit of science, in order to force philosophers to make statements that were testable. Perhaps this is an unduly Popperian way of expressing what Peirce was about, but I think a careful reading of his paper "How To Make Our Ideas Clear" (1878) confirms that he was not far removed from the spirit of your own writings, Sir Karl. I recognize that you have not claimed that philosophical or metaphysical statements must be testable—you use refutability as the criterion of *science*, not of philosophy or metaphysics. But in effect Peirce was close to you: if philosophers purport to be saying things about the world, then what they say must satisfy a similar criterion. By the way, I recall that in *Objective Knowledge* you compliment Peirce as a brilliant philosopher.

Popper: Well, there might be some superficial similarities, but I would insist that what seem like small differences to the untutored eye really are very significant. While I admire the attempt to make anyone's hypotheses testable, I regard it as a mistake to do this by way of a criterion of meaning as the positivists (and perhaps Peirce) have done. (See also Chapter 7.) You see, the positivist dislikes the idea that there should be meaningful problems outside the field of "positive" empirical science— problems to be dealt with by a genuine philosophical or metaphysical theory. He dislikes the idea that there should be a genuine theory of knowledge. He wishes to see in the alleged metaphysical problems mere "pseudo-problems" or "puzzles". Now this wish of the positivists— which, by the way, he does not express as a wish or a proposal but rather as a statement of fact—can always be gratified. For nothing is easier than to unmask a problem as "meaningless" or "pseudo". All you have to do is to fix upon a conveniently narrow meaning for "meaning", and you will soon be bound to say of any inconvenient question that you have been unable to detect any meaning in it! (Popper, 1959, p. 51). In short, I absolutely reject the stratagem of classifying metaphysics as meaningless— metaphysics, being non-testable, is not science, but that does not make it meaningless!

Furthermore, Professor Dewey, I do not accept the pragmatist's notion (which comes from William James) that theories or ideas which "work" are true. I have specifically stated that I accept the common sense theory (defined and refined by Alfred Tarski) that truth is correspondence with the facts (or with reality); or, more precisely, that a theory is true if and only if it corresponds to the facts (Popper, 1972, p. 44).

Dewey: I'm afraid you have played right into my hands. You see, pragmatists *also* subscribe to the "common sense theory". Let me quote William James:

> Truth, as any dictionary will tell you, is a property of certain of our ideas. It means their "agreement", as falsity means their disagreement, with "reality". Pragmatists and intellectualists both accept this definition as a matter of course. They begin to quarrel

only after the question is raised as to what may precisely be meant by the term "agreement", and what by the term "reality", when reality is taken as something for our ideas to agree with (James, 1960, p. 132).

It is my contention that in this passage James is saying very much the sort of thing that you just said, Sir Karl. The common sense definition of truth may be acceptable as a definition, but it offers no *practical* guide as to which particular ideas may be true. What is required for this latter task is a *criterion* of truth, and it is this that James (and I suppose that I myself) attempted to give. You deny that a single criterion exists, Sir Karl, but in practice you have taken a stand very similar to the one advocated by James in the following passage:

Pragmatism, on the other hand, asks its usual question. "Grant an idea or belief to be true", it says, "what concrete difference will its being true make in any one's actual life? How will the truth be realized? ... What, in short, is the truth's cash-value in experiential terms?"

The moment pragmatism asks this question, it sees the answer: *True ideas* are those that we can assimilate, validate, corroborate and verify. False ideas are those that we cannot (James, 1960, p. 133).

This passage is not quite so marred by excessively popular figures of speech as were many of James's other expositions of the same general theme. It is clear that when he wrote this in 1907 he was on the road leading to the major breakthrough you made many years later, Sir Karl. I see nothing in James that is in serious conflict with your own emphasis on refutation or error-elimination in science and the closer and closer approximation to truth. I feel sure that if James were with us now he would embrace your work as an important development of pragmatism.

Popper: Good Lord! Once again I must stress that there are similarities and differences, and the latter are quite important. Of course I believe that the aim of science is to get closer and closer to the truth—why, I even developed a theory of verisimilitude to make this notion more precise. But I strenuously deny that there can be a criterion—an infallible indicator— that we have discovered the truth. Certainly we cannot validate or confirm or verify that we have discovered the truth! From 1934 onwards I have insisted that theories are *not* verifiable, but they can be "corroborated"— by which I mean only that they have stood up to severe tests (Popper, 1959, p. 251). But a theory corroborated today may fail a severe test tomorrow; for the point is that theories make *universal* claims which go beyond the finite bodies of evidence that we have available to us at any given time. There is no way to be absolutely certain that future experience will confirm the views we hold today. (There is *no* solution to the problem of induction as traditionally conceived.) (Popper, 1965, ch. 1; and Popper, 1976, section 32.)

Inter: And I also cannot let your remarks pass without a protest, Professor Dewey! What you have said goes against the consensus of opinion in the voluminous literature on pragmatism and on truth.

Dewey: Certainly there have been a great many wrong-headed views expressed about pragmatism, so you can't judge my remarks by their lack of agreement with *that* literature. James himself was staggered by the incredible interpretations placed on his words in his book *Pragmatism*, and over the years I, too, have been amazed. Take G. E. Moore's famous attack on James on truth; do you realize that it was only in the last few years that his weak arguments have been exposed for what they were? (Hertz, 1971; Phillips, 1984).

Inter: I'm still a bit doubtful, but perhaps I am only cautious because it is always fairly easy to show that there are some similarities between any two writers one cares to select, even a James and a Popper.

Dewey: I take your point. But the time is ripe for a fresh and unbiased appraisal of what James and I have said about truth, and for a comparison of it with Sir Karl's work. But let me turn to the second way of viewing pragmatism that I foreshadowed earlier. My account must again start with William James; there is an important passage in a critique he wrote of Herbert Spencer's work in 1878. It was really an evolutionary point, Sir Karl, for James noted that Spencer did not stress enough the active nature of the inquiring mind.

> I, for my part, cannot escape the consideration, forced on me at every turn, that the knower is not simply a mirror floating with no foot-hold anywhere, and passively reflecting an order that he comes upon and finds simply existing. The knower is an actor.... In other words there belongs to mind, from its birth upward, a spontaneity, a vote. It is in the game, and not a mere looker-on (James, 1920, p. 67).

There are good grounds for saying that the central thesis of pragmatism has turned out to be this view of the knower—certainly it has been central in my own work (Hill, 1942).

Inter: If I'm not mistaken, the view that you and James oppose is what is referred to as the "spectator theory of knowledge".

Popper: I think I follow what is being said, but perhaps you ought to explain the spectator theory a little more, Professor Dewey, together with James's and your own opposition to it.

Dewey: In fact my opposition to it has been so marked that one commentator has said that my theory of knowledge was developed to combat the spectator theory and can't be understood apart from it. He says this is why I keep digging up, and then re-burying, the spectator theory (Murphy, 1951, p. 207). Perhaps the best way of explaining matters is by way of an analogy suggested by James's remark that the knower "is in the game", namely the analogy of a game of football (see Phillips, 1971). I think you will find that the analogy applies quite well to the scientific researcher. According to the spectator theory, the way a knower or inquirer obtains knowledge is analogous to the way in which a person can learn about football by being a spectator at a game. Whilst he is learning, the spectator is quite passive; he does not affect the course of the game in any way. Thus the spectator theory of knowledge held that a knower was a spectator, passively observing the material that was to become known, and in no way affecting this material. The classic example would be Plato's metaphor of the cave, where the knower is like a prisoner released from gazing at shadows on the wall of the cave. Although the eyes of the prisoner are turned so that he eventually comes to see reality (the light of the sun), the prisoner is a spectator who exerts no influence upon the reality about which he is gaining knowledge. The same passive view of the knower or inquirer is found in the Lockean or traditional empiricist tradition. In the view put forward by James and myself, however, the inquirer is like the person who learns about football not by watching but by playing the game—he affects the game and in the process obtains knowledge about the game. In 1929, in my book *The Quest for Certainty* (which was subtitled "A study of the relation of knowledge and action"), I argued that all the difficulties connected with the philosophical problem of knowledge grow from a single root. They spring from the assumption that the true and valid object of knowledge is that which has being prior to and independent of the operations of knowing. They spring from the doctrine that knowledge is a grasp or beholding of reality without anything being done to modify its antecedent state—the doctrine which is the source of the separation of knowledge from practical activity. If we see that knowing is not the act of an outside spectator but of a participator inside the natural and social scene, then the true object of knowledge resides in the consequences of directed action (Dewey, 1960, p. 196).

Inter: This view of knowledge certainly seems to fit the case of the scientist, who surely is no passive spectator, but is active in acquiring his or her knowledge. Now, Sir Karl, it would seem that you *are* in this same pragmatic tradition of opposition to the spectator theory—you may not be as marked an opponent as James or Professor Dewey, but you are more an ally of theirs than an enemy.

Popper: I realize that there are passages in my writings that could have given you that impression. I remember saying in *Conjectures and Refutations* that I was led by purely logical reasons to hold the following view: Without waiting, passively, for repetitions of phenomena in nature to impress or impose regularities upon us, as scientific inquirers we actively try to discover similarities in it, and to interpret it in terms of laws invented by us. Without waiting for premises we jump to conclusions. These may have to be discarded later, should observations show that they are wrong. This was a theory of trial and error—of conjectures and refutations (Popper, 1965, p. 46). This, I suppose, is very much the procedure that would have been followed by the novice footballer in your analogy, and of course I intended my account to apply directly to the scientist.

Dewey: Yes. It certainly wasn't a procedure that was followed by Plato's prisoner or by Locke's *tabula rasa*! And I recall another pertinent passage a little later in your book.

Popper: I asked my readers to assume that we have deliberately made it our task to live in this unknown world of ours; to adjust ourselves to it as well as we can; to take advantage of the opportunities we can find in it; and to explain it, *if* possible, with the help of laws and explanatory theories. *If we have made this our task, then there is no more rational procedure than the method of trial and error—of conjecture and refutation*: of boldly proposing theories; of trying our best to show that these are erroneous; and of accepting them tentatively if our critical efforts are unsuccessful (Popper, 1965, p. 51).

Inter: Your mention of rationality gives me the chance to return to an issue I foreshadowed earlier in our conversation. A number of critics, Sir Karl, have called you an *irrationalist* who disguises himself as a rationalist (see Newton-Smith, 1981; and Stove, 1982). Their point is that you do not give us any rational grounds for supposing that the beliefs scientists corroborate today will hold true tomorrow—for although corroborated, these beliefs are not true at all! Corroboration merely means they have passed all *current* tests. You face this problem for two reasons: because you strenuously deny that our knowledge is founded on anything certain; and because you oppose inductive reasoning, and assert that the surviving of past tests does not increase the probability that the belief or theory or conjecture is true and will continue to hold in the future.

Popper: All I can do to answer such criticisms is to repeat what I have said in many of my writings. Those conjectures which, in principle, can be overthrown by criticism (including, of course, criticism by way of finding conflicting evidence), but which yet resist all our critical efforts to do so may quite possibly be false, but are at any rate not unworthy of being seriously considered and perhaps even of being believed—though only tentatively (Popper, 1965, p. 228). In short, we tentatively accept corroborated conjectures because we have not yet been able to find what is wrong with them.

Dewey: If I'm not mistaken, Sir Karl, you also hold that unfalsified conjectures have greater verisimilitude than falsified ones; that is, they are nearer to the truth. And I suppose that if we can't be sure we have arrived at the truth, it is rational for us to believe those conjectures that are *close* to the truth—we are acting rationally when we act upon those views that as yet we have not been able to fault.

Inter: But this doesn't quite resolve the difficulty. It is not rational to believe a successfully tested conjecture if we are no surer than we were before the test that it will continue to hold in the future—and to have rational grounds for this we must use some form of inductive reasoning, which of course Sir Karl rejects. In other words, to act rationally upon some item of knowledge, we must hold that views which seem true today are at least highly likely to hold true in the future (and this, of course, involves inductive reasoning).

But since you have broken in, Professor Dewey, what grounds does your epistemology give us for thinking that our ideas, upon which we are acting, are in fact likely to hold in the future?

Dewey: From my perspective you have mis-stated the whole issue. The future does not yet exist: it is not sitting out there, ready made. The world is an *open* world (Dewey, 1957, p. 54). We cannot expect *any* guarantees about which of our beliefs will continue to hold up. The whole point is that our knowledge is not backward looking, but it projects "our best bets" into the future. I have argued in my writings that notions, theories, systems, no matter how elaborate and self-consistent they are, must be regarded as hypotheses. They are to be accepted as bases of actions which test them, not as finalities. *They are tools* (Dewey, 1957, p. 145). *If* ideas, meanings, conceptions, notions, theories, systems are instrumental to an active reorganization of the given environment, to a removal of some specific trouble and perplexity (i.e., a problem), then the test of their validity and value lies in accomplishing this work. Confirmation, corroboration, verification lie in works, consequences. That which guides us truly is true! (Dewey, 1957, p. 156). In short, we *cannot* tell beforehand if some conjecture is true.

Inter: Well, at last we have a point of agreement between the two of you: You both acknowledge that our current best ideas might not project successfully into the future, so neither of you has an epistemology that is successful!

Dewey: Nonsense! You neglect the crucial fact that the traditional inductivist epistemology you seem to favor fails as well—the history of science, and of course everyday life experience, can provide countless examples of supposed "truths" that turned out to be false when tested further! (See the discussion of the "pessimistic induction" in Newton-Smith, 1981.) The difference is, traditional epistemology likes to *pretend* that current ideas are "true" or "highly probable", but abandons them when they fail (as they so regularly do), whereas Popper and I have epistemologies that *account* for this fact of failure. We claim that no epistemology can be taken seriously when it claims to show that it has grasped the truth, or has grasped things that are highly likely to be true! Our epistemologies are both forward looking—it is the future that determines the fate of our ideas held now, not the past that determines the future truth of our ideas.

Popper: I want to go further— I want to suggest to Professor Dewey that he retract his earlier assertion that you are a woman with insight!

§ Reprinted with permission from *Educational Theory*, 25(1). Phillips, D. C. "Popper and Pragmatism: A Fantasy", © 1975, pp. 83-91.

References

Cohen, Morris (1940). Some difficulties in John Dewey's anthropocentric naturalism. *Philosophical Review*, v, 49.

Dewey, John (1910). *How We Think*. London: Heath.

Dewey, John (1917). The need for a recovery of philosophy. In John Dewey (Ed.), *Creative Intelligence*. NY: Holt.

Dewey, John (1953). *Essays in Experimental Logic*. NY: Dover.

Dewey, John (1957). *Reconstruction in Philosophy*. Boston: Beacon.

Dewey, John (1960). *The Quest for Certainty*. NY: Capricorn.

Dewey, John (1966). *Logic: The Theory of Inquiry*. NY: Holt, Rinehart & Winston.

Hertz, Richard (1971). James and Moore: two perspectives on truth. *Journal of the History of Philosophy*, v, 9.

Hill, Walker (1942). The founder of pragmatism. In B. Blanshard and H. Schneider (Eds.), *In Commemoration of William James 1842-1942*. NY: Columbia University Press.

James, William (1920). *Collected Essays and Reviews*. London: Longmans, Green and Co.

James, William (1960). *Pragmatism: and Four Essays from the Meaning of Truth*. NY: Meridian.

Lakatos, Imre (1971). Falsification and the methodology of scientific research programmes. In I. Lakatos and A. Musgrave (Eds.), *Criticism and the Growth of Knowledge*. London: Cambridge University Press.

Moore, G. E. (1960). *Philosophical Studies*. London: Routledge and Kegan Paul.

Murphy, Arthur E. (1951). Epistemology and metaphysics. In P. A. Schilpp (Ed.), *The Philosophy of John Dewey*. NY: Tudor.

Newton-Smith, W. H. (1981). *The Rationality of Science*. London: Routledge and Kegan Paul.

Phillips, D. C. (1971). John Dewey and the organismic archetype. In R. J. W. Selleck (Ed.), *Melbourne Studies in Education 1971*. Melbourne: Melbourne University Press.

Phillips, D. C. (1984). Was William James telling the truth after all? *The Monist*, **67**, 3.

Popper, Karl (1959). *The Logic of Scientific Discovery*. London: Hutchinson.

Popper, Karl (1965). *Conjectures and Refutations*, 2nd edition. London: Routledge and Kegan Paul.

Popper, Karl (1972). *Objective Knowledge*. London: Oxford University Press.

Popper, Karl (1976). *Unended Quest: An Intellectual Autobiography*. LaSalle, Illinois: Open Court.

Rorty, Richard (1979). *Philosophy and the Mirror of Nature*. Princeton, NJ: Princeton University Press.

Russell, Bertrand (1946). *A History of Western Philosophy*. London: Allen and Unwin.

Stove, David (1982). *Popper and After: Four Modern Irrationalists*. Oxford: Pergamon Press.

7

Positivism

NOWADAYS the term "positivist" is widely used as a generalized term of abuse. As a literal designator it has ceased to have any useful function—those philosophers to whom the term accurately applies have long since shuffled off this mortal coil, while any living social scientists who either bandy the term around, or are the recipients of it as an abusive label, are so confused about what it means that, while the word is full of sound and fury, it signifies nothing.

The anti-positivist vigilantes, who realize nothing of this, still claim to see positivists everywhere. (When one is confused, or suffering from delirium, it is possible to see *anything*.) Displaying what often amounts to an embarrassing degree of philosophical illiteracy, the vigilantes rarely bother to distinguish between classical (or Comtean) positivists on the one hand, and the even more nefarious logical positivists on the other; furthermore, they use a number of faulty criteria, either singly or in combination, to identify their illusory foe. The general fantasy is that anyone who is impressed by the sciences as a pinnacle of achievement of human knowledge, anyone who uses statistics or numerical data, anyone who believes that hypotheses need to be substantially warranted, anyone who is a realist (another unanalyzed but clearly derogatory word), is thereby a positivist. The following discussion has as its aim the clarification of these delusions.

As a preliminary, however, it needs to be affirmed that the corpus of the sciences *does* constitute a magnificent achievement. The issue is, for those who want somehow to learn from—and to emulate—the sciences: What precisely has been the source of their success? Before we heap outright condemnation upon those who wish to use the successful natural sciences as a model for their own investigations in the social sciences, it seems a counsel of wisdom to examine the analysis of science that they give—for while some accounts may be narrow and deficient, and deserving of abuse, other accounts might be such that we are likely to profit from them! It is in this spirit that we should approach the work of the classic positivists and logical positivists.

Classical or Comtean Positivism

With respect to positivism, the truth is less straightforward than the fantasy. The term itself was coined by the French philosopher Auguste Comte, who published his six-volume work *Cours de Philosophie Positive* in fits and starts between 1830 and 1842. In this work Comte argued several different things. First, he held that each branch of knowledge, by an "inevitable necessity", passes through "three different theoretical states"—"the theological or fictitious state, the metaphysical or abstract state, and the scientific or positive state" (Comte, 1970, p. 1). (It is interesting to note, in passing, that there is a similarity between this aspect of Comte's work, and the views of the American pragmatist C. S. Peirce on the stages that human communities pass through with respect to the "fixation of belief"; see Peirce, in Konvitz and Kennedy, 1960, pp. 82-99.) The development of the modern discipline of biology would be a good example here; at first the behavior of living things was explained in terms of souls or spirits, then in terms of wildly metaphysical notions such as "vital forces" or "entelechies" (hardly an improvement), and then finally in terms of the biochemical mechanisms expounded in modern science. Clearly Comte's and Peirce's belief in intellectual stages reflected the nineteenth-century conviction that intellectual progress had occurred, and that "scientific" modes of explanation and description were an advance over earlier forms.

Second, Comte offered a classification of the "positive sciences" which attempted to clarify "the arrangement of the sciences in the order of their natural connection, according to their mutual dependence, so that one might be able to present them successively ..." (Comte, 1970, p. 46). Comte realized that the sciences could be classified in many ways—indeed, if there were six general types of science, he pointed out there were 720 distinct classifications possible (Ibid., p. 51). But he was after a classification that reflected the way in which each successive science was "founded on a knowledge of the principal laws of the preceding one while serving as the basis of the following one" (Ibid., pp. 51-52). (Why it should even be possible to produce such a classification, he really does not adequately say; a view such as Comte's requires that many thorny issues relating to reduction be resolved. Comte's younger contemporary, the British essayist Herbert Spencer, offered a dry but detailed set of other criticisms; see Spencer, 1949.) At any rate, Comte reached the "final result that we have (in order) mathematics, astronomy, physics, chemistry, physiology, and social physics" (Comte, 1970, p. 67)—the latter being, of course, Comte's way of referring to what we now call the social sciences (and sociology in particular).

Finally—and for our purposes most significantly—Comte advanced a type of Humean empiricism that led in the direction of anti-realism with respect to the underlying entities of the physical sciences, and which also led in the direction of a type of instrumentalism according to which talk about such underlying entities—atoms and the rest—is only shorthand to replace more accurate but more cumbersome talk in terms of the data of direct experience.

This last set of issues is complex, and the material needs to be spelled out more fully; a good place to start is a key passage that occurs in Comte's *Introduction*:

> Finally, in the positive state, the human mind, recognizing the impossibility of obtaining absolute truth, gives up the search after the origin and hidden causes of the universe and a knowledge of the final causes of phenomena. It endeavors now only to discover, by a well-combined use of reasoning and observation, the actual laws of phenomena—that is to say, their inevitable relations of succession and likeness (Ibid., p. 2).

In these two sentences Comte dispels, for the careful reader, a number of the myths about positivism: he eschews the pursuit of "absolute truth", and he disavows the quest for unobservable ("hidden") scientific entities and resolves to stick to the realm of observable phenomena. Whether his arguments are powerful enough to sustain these positions is a different matter—the point is, the fantasy about positivists is that they were/are realists, who believe in absolute truth—and who regard scientific investigation as being the "royal road" to attaining it. To reinforce this important point it is appropriate to quote from Popper:

> For the commonsense theory of knowledge is liable to lead to a kind of anti-realism. If knowledge results from sensations, then sensations are the only *certain* elements of knowledge, and we can have no good reason to believe that anything but sensation exists (Popper, 1985, p. 106).

To say a little more about Comte's empiricism and the difficulties it entails for him and his successors: The classical empiricists regarded knowledge (knowledge about the physical universe, but not necessarily knowledge of mathematics and logic) as being based on sense experience— there is nothing that we know about the world that did not "enter" the "understanding" except through the senses. The seventeenth- and eighteenth-century figures John Locke and David Hume argued this position in great detail. Hume, consistently with this basic orientation, raised important problems about causation and induction: What do we experience, when we experience two events, that entitles us to identify one as the "cause" of the other? For what we see is the two events, and the temporal and spatial relations between them; but we experience nothing more—certainly we do not experience a necessary connection or link establishing that the one *produces* the other. So, on this skeptical line of thought, the Humean empiricist has to abandon (or recast as mere constant correlation) the notion of causation. Similarly, when we see that one event follows another, what do we experience that allows us to make the induction that the one will *always* follow the other, or will follow the other on some particular future occasion? For our experience is limited to what we *can* experience; we cannot experience "necessity", nor the future, so we cannot say (on the basis of experience) that one event will always and necessarily follow the other! This line of thought throws into question the warrant for our belief that the laws and theories of science will hold true in the future (or in those parts of the universe where we have not yet had experience).

This empirically-based skepticism is far-reaching. The entities postulated in scientific theories—including atoms, quarks, social forces, psychological drives, and cognitive structures, to mention only a few—are not experience-able in any direct form that would be acknowledged by Hume or Comte, and so their status as *things*, as "furniture of the world", becomes dubious. Perhaps, at best, they can be regarded as convenient fictions, as shorthand ways of referring to what *can* be experienced (readings on measuring instruments, or performance in psychological tests, and so forth).

It is hard to live as a skeptic, although some folk manage to do so consistently. It is not clear that Comte was such a one. In the passage cited above, for example, he clearly departed from the "straight and narrow" when he stated that the positivists endeavor to discover "the actual laws of phenomena", that is, their "invariable relations of succession" for, according to the empiricist argument cited above, *no* experience can establish "invariable relations". Similarly, Comte was critical of those who wished to determine what weight and gravitational attraction "are in themselves, or what their causes are" (Ibid., p. 9), for such matters lie beyond experience; and yet, in virtually the same breath, he is admiring of "the Newtonian law of gravitation" (Ibid., p. 8), which—because of its universal pretentions—clearly takes us beyond the experiential realm. There is thus some justice in John Stuart Mill's judgment, a few years later, that Comte "had not lived up sufficiently to his positivist principles" (Keat and Urry, 1982, p. 75). Neither did Comte find it necessary to discuss in great detail what, precisely, we *can* experience—some later writers (including psychologists as well as philosophers) would claim that we experience *things* and not mere "sense data" such as patches of color. (John Dewey and William James, for example, claimed that experience was much more richly populated than the classic positivists would allow— James even called his own position "radical empiricism", and Dewey explicitly stated that "direct experience contains, as a highly important direct ingredient of itself, a wealth of *possible* objects". (See Dewey, 1941, p. 539.) This is a non-trivial matter for contemporary social scientists; do we experience, for example, social phenomena or do we only experience individual people acting in certain ways (which leaves "social phenomena" as empirically illegitimate inferences or "constructions")? And, for that matter, do we actually experience people, or are these also "constructions" from our data of raw sense experience?

Comte's legacy, therefore, was a complex one. He bequeathed to subsequent generations the conviction that religious or metaphysical modes of explanation were not satisfactory when applied to empirical phenomena, for their key concepts were not adequately warranted by empirical data; and together with this he passed on his great admiration for the procedures that he believed were followed in science (or, in successful instances of science). But, clearly, his empiricism left a difficult skeptical legacy, and (arguably) an impoverished account of experience and of the nature of science.

Although many of Comte's specific arguments have become less apposite with the march of time, it remains difficult not to sympathize with his main concerns (and with Peirce's concerns in his essay "The Fixation of Belief"). Belief systems that do not incorporate some form of observational testing or empirical constraint give rise to "chimerical hopes" and "exaggerated ideas of man's importance in the universe" (Comte, 1970, p. 6), and they make use of metaphysical concepts that become "so empty through oversubtle qualification that all right-minded persons considered them to be only abstract names of the phenomena in question" (Ibid., p. 8). Neither can Comte be blamed for being interested in determining the intellectual method that has made science so successful, although we might not be so confident as he was regarding the outcome of the deliberations:

> The first great direct result of the positive philosophy is then the manifestation by experience of the laws that our intellectual functions follow in their operations and, consequently, a precise knowledge of the general rules that are suitable for our guidance in the investigation of truth (Ibid., p. 24).

Logical Positivism

Somewhat similar motivations seemed to have been at work in the logical positivists of the 1920s and 1930s. Centered around Vienna, and thereby also called "the Vienna Circle", the group was made up of people with a range of interesting backgrounds: Schlick and Frank from physics, Carnap and Waissman from mathematics and philosophy, Neurath from sociology, Gödel and Hahn from mathematics, and Kraft from history. Later Reichenbach, Hempel, Ayer and others were associated with the group. As a group they exerted a powerful influence over the image of science that was held by many physical and social scientists of the following decades. Their influence was particularly marked in the English-speaking world, due to their being scattered there when they escaped from Nazi persecution. The physicist Percy Bridgman (Bridgman, 1927) developed his ideas on operational definitions under this influence (it was an interesting twist of fate that his operationism survived, and even flourished, in the social sciences long after it had been passed by in the physical sciences); and B. F. Skinner met logical positivism while in graduate school, and his behaviorism can be interpreted as an application of this philosophy to the realms of psychology. (John B. Watson's behaviorism predated the work of the logical positivists, although it might have been indirectly influenced by C. S. Peirce.)

The logical positivists are notorious for their development of the "verifiability principle or criterion of meaning". Their idea, of course, was to rule out of serious consideration (by means of defining them as meaningless) any statements the method of verification of which cannot be specified in terms of sense experience. (Clearly this was an extension of the skeptical empiricism inherent in Hume and Comte.) Attempts to state this principle became very complex, but a simple form read as follows: "A statement is held to be literally meaningful if and only if it is either analytic or empirically verifiable" (Ayer, 1960, p. 9)—the "analytic" being necessary here in order to exclude logic and mathematics from the requirement of empirical verification. Colloquially, the principle can be stated as: "If it can't be seen or measured, it is not meaningful to talk about."

Here again the American pragmatists were close to the logical positivists in spirit. Peirce, too, wanted to find a way of "settling metaphysical disputes that otherwise might be interminable" (see Peirce, "How To Make Our Ideas Clear", in Konvitz and Kennedy, 1960; the nice phrase here is actually taken from William James, in Ibid., p. 29). And so Peirce, anticipating the logical positivists by half-a-century, devised the pragmatic maxim of meaning that was, in thrust, very similar to the verifiability principle of meaning. Peirce illustrated how such a principle or maxim could wreak havoc with fanciful metaphysical problems—for example, he argued that the theory that a diamond is soft until it is actually scratched, whereupon it becomes hard, is identical in meaning with the theory that diamonds are always hard, because there are no circumstances whatever when the two theories would lead to different testable consequences. To cite another example: John B. Watson may well have known of Peirce's pragmatic maxim of meaning, as he studied under Dewey at the University of Chicago, and Dewey certainly knew of it and had been influenced by it. But whatever the source, Watson's classic paper of 1913 that founded the behaviorist movement in psychology contained a major thread of ideas that would have delighted Peirce, Comte, and the (later) logical positivists. Watson urged psychologists to abandon the notion of "consciousness" because there were no clear-cut observational criteria for using it; he wrote that so far as making observations was concerned it mattered neither "jot nor tittle" whether one supposed consciousness was present or not. Only behavior is observable, and only by focusing on this could psychology become scientific. The opening lines of Watson's revolutionary paper of 1913 are notorious:

> Psychology as the behaviorist views it is a purely objective experimental branch of natural science. Its theoretical goal is the prediction and control of behavior (Watson, 1948, p. 457).

The philosopher and social scientist Michael Scriven summarized the positivists' use of the verifiability criterion of meaning as follows:

> The Vienna Circle or *Wiener Kreis* was a band of cutthroats that went after the fat burghers of Continental metaphysics who had become intolerably inbred and pompously verbose. The *kris* is a Malaysian knife, and the *Wiener Kreis* employed a kind of Occam's Razor called the Verifiability Principle. It performed a tracheotomy that made it possible for philosophy to breathe again (Scriven, 1969, p. 195).

Scriven illustrates that it is possible for a non-positivist to be sympathetic with at least part of the logical positivist program. Karl Popper, too, has been extremely critical of the verbal excesses of Continental philosophers, and, using prose that the logical positivists would have admired, he has accused the leader of the Frankfurt School, Jurgen Habermas, of fostering a cult of "un-understandability" (Popper, 1976). Popper also wanted to clearly demarcate metaphysics from science, and his early work was driven by the so-called criterion of demarcation which, to a careless reader, looks like a close variant of the logical positivists' criterion of meaning. Popper argued that science and metaphysics were demarcated by the principle of testability: If a proposition could not be tested (and hence face the possibility of refutation) then it was not scientific, and therefore it was metaphysical (for Popper only recognized the two categories). However—and this is a crucial difference—Popper did not regard metaphysics as *meaningless*; it simply was *not* science. The logical positivists, on the other hand, not only demarcated science and metaphysics, but labeled the latter category as containing—literally—non-sense! Popper, in contrast, insisted that metaphysics was an important field, and he suggested that in fact many scientific ideas start life as metaphysical. Not only, then, is Popper not a positivist, he also claims to have been the person who destroyed logical positivism (Popper, 1974, esp. p. 69). But the rumor persists that he is a fellow-traveler, fueled probably by the fact that he lived in Vienna in his youth and had contact with the Circle, and even had his first book published by them (an act of intellectual charity that both parties probably lived to regret).

The verifiability criterion of meaning raises, in a particularly virulent way, the dilemma about laws and the theoretical entities of science that we saw Comte did not deal with in a fully consistent manner. The first set of problems that arose here for the logical positivists concerned the issue of what will count as a satisfactory verification procedure in any given case. Their answers usually involved reference to a class of elementary "observation statements"; that is, in discussing how a given term or proposition could be "verified" and hence given meaning, the logical positivists usually claimed that the verification had to be in terms of simple, "rock bottom", direct and indubitable descriptions of sense experience. (There is a temptation, of course, to allow *indirect* observations, such as observations via instruments, but this only opens the floodgates.) This doctrine had a checkered history, and the logical positivists were not always in full agreement about it. Rudolf Carnap's formulation was as follows:

> we have to proceed from what is epistemically primary, that is to say, from the "given", i.e., from experiences themselves in their totality and undivided unity.... The elementary experiences are to be the basic elements of our constructional system. From this basis we wish to construct all other objects of prescientific and scientific knowledge (Carnap, 1969, pp. 108-109).

This doctrine was eventually undermined by the realization (found in the work of Wittgenstein, Dewey, Popper, and Hanson; see Hanson, 1956, ch. 1) that perception is theory-laden. Sense experience, in other words, is not a secure, theory-neutral foundation of our knowledge, for our theories and our knowledge influence both what we see and how we see it. (It is another interesting twist of fate that Comte shared this realization, at least in elementary form, but evidently did not realize its key significance. Thus he wrote, almost as a throw-away line: "For if, on the one hand, every positive theory must necessarily be founded upon observations, it is, on the other hand, no less true that, in order to observe, our mind has need of some theory or other." See Comte, 1970, pp. 4-5.) The logical positivists—less prescient than Comte—would these days be classified as holding a version of foundationalist epistemology (knowledge is built upon a foundation of theory-free, or "neutral" sense experience), whereas it presently seems that non-foundationalism is a stronger position.

Now, given the way the logical positivists typically treated verification, it is no surprise that, on the whole, they took the skeptical path opened by Hume and Comte and were not realists with respect to the status of the entities referred to in scientific theories. (Of course, they might not have seen this position as skeptical!) Consider the entities postulated in subatomic theory; these are not directly observable, and even indirect confirmation is a complex business. So, rigorous use of the verifiability principle of meaning poses a problem here—what do we mean when we speak of protons, electrons, or quarks? Can they be regarded as real entities if there is a problem with respect to their verification in terms of direct sensory experience? Alternatively, should they be interpreted as theoretical fictions? (For further discussion, see Chapter 2.) There is a parallel problem about the laws of nature, for, as we saw in regard to Comte, universal generalizations of the form "all X are Y" cannot be verified (for usually we cannot observe all members of the class X).

So, to repeat, many of the logical positivists were led to take a non-realist or anti-realist stand. Even as late as 1956 Rudolf Carnap was still grappling with this issue, and he wrote that a major concern was still

> the problem of a criterion of significance for the theoretical language, i.e., exact conditions which terms and sentences of the theoretical language must fulfill in order to have a positive function for the explanation and prediction of observable events and thus to be acceptable as empirically meaningful (Carnap, 1956, p. 38).

Carnap was still confident, at this late stage in the history of logical positivism, that he would be able to draw the line "which demarcates the scientifically meaningful from the meaningless" (Ibid., p. 40). Six short years later Grover Maxwell was scathing about this position:

> that anyone today should seriously contend that the entities referred to by scientific theories are only convenient fictions, or that talk about such entities is translatable without remainder into talk about sense contents or everyday physical objects ... strike(s) me as so incongruous with the scientific and rational attitude and practice that I feel this paper should turn out to be a demolition of straw men (Maxwell, 1962, p. 3).

Thus there is little comfort here for the anti-positivistic vigilantes with whom the present discussion opened. Typically these folk have themselves accepted the anti-realism, relativism, and even subjectivism that is not uncommon today across the pure and applied social sciences and which is traceable, at least in large part, back to the influence (and/or mis-interpretations) of the work of Thomas S. Kuhn. But whatever the source, their beliefs place them much closer to the spirit of the logical positivists than they suppose in even their wildest dreams! For the logical positivists, as we have seen, were also anti-realist, they did not have much time for the notion of absolute truth, and they wanted to remain close to the raw phenomena of experience. Thus it is clear that the vigilantes are fundamentally confused—logical positivism may be indefensible, but it is not indefensible for the reasons that the vigilantes suppose; rather, it is indefensible for much the same reasons as is the position of many of the vigilantes themselves! In turning on the logical positivists, the vigilantes are turning on their own kind.

Respect for Scientific Method

A little more needs to be said, however, about the respect for scientific method that was part, at least, of the positivists' credo. This is often what offends the vigilantes—they see the slavish imitation of science as being detrimental to the progress of the social sciences. And so it is—if the view of science that is held is an indefensible one.

Here the vigilantes are both right and wrong. They are right to be critical of the positivists' analysis of science; but they are wrong to set up a "straw man" and to act as if all admiration of science is beyond the pale simply because the positivists turned out to have admired something of a monster. As indicated earlier, Comte and his successors regarded the key method of science as being the primacy given to sense experience, to which Comte added the quest to find the (observable) laws of phenomena. By the light of our contemporary understanding this is a considerable oversimplification, if not worse.

There has been no dearth of others who have admired science, and who have given analyses of it that differ markedly from the one provided by the positivists and logical positivists. This is not the place to recount the Popperian analysis, nor the Deweyan (to pick two that are particularly interesting and compatible with my own predilections, and which are discussed elsewhere in this volume). But it can be said that there are substantial reasons for believing that *all* effective thinkers, across a very broad range of disciplines—including the humanities—use similar intellectual methods. Whether these are collectively called the "scientific method", or the method of "effective thinking", is a matter of personal preference. Both Dewey and Popper give strikingly similar analyses of this "method"; which of course is not a *method* in the sense that an algorithm is put forward, the slavish following of which is guaranteed to lead always to a happy outcome—their "method" is much more open-ended than that. Basically, effective thinking, in science and elsewhere, involves the identification and clarification of problems, the formulation of tentative solutions, and the practical (or theoretical) testing of these and the elimination of those that are not successful in resolving the original problem. For all intents and purposes this "method" is a "soft" extension of what has come to be labeled as the hypothetico-deductive method in science.

The anti-positivistic vigilantes, if indeed they are seriously interested in thinking effectively about the empirical realm, have nothing to fear from such an account of "scientific method"—it is quite un-positivistic (although it is, one supposes, compatible with Comte's desire to commandeer scientific method for wider use among those who study human affairs). Furthermore, as philosophers like Dagfinn Follesdal have pointed out, this method is used even in areas such as hermeneutics, which are typically regarded as being far removed from the field of science (Follesdal, 1979; and also the literary theorist E. D. Hirsch, Jr., 1978, pp. 151-152, for a similar point).

Perhaps it is fitting, by way of conclusion, to recall that among all the defects, the positivists and logical positivists were interested in serious questions, and they gave an interesting (but flawed) series of answers. R. W. Ashby has reminded us that the

> logical positivists contributed a great deal toward the understanding of the nature of philosophical questions, and in their approach to philosophy they set an example from which many have still to learn. They brought to philosophy an interest in cooperation.... They adopted high standards of rigor.... And they tried to formulate methods of inquiry that would lead to commonly accepted results (Ashby, 1964, p. 508).

References

Ashby, R. W. (1964). Logical positivism. In D. J. O'Connor (Ed.), *A Critical History of Western Philosophy*. NY: The Free Press.

Ayer, A. J. (1960). *Language, Truth, and Logic*. London: Gollancz.

Bridgman, P. W. (1927). *The Logic of Modern Physics*. NY: Macmillan.

Carnap, Rudolf (1956). The methodological character of theoretical concepts. In H. Feigl and Michael Scriven (Eds.), *Minnesota Studies in the Philosophy of Science*, Vol. 1. Minneapolis: University of Minnestoa Press.

Carnap, Rudolf (1969). *The Logical Structure of the World and Pseudoproblems in Philosophy*. Berkeley: University of California Press.

Comte, Auguste (1970). *Introduction to Positive Philosophy*. Tr. by Frederick Ferre. Indianapolis and NY: Bobbs-Merrill.

Dewey, John (1941). The objectivism-subjectivism of modern philosophy. *The Journal of Philosophy*, xxxviii, 20, Sept. 25.

Follesdal, Dagfinn (1979). Hermeneutics and the hypothetico-deductive method. *Dialectica*, 33, 319-336.

Hanson, N. R. (1958). *Patterns of Discovery*. Cambridge: Cambridge University Press.

Hirsch, E. D., Jr. (1978). *The Aims of Interpretation*. Chicago: University of Chicago Press.

Keat, Russell and Urry, John (1982). *Social Theory as Science*, 2nd edition. London: Routledge.

Konvitz, Milton and Kennedy, Gail (Eds.) (1960). *The American Pragmatists*. NY: Meridian.

Maxwell, Grover (1962). The ontological status of theoretical entities. In H. Feigl and G. Maxwell (Eds.), *Minnesota Studies in the Philosophy of Science*, Vol. III. Minneapolis: University of Minnesota Press.

Popper, Karl (1974). Autobiography. In P. A. Schilpp (Ed.), *The Philosophy of Karl Popper*. La Salle: Open Court.

Popper, Karl (1976). Reason or revolution? In T. Adorno *et al.* (Eds.), *The Positivist Dispute in German Sociology*. NY: Harper and Row.

Popper, Karl (1985). In David Miller (Ed.), *Popper Selections*. Princeton, NJ: Princeton University Press.

Scriven, Michael (1969). In P. Achinstein and F. Barker (Eds.), *The Legacy of Logical Positivism*. Baltimore: Johns Hopkins Press.

Spencer, Herbert (1949). On the genesis of science. In his *Essays on Education*. London: Dent/Everyman.

Watson, J. B. (1948). Psychology as the behaviorist views it. In Wayne Dennis (Ed.), *Readings in the History of Psychology*. NY: Appleton-Century-Crofts.

8

Qualitative Research and Its Warrant *

It is generally held that William Topaz McGonagall (d. 1902) was the worst poet ever to have been published in the English language. One commentator has written:

> He was so giftedly bad that he backed unwittingly into genius. Combining a minimum feel for the English language with a total lack of self-awareness and nil powers of observation, he became a poet (Pile, 1980, p. 123).

We can thank our lucky stars that he did not become a naturalistic qualitative researcher—another profession for which he would have been singularly unqualified.

Unlike McGonagall, but like genuine poets, qualitative researchers are supposed to have keen powers of observation, heightened self-awareness and realization of how their own personalities can shape their work, and a sensitive command of the language in which they are going to report their observations. There is, however, one important respect in which poets and qualitative researchers differ—the works produced by poets may be intended to be enjoyable, insightful, and stimulating, but usually it is not necessary that they be *accepted as true*. "Half a league, half a league, half a league onward ...", and the rest, is a poetic rendering of the charge of the Light Brigade, but only the innocent (or the Hollywood scriptwriter) would take it to be a factual description of what actually happened on that fateful day in the Crimea. Indeed, in many cases the notion of "truth" does not seem applicable to poetry at all; consider the lines of John Keats: "Thou still unravish'd bride of quietness. Thou foster-child of Silence and slow Time". These words are magical—they are evocative and communicate a great deal; to ask whether they are true or not is to make a serious "category mistake".

On the other hand, qualitative researchers generally *do* intend for their findings to be taken as veridical. To say that a description of a classroom, life in an urban gang, or village life in some exotic culture, is evocative but is not meant to be true or false, is merely another category mistake

106

(it is to identify qualitative research as being poetry, or something similar). Moreover, it is a mistake that is fatal for qualitative research; if a qualitative description or analysis is not true or false (i.e., if in principle these terms are not applicable to it), then the issue of whether that description or analysis is to be believed or acted upon cannot arise—it is not sensible to say that one believes the lines by Keats, just as it is not sensible to say that one believes Mozart's clarinet concerto and is prepared to base policy or social intervention upon it.

Thus, in order to be believed (or disbelieved), and in order to be (or not to be) the basis for intervention or for policy, it is absolutely necessary to have the property of being true or false; and to have one or other of these properties the statement, finding, theory or whatever must make some claim about some state-of-affairs. (This is not to say that we can always, or even often, determine whether the item under consideration is *actually* true or false.) All of this seems to have been acknowledged by Miles and Huberman, authors of what is fast becoming a standard volume on naturalistic qualitative methodology; in an earlier paper they wrote:

> The results (of qualitative research, especially the "connoisseurship" approach) are expected to be taken seriously, to be accepted as plausible, even valid, beyond the corps of people using the critical perspective. Otherwise, no one beyond the observer would be illuminated, and no serious claims of connoisseurship could be made that other publics could acknowledge (Miles and Huberman, 1984, p. 21).

The foregoing argument establishes that truth is necessary for certain societal functions to be carried out; but it is also necesary to point out that people have surprising "hangups" about it. Today truth has a similar status to that occupied by the topic of sex in the bygone Victorian era—it is not a topic that refined folk like to discuss, at least in public. (In private, of course, both topics have been the focus of much attention and have been the butt not only of words, but of deeds.) In both cases euphemisms have been used, as if the embarrassing topics would vanish if they were not referred to in a direct and forthright manner. Thus expressions like "X is true" and "X is the truth" are often avoided by qualitative researchers, and get replaced by "X is to be believed" or "X can be assented to"—a harmless enough verbal ploy, because most folk realize that, in general, to *believe X* is to *accept X as being true*. The practice only becomes pernicious when some qualitative researchers claim that there is no "truth", but still want their account of X to be believed! (It is worth stressing that not *all* qualitative researchers are guilty of this; and it is not all qualitative researchers who are the butt of criticism in the following discussion. In general, the negative points to be made do not apply to those who work in the anthropological or ethnographic tradition, but rather it is the newer modes of qualitative work that are the targets here.)

Other euphemisms are common as well; questions about truth are often stated in terms of validity or justification. "Is this conclusion valid?", "Is it justified?", "Can this result be trusted?" are questions posed by researchers from different poles of the "newer" qualitative continuum. This word-game is somewhat more dangerous, for, if it is not played carefully, it can very easily lead to pernicious results. Before pursuing this discussion, however, some clearing of the terrain needs to take place.

Some Truths About Truth

1. There is one euphemism that has a great deal to be said in its favor. John Dewey was reluctant to use the term "truth", and he decided to replace the term by "warranted assertibility". The reasoning is complex (it is to be found scattered through the pages of *Logic: The Theory of Inquiry*), but it is clear Dewey recognized that when truth-claims are made, to be taken seriously they must be supportable with appropriate arguments or evidence. It is, indeed, the strength of the warranting argument or evidence that *allows* a truth to be recognized and labeled as such. This approach, too, can easily accommodate those cases where what was formerly regarded as truth is re-identified as non-truth—what has happened here is that the warrant for assertion has been withdrawn, it has been found to be in error. The great merit of Dewey's language, then, is that it highlights the necessity to have an adequate warrant—which in his view can come only from "competent inquiries" (Dewey, 1966, p. 8). What should count as the criteria of adequacy and competency is, of course, a sticky question.

2. It is held by many—including some in the qualitative camp who have been eager to latch onto this—that recent developments in philosophy of science have made the notion of truth otiose. (The argument here is that if philosophers have shown that the notion of truth has to be abandoned in the physical sciences, then qualitative researchers should have no concerns about it at all.) This is a misinterpretation of the contemporary scene. Certainly there has been a great freeing-up with respect to what counts as evidence for and against the truth of a scientific hypothesis; it can no longer be held that any single test result can be definitive one way or the other. The role of theories in influencing observations, the relation between theory and evidence, the role of auxiliary and *ad hoc* assumptions—all of these have been elucidated in the recent literature (see Phillips, 1987 and also Chapter 4 of the present volume). It is now recognized more clearly than ever before that our human judgments about what *is* true are fallible, and subject to constant revision. And it is recognized that we cannot even be sure that our constant revisions are

bringing us nearer to the truth; Popper's great attempt to produce a theory of verisimilitude is acknowledged as being a failure, even by his closest admirers.

But nowhere in the mainstream of philosophy (anything can happen, of course, in the "lunatic fringe") is it held that we are free to believe whatever we want, that there are no constraints on belief. Even Kuhn, who has been seen by some as the apostle of rampant relativism, does not believe in intellectual anarchy. (He sees most investigators in any particular field of natural science, at most times in history, as being in one paradigm, but during revolutionary periods they are spread over two. Kuhn certainly does not see every investigator being in his or her *own* paradigm. In other words he does not do away with truth, but sees judgments about what is true as being made internally to a paradigm.) And Richard Rorty, who wants to do away with Truth (note the capital T), does not want to abandon truth (note the lower-case t) or standards for warrants; towards the end of his influential *Philosophy and the Mirror of Nature* he writes of "knowing" as being "a right, by current standards, to believe" (his acknowledged debt to Dewey is quite evident here), and he goes on to say that more attention should be given

> to the relation between alternative standards of justification, and from there to the actual change in those standards which make up intellectual history (Rorty, 1979, pp. 389-390).

To say that standards change or evolve is not to say that there are no standards or that there should not be any!

3. The Kuhnian-inspired notion that there may be rival paradigms, with their own views of what is true, has led to the development of a more extreme position—there are *multiple realities*, so there are multiple sets of truths, all of which are true at the same time (see the discussion in Chapter 4). Several of the newer apologists for qualitative methods of research have held this; William Filstead, for example, claims that this view is related to the philosophical position of idealism, and he states:

> The qualitative paradigm does not conceive of the world as an external force, objectively identifiable and independent of man. Rather, there are multiple realities (Filstead, 1979, pp. 35-36).

A similar statement is to be found in Guba and Lincoln:

> Naturalistic inquirers (their name for qualitative researchers) make virtually the opposite assumptions (to positivistic, scientific inquirers). They focus upon the multiple realities that, like the layers of an onion, nest within or complement one another. Each layer provides a different perspective of reality, and none can be considered more "true" than any other. Phenomena do not converge into a single form, a single "truth", but diverge into many forms, multiple "truths" (Guba and Lincoln, 1982, p. 57).

On one interpretation, Guba and Lincoln and the others who hold similar positions are saying something rather trite, and they are mistaken in thinking that there is a conflict here with what "traditional" or "non-naturalistic" scientists believe. Of course a phenomenon can be examined from different perspectives; a motor accident can be approached in terms of the physics of the collision, in terms of economics, in terms of the psychological states of the drivers, in medical terms, and so on. Such accounts may all be true; they are complementary or orthogonal, not conflicting. But it seems as if Filstead, and Guba and Lincoln, have something else in mind—possibly they envision multiple but conflicting truths that can, nevertheless, all be true. The discussion here can best progress in terms of an analogy: Consider rival religions, which give quite incompatible accounts of the nature of the Deity (one says He or She has property P, and the other holds the opposite). Each religion has its devotees who regard it as true, but it is hard to conceive that *all* accounts are true at the same time. (Of course, *which* account is true is not the issue here.) Even a Deity would be hard pressed to both have, and not have, property P, at the one instant. There is a strong tradition in the philosophy of religion that even a Deity must conform to the laws of logic; it is sobering that according to Filstead, and Guba and Lincoln, the physical realm outstrips the power of a Deity here (for according to them it can have opposing properties)! Certainly they owe their readers further discussion on this extraordinary point. (This issue is pursued further in Chapter 4.)

Whatever these various writers mean, they cannot coherently hold that any view which anyone cares to assert must be accepted as being true. They do not want to eradicate the need to put forward warrants for belief (indeed, this and other books by Guba and Lincoln deal with how to produce effective warrants in social program evaluation settings). They seem to realize that not everyone who postulates an alternative reality is right—it is possible for such a person to be paranoid, deluded, or simply in error. So, then, there must be criteria for judging the warrants that are advanced on behalf of claims to have detected new realities. Guba and Lincoln raise this issue in the following terms, using "scare marks" around the word "truth" to warn their readers that they are unhappy with it and intend to replace it by "credibility"; nevertheless, the concern with warrant is still apparent:

> How can one establish confidence in the "truth" of the findings of a particular inquiry for the subjects with which—and the context within which—the inquiry was carried out? (Ibid., p. 103).

This, then, is the moral of the discussion so far: The worry about what will count as a satisfactory qualitative warrant for beliefs or truth-claims will not wane. On all but the most exotic (and incomprehensible) views of the nature of truth and knowledge, there arises the issue of why the account of some phenomenon that is given by a qualitative researcher (or, for that matter, any researcher) should be believed.

Is Qualitative Work More Suspect than Quantitative or Experimental?

The points made so far apply to *all* research. All truth claims, in all areas, need to have warrants; and all truth claims, in all areas except perhaps logic and mathematics, are never absolutely established—they may be strongly supported by warrants, but they never reach the stage where they are immune from revision in the light of the results of further inquiry. So why, then, should qualitative research be singled out for especial attention?

There are a number of methodological problems that, while not entirely confined to the province of qualitative research, are especially serious here. They are somewhat interrelated, so the following listing should not be taken too seriously; the categories could easily be collapsed or expanded:

(a) As N. R. Hanson and many others have shown, observation is theory-laden. It is somewhat easier to correct for (or control) the biasing effects of prior knowledge and beliefs when one is observing inanimate nature than it is when observing human or social phenomena. For we ourselves are human, and our beliefs about humankind are strongly held, and are bound up with our feelings and our valuations.

(b) It is unlikely that an observer will enter into social relationships with any inanimate or subhuman entities that are under study; this is quite likely to occur in the human or social domains. The point, of course, is that in social relationships the behaviors, beliefs, and perceptions of the parties concerned are likely to be affected; people do and say things partly with the likely reactions of the other actors in mind; and emotional bonds start to form. It is hard to know what to make of observations that are made under these conditions, unless the observer has been especially sensitive and has taken careful precautions.

(c) An observer does not have to make especial efforts to understand or empathize with inanimate objects, but there are good grounds to believe that if observation of human and social phenomena is to be sensible then it is often unavoidable that the reasons held by the people being observed must be comprehended (see the discussion in Chapter 1). But attainment of this understanding of the reasons and beliefs held by other people often results in some fellow-feeling with them—it is difficult to be distant and unconcerned; in short, it is difficult to be objective.

These problems are widely understood by qualitative methodologists; and Miles and Huberman, and of course many writers in the ethnographic tradition, offer many positive suggestions. Others take these problems as indications that the study of human or social affairs can never be "scientific", or argue that objectivity is an unattainable—and perhaps even a misplaced—ideal.

(d) Insofar as qualitative researchers rely on non-formal or "intuitive"modes of data-processing, they have to face squarely the fact that "whatever its other strengths, the mind is apt to make errors of judgment and inference" (Royce Sadler, 1982, p. 199). For example, human observers are quite prone to be unduly influenced or "anchored" by their first impressions of a situation, they are over-influenced by positive instances supporting an hypothesis or bias but undervalue negative instances, they incorrectly estimate "base-rate" frequencies of behaviors they are studying, they do not allow properly for missing data even when they know it is missing, and so forth. Again some—but by no means all—qualitative methodologists are sensitive to the problems here, and they take care to minimize the threats to the validity of their studies (while others call such precautions the illicit remnant of positivism) (see Bryman, 1984, esp. p. 85).

(e) There is an especially difficult problem that can arise in some—but not all—qualitative research. It does not arise if the aim of the research is to catalogue the beliefs that are held by the people who are being studied, and it also does not arise if the purpose is entirely descriptive. But it does arise when qualitative research aims to uncover causes—and this is not uncommon, especially in research that hopes to result in advice on how to improve performance (e.g., how to improve effectiveness of teaching or how to combat juvenile delinquency), or in research that is related to evaluation of programs or settings. Causes are not always accessible to unaided observation; in most settings there are many inter-acting factors at work, and to tease out those that are causally responsible for effects is no easy task. Usually a degree of control will have to be exercised—some factors will have to be held constant, while others are varied. The classic statement of this is in the work of John Stuart Mill:

> In every instance which comes under our observation, there are many antecedents and many consequents. If those antecedents could not be severed from one another except in thought or if those consequents never were found apart, it would be impossible for us to distinguish (a posteriori, at least) the real laws, or to assign to any cause its effect, or to any effect its cause. To do so, we must be able to meet with some of the antecedents apart from the rest and observe what follows from them, or some of the consequents and observe by what they are preceded. We must, in short, follow the Baconian rule of *varying the circumstances* (Mill, 1950, p. 210).

The qualitative researcher who seeks causes thus has to become an experimenter (even if the experiments are not true, randomized ones)—a matter that those in the anthropological tradition have long recognized. In short, naked observation is generally a poor device for warranting causal claims, or for warranting advice on intervention or on future policy (for such advice itself is dependent upon having causal knowledge of situations). Many of the newer qualitative methodologists have not seriously grappled with the difficult problems here.

By way of summary of this section of the discussion, it seems appropriate to cite the assessment given by Martin Hammersley of the work of the influential Chicago qualitative sociologist Herbert Blumer. Hammersley writes that nowhere is

> Blumer clear about the nature of the process of testing that he claims is involved in naturalistic (i.e., his form of qualitative) research. He seems to place faith in the idea that by "going directly to the social world" and examining it we will discover its nature. I think he sees any fixed procedure as a barrier to such discovery because it impairs the flexibility of the researcher. The latter must be free to adapt to, to be moulded by, the world. In my view, though, while exploration, flexibility, and creativity are necessary, the idea that if one adopts a flexible attitude towards the world in one's interactions with it, one will come to discover its nature amounts to a naive form of realism. It underestimates the potential for bias and error (Hammersley, 1989, p. 189).

Hammersley could have added that observation, or even "flexible" inter-action with the world, is not sufficient to sort out the causal chains that operate in the social world. The point, simply, is this: the social world can be given *many* descriptions, and the issue arises as to why we should accept the description that a particular researcher happens to favor. The fact that the researcher happens to favor it is not a sufficient warrant.

In the light of all these complexities, the issue again arises as to how well the warrants that are suggested in the literature fare—will the warrants favored by qualitative researchers (when, indeed, they explicitly favor a warrant) stand up to scrutiny?

Will the Suggested Warrants Work?

Qualitative methodology has won a foothold in many branches of the "pure" and "applied" social sciences; it has, of course, long been a feature of some branches, such as anthropology. But the foothold was not always won easily in the other branches. In sociology, for example, several journals ran symposia in the late 1970s (see Bryman, 1984, p. 76); and there was an attendant amount of name-calling and labeling:

> In some cases writers have chosen not to use the quantitative/qualitative distinction and have instead used terms which have been used as synonyms. The terms "positivist" and "empiricist" often denote the same fundamental approach as "quantitative", while "naturalistic" field research, "ethnographic", "interpretivist", and "constructivist" are sometimes used instead of "qualitative" (Bryman, 1984, p. 77).

A strikingly similar debate has raged in the field of educational research during the decade of the eighties, chiefly in North America; some of the contributors here (including Miles and Huberman, and Guba and Lincoln) have been influential more broadly across the applied social sciences. To make the following discussion manageable, it is this more recent debate that shall be the focus of attention—the points are applicable across the social sciences.

The literature on qualitative methodology in the educational research domain contains a variety of suggested warrants, and a host of ways of conceptualizing warrants—ways that are generally notable for their avoidance of the embarrassing term "truth". Some writers admit that there is a problem here, that is, they acknowledge that the warrants which have been suggested are not adequate for the task in hand. In the work of Miles and Huberman referred to earlier, this concern about qualitative methodology has been raised, and they have written that "As we have said often, qualitative analyses can be evocative, illuminating, masterful, and downright *wrong*" (Miles and Huberman, 1985, p. 230). In the discussion that follows, their own suggestions concerning warrants will be examined, as will the views of the Stanford researcher Elliot Eisner, and Egon Guba and Yvonna Lincoln. (These three sets of authors are considered because between them they seem to cover the whole spectrum of the newer qualitative methodologies. At one pole, Eisner is a self-declared electicist, relativist, and instrumentalist (Eisner, 1983, p. 14); Miles and Huberman are at the other pole—they call themselves "right wing" qualitative researchers, or "soft-nosed positivists" (Miles and Huberman, 1985, p. 23); and Guba and Lincoln are—perhaps—somewhere in between.) For want of a better criterion, the discussion will proceed alphabetically.

(i) Elliot Eisner. Eisner sees the issue of the truth of qualitatively-generated findings in terms of "validity" and "trustworthiness". He asks, "How can we know if educational criticism (his version of qualitative investigation) can be trusted?" (Eisner, 1979, p. 213). He goes on to provide three criteria—structural corroboration, referential adequacy, and multiplicative replication.

The first of these, structural corroboration, is easily dealt with. Eisner himself admits—after advocating its use—that it is not a reliable yardstick. For structural corroboration is the process in which various parts of the account or description or explanation give each other mutual support, it is a process of "gathering data or information and using it to establish links that eventually create a whole that is supported by the bits of evidence that constitute it" (Ibid., p. 215). Possession of this type of corroboration, of course, shows that the account is coherent, but coherence is not correlated with truth. As Eisner notes, a swindler's story is coherent and convincing!

Turning to the second criterion: A work (for example, a description of a classroom) has referential adequacy, when it enables us to see features that it refers to but which we may not ourselves have noticed:

When the critic's work is referentially adequate we will be able to find in the object, event, or situation what the cues point to (Ibid., p. 216).

The problem here, of course, is that seeing what the critic or qualitative researcher is talking about, does not mean that the account is *true*. Thus, I can read Hitler's description of (among other things) the post-World War I Germany in *Mein Kampf*, and had I been alive at the time I might—with a little effort—have been able to see the world through his eyes, but this does not mean that his account would have been veridical. Or, to take a less loaded example, it is possible to look at an autistic child after having studied the Freudian theory about this condition; one can see what the Freudians are talking about. (One can do the same with the behaviorist theory.) The fact that this can be done does not establish the *truth* of the theory.

An argument drawn from contemporary philosophy of science can be used to bolster this conclusion. For any data set, no matter how large, an infinite number of theoretical explanations can be given—a phenomenon that has come to be called "the under-determination of the theory of nature". So the fact that we may all see the same things does not speak to the truth of any one theoretical account. But it must be stressed again that there are problems for Eisner's criterion at less lofty levels than the realms of theory—the actual *description* of the situation that is observed may be challengeable. Just because I can see what the Freudian is referring to, does not mean that I thereby endorse that his or her description is the correct one. (After all, I can also see what the rival behaviorist is referring to.)

So Eisner is down to one last criterion, which involves other people having seen the same things; he calls this "multiplicative replication", and he himself does not place much weight on it. For consensual validation (which is what the criterion amounts to) is a two-edged sword; all sorts of cults and fads have been "corroborated" in this way, but one would be hard pressed to say this was a sign of their truth. (On occasion Eisner bravely bites the bullet, and suggests that there is no such thing as truth, it is *only* a matter of what a community believes. This, of course, has the consequence that it is true that the earth is both spherical and flat, because there are communities who believe either thing. On the positive side, it must be acknowledged that this nicely solves the problem with which this chapter began—there is no problem about the truth of qualitative research findings, because *each one* of them is true, providing that a community can be found that will subscribe to it!)

In case, however, there are some readers who do not find this satisfactory, the discussion will turn to the work of Guba and Lincoln.

(ii) Guba and Lincoln. These writers argue that the question of "truth value" can be reduced to the question of "credibility" (Guba and Lincoln,

1982, pp. 104-105). They suggest various techniques, such as reducing involvement with the human subjects the fieldworker is interacting with; they also build upon Eisner's notion of structural corroboration. However, after a detailed discussion of techniques that are useful here, they make a significant remark:

> the techniques discussed above do not themselves establish credibility—at best they simply increase the probability that data and interpretations will be found credible.

What then *is* their answer?

> The determination of credibility can be accomplished only by taking data and interpretations to the sources from which they were drawn and asking directly whether they believe—find plausible—the results. This process of going to the sources—often called "member checks"—is the backbone of satisfying the truth-value criterion (Ibid., p. 110).

It is worth noting that this same procedure is standardly used by ethnographers working within the anthropological tradition.

In one sense this is no advance, indeed it is a retrograde suggestion; but in another sense it is sound. The heart of the matter here is the precise nature of the findings or account the "credibility" of which is being probed. If the account that the qualitative researcher is dealing with is an account of the beliefs held by an individual or by a group of subjects—and this is the central focus in ethnographic work—then the appropriate criterion *is* whether or not these subjects agree that the researcher has indeed accurately recorded their beliefs. But this is not central in most of the work done by qualitative researchers of an Eisnerian or Guberian stamp. When the account produced by the qualitative researcher is an account of a classroom, or of the effects of some educational or social program, or the like, then it is clear that the endorsement of the participants in the classroom or program in question has little or nothing to do with the truth of the account. A qualitative researcher's account of an interaction between a therapist and an autistic child might be true or false quite independently of the assent or dissent of the two participants; similarly, an account of a classroom might be true even though the teacher (or the pupils) disagree with it.

This is such a major point that it is worth stating in another way. If the purpose of a piece of qualitative work is *emic*, that is, if the intent is to give an account of how the participants in a situation see it, then checking the account with the participants (or with a selected "informant") is a vital step. On the other hand, if the intent is *etic*, that is, if the purpose is *not* to describe a situation from a participant's viewpoint but from, say, an Eisnerian connoisseur's outside perspective, then getting the imprimatur of the participants is beside the point—their judgments about "credibility" are irrelevant.

Guba and Lincoln are paying the price, here, of misidentifying truth with credibility. Credibility is a scandalously weak and inappropriate surrogate for truth or veracity—under appropriate circumstances any nonsense at all can be judged as "credible". It is time, then, to turn to the next set of authors to see if they fare any better.

(iii) Miles and Huberman. These writers start in a promising way by noting that qualitative analyses can be illuminating, masterful, and evocative, but also *wrong* (Miles and Huberman, 1984, pp. 27 and 230). They also use the expression "truth space". But then they start to drift off target by identifying the attainment of truth with the possession of certain data-processing methods:

> The problem is that there is an insufficient corpus of reliable, valid, or even minimally agreed-upon working analysis procedures for qualitative data (Miles and Huberman, 1984, p. 22; see also 1985, p. 230).

Of course a lot depends upon what procedures they have in mind to recommend, and as will be seen shortly they undoubtedly have some important ideas. But in general it must be recognized that there are *no* procedures that will regularly (or always) yield either sound data or true conclusions. If there were such procedures, then steady progress in human understanding would be guaranteed—indeed, it would probably become a matter of following routines, and eventually knowledge generation could be taken over by computers. The words of philosopher of science Paul Feyerabend are worth quoting in this context:

> The idea of a method that contains firm, unchanging, and absolutely binding principles for conducting the business of science gets into considerable difficulty when confronted with the results of historical research. We find, then, that there is not a single rule, however plausible, and however firmly grounded in epistemology, that is not violated at some time or another. It becomes evident that such violations are not isolated events.... On the contrary, we see they are necessary for progress.... More specifically, the following can be shown: considering any rule, however "fundamental", there are always circumstances when it is advisable not only to ignore the rule, but to adopt its opposite (Feyerabend, 1970, pp. 21-22).

Feyerabend states that, in fact, there *is* one rule: "Anything goes."

The point of this is not to strengthen the skepticism (or Feyerabendian "anarchism") that is already rampant in the modern academic world. The point is merely to issue a caution to those who read Miles and Huberman as saying that the formulation of true belief is simply *a matter of finding, and following, certain analytic procedures*. They themselves recognize this danger, and they warn against "overpreoccupation with method rather than substance and the development of a crippling, mechanical orthodoxy" (Miles and Huberman, 1984, p. 28).

Miles and Huberman suggest a dozen "verification tactics", many of which have already been alluded to—they draw liberally on Eisnerian and Guberian ideas. Mostly, their suggested procedures, if followed, would produce consensus among investigators (i.e., multiplicative replication) rather than truth. This direction in their work is clearly revealed in the preamble to their list of tactics:

> How do we know whether a conclusion is surreal or real? By "real" we mean another competent researcher, working independently at the same site, would not come up with wholly contradictory findings (Ibid., p. 27).

It must be stressed that no objection is being made here to having researchers, as far as possible, independently check each other's work. On the contrary, this is a counsel of wisdom. But the point is that this is a relatively weak guarantee of "reality" or "truth" (as the history of anthropology and of physics bear witness). It may be the best that we can hope for, but it should be recognized for what it is, warts and all.

In fact, Miles and Huberman succeed in doing a little better. One of their twelve tactics is "looking for negative evidence", and while this is not absolutely foolproof, and cannot establish that a finding or conclusion is right, it can help in what Popper has called "error elimination". Indeed, this tactic is worthy of elaboration, and deserves a much more central place than they given it—it is buried as number eleven in their list, and does not seem to play a role at all in the methodology recommended by Eisner or Guba and Lincoln (Ibid., p. 28). Popper, in various places, makes the telling point that any fool can find confirmations for an hypothesis, but what is crucial is whether or not refuting evidence can be found. (Of course, it has to be actively sought.) Again this does not *guarantee* truth, but if believability is important—and all the qualitative methodologists considered in this chapter regard it as such—then surviving a serious attempt at refutation provides the strongest basis that probably can be attained for belief. Dewey, too, regarded the testing of hypotheses as a vital step in effective inquiry resulting in the warranting of belief; and like Popper he saw that conclusions cannot be proven as true, but they can be eliminated as false (he should have said: probably false):

> Denial of the consequent grounds (i.e., warrants), however, denial of the antecedent. When, therefore, operations yield data which contradict a deduced consequence, elimination of one alternative possibility is effected.... Elimination of other possibilities progressively reduces the likelihood of fallacious inference (Dewey, 1966, pp. 318-9).

Those readers who do not find Dewey and Popper convincing about the relationship between refutation and growth of knowledge (warranted belief), may find the following statement authoritative—in Proverbs, 12:1, it is written that "Whoso loveth correction loveth knowledge, but he that hateth reproof is brutish."

Unsatisfying Conclusion

The worry about the warrant for conclusions drawn from a qualitative inquiry will not wane, largely because the worry about the warrant for conclusions drawn from *any* inquiry will not wane. But we should not be fobbed off by *purported* resolutions to this worry that really do not address the relevant issues. Believability, credibility, consensus, coherence—all these things are no doubt important, and a piece of research would be the better for possessing them; but these things do not guarantee the truth of the research conclusion, indeed, they might not even be indicators of truth. Nevertheless, truth is a *regulative ideal*; it is much better to strive for it, even though it is akin to the impossible dream of the Man from La Mancha, than it is to strive for something less worthy.

Qualitative research is hard work, and, as indicated, it is work that is not always destined to meet with success. But it may not be as hard as writing poetry. McGonagall immortalized the pain and effort that is involved in the terrible lines he penned in tribute to his physician, Dr Murison:

> He told me at once what was ailing me;
> He said I had been writing too much poetry,
> And from writing poetry I would have to refrain,
> Because I was suffering from inflammation on the brain.
> (McGonagall, 1980, p. 45)

Qualitative researchers need to have a much clearer understanding of their own limitations than McGonagall had.

* Reprinted with permission from *Education and Urban Society*, 20, 1, November 1987. Phillips, D. C. "Validity in Qualitative Research". © 1987.

References

Bryman, Alan (1984). The debate about quantitative and qualitative research: a question of method or epistemology? *British Journal of Sociology*, **xxxv**, 1, 75-92.

Dewey, John (1966). *Logic: the Theory of Inquiry*. NY: Holt.

Eisner, Elliot (1979). *The Educational Imagination*. NY: Macmillan.

Eisner, Elliot (1983). Anastasia might still be alive, but the monarchy is dead. *Educational Researcher*, **12**, 5, May.

Feyerabend, P. (1970). Against method. In M. Radner and S. Winokur (Eds.), *Analyses of Theories and Methods of Physics and Psychology*. Minneapolis: University of Minnesota Press.

Filstead, W. (1979). Qualitative method: a needed perspective in evaluation research. In T. Cook and C. Reichardt (Eds.), *Qualitative and Quantitive Methods in Evaluation Research*. Beverly Hills: Sage.

Guba, E. and Lincoln, Y. (1982). *Effective Evaluation*. SF: Jossey-Bass.

Hammersley, Martin (1989). *The Dilemma of Qualitative Method: Herbert Blumer and the Chicago Tradition*. London and NY: Routledge.

McGonagall, W. T. (1980). *Yet Further Poetic Gems*. London: Duckworth.

Miles, M. and Huberman, A. M. (1984). Drawing valid meaning from qualitative data. *Educational Researcher*, **13**, 5, May.

Miles, M. and Huberman, A. M. (1985). *Qualitative Data Analysis*. Beverly Hills: Sage.

Mill, John Stuart (1950). In E. Nagel (Ed.), *Philosophy of Scientific Method*. NY: Hafner.

Phillips, D. C. (1987). *Philosophy, Science, and Social Inquiry*. Oxford and NY:. Pergamon Press.

Pile, Stephen (1980). *The Book of Heroic Failures*. London: Futura Publications.

Rorty, Richard (1979). *Philosophy and the Mirror of Nature*. Princeton: Princeton University Press.

Royce Sadler, D. (1982). Intuitive data processing as a potential source of bias in naturalistic evaluations. In E. House *et al.* (Eds.), *Evaluation Studies Review Annual*, Vol. 7.

9

Theories and Laws

Questioner: As a social scientist I try to produce theories in my areas of interest. But it has occurred to me that I don't know what characteristics a set of statements must possess in order to count as a theory—I guess up to now I have just gone on intuition. That is, if it felt as if something was a theory, I called it a theory (not that I have had overmuch success in satisfying my ambitions to produce them, I must admit). At any rate, my opening question is this: What *is* a theory?

Respondent: My response is to quote a contributor to the periodical *New Scientist* who wrote that "I have yet to see any problem however complicated which, when you look at it in the right way, did not become still more complicated" (cited in Matthew, 1991, p. 112). Let's take first things first in this enormously complex issue—there is a kind of "chicken and egg" problem that can get us derailed right at the start. Arthur Caplan recently put the point this way: he said that

> the domain of examples governing philosophical reflection about science is highly determinative of how the conceptual evolution and change is understood and explained ... the extent to which theories can be axiomatized, and the deductive or nondeductive nature of relationships between theoretical statements are closely tied to the examples of scientific theories that are selected for analysis (Caplan, 1990, p. 25).

Let me enlarge on what I take his point to be. You could, as one strategy, define a theory as anything that has a set of characteristics C (you, and certainly many of my philosophical colleagues, have lots of presuppositions about what a theory should be like); this strategy would allow you to exclude anything that does not have these features—in other words no matter how interesting it might be, it couldn't possibly be a theory. (This, of course, would always allow you to maintain *your* account of the nature of theory, because no counterexample could be found—at least none that was allowable!). On the other hand, you could collect (without any censorship) a reasonable number of things that folk across the social sciences have at one time or another called theories, and you could then do an analytic job to find, as it were, the lowest common factor, and this would become your set of defining features. (In philosophical terminology, the two strategies boil down to giving either a stipulative or a reportive definition.)

Q: It doesn't seem unfair to say that one of these strategies guards against what statisticians call the "type one" error, and the other defends against the "type two" error, in the sense that one strategy is quite conservative about what will be allowed to count as a theory and might exclude some genuine cases, while the other is quite liberal and might allow a few imposters to slip in! I am drawn more to the second strategy, but it occurs to me that a melange of things have been called theories in the social sciences—some of my colleagues talk about theories of why Hitler or Napoleon acted in certain ways on specific occasions, or of theories of social mobility, or of theories of the labor market, or theories about such things as the origin of World War I or of causes of the Great Depression, or theories about Ronald Reagan's presidential election victory over Jimmy Carter, or theories of the causes of the enormous high school dropout rate among minority students. The lowest common factor here indeed would be very low—does it make any sense to think that one might find any significant commonalities from such a diverse group?

R: I share your concern. Perhaps we should remember that the word "theory" is not a technical word in the vocabulary of the social sciences (unlike "free market" or "intelligence quotient"). The term does not label what philosophers would call a natural kind. It is simply a general term that is used rather loosely, and can cover anything from an hypothesis about something ("my theory about who committed the murder is ...") to a highly abstract thing such as Einstein's special theory of relativity. There is no divinely ordained *correct* usage, but we can strive to use the word consistently and to mark distinctions that we feel are important. But this of course brings us back to square one again.

Q: Perhaps we could take a completely different tack, at least to get us going. I have noticed that some of my fellow social scientists want to produce theories in what they take to be the natural science sense, and before I make up my mind about this, I ought to find out what that sense is! Now, I have noticed that these colleagues have a strange fondness for, of all things, the kinetic theory of gases. Robert Merton is one case in point; he sees this theory as an admirable model for what he calls "theories of the middle range" in the social sciences (see Merton, 1967, esp. pp. 39-40). Another and more recent example is the sociologist Arthur Stinchcombe; in a paper of great philosophical interest that investigates the types of mechanisms to be found in social science theories, he constantly makes comparisons with kinetic theory (Stinchcombe, 1991). Not having done any physics or chemistry since high school, I must admit to being a bit rusty. Why is this so attractive, and what features does it illustrate about theories, at least in the natural sciences?

R: I warn you that this is not going to be a short answer; and I stress that I will be simplifying matters out of deference to your acknowledged lack of background. That understood, here goes; I'm about to launch into an exposition of what some philosophers have called "the received view" of the nature of theories. (See Suppe, 1974 and later editions, for the standard discussion of these matters.)

Q: I'm sorry to interrupt when you were hardly started, but the fact that it is labeled as the "received view" suggests to my suspicious mind that not everyone actually *does* receive it!

R: You're absolutely right. But almost everyone would accept *much* of the account I'm about to give, at least so far as kinetic theory goes. We can get to the dissenters later. So, back to the main theme: The field of gas behavior illustrates a number of important points. First, the field nowadays is one that is quite well understood, in the sense that we have a number of empirical laws, and a body of theory that has stood the test of time. So, textbooks tend to present a picture of the field, a picture of the relations between these elements, which is of necessity somewhat static and which represents what might be called the logical state of the field now that the tumult and the shouting have died. The naive reader sometimes goes away with the impression that the neat account that is given is also an accurate account of the history of the field, i.e., that it represents the order in which or the manner in which advances were made.

Q: Could you clarify this a little?

R: Let me start with a quotation from the philosopher R. B. Braithwaite:

> an advanced science like physics is not content only with establishing lowest-level generalisations covering physical events: it aims at, and has been largely successful in, subsuming its lowest-level generalisations under higher-level hypotheses, and thus organising its hypotheses into a hierarchical deductive system—a scientific theory—in which a hypothesis at a lower level is shown to be deducible from a set of hypotheses at a higher level (Braithwaite, 1973, p. 47).

The situation Braithwaite was describing can be captured in the form of a diagram depicting the "structure" of the field of gas behavior (I should say as an aside that social scientists sometimes draw similar diagrams in their own fields; see Kerlinger, 1973).

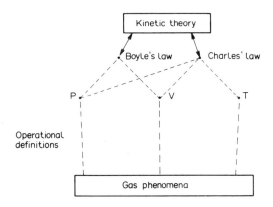

Fig. 9.1

Now, both Braithwaite's words (if read uncautiously) and this diagram (if it is read from the bottom up) might leave the impression that a scientist first identifies some phenomena that are of interest, then he or she makes observations and measurements of such things as pressure, volume and temperature (to do which, one needs to have constructed operational definitions of these variables), then the relationships between these variables are found (or, in social science terms, the researcher does a series of correlational studies), and finally, when enough results are in hand, the scientist "puts on the theoretical hat" and produces the theory that accounts for whatever relationships (laws or correlations) have been found. I guess this is the account Merton is proposing when he cautions that one should not theorize until enough data (in the form of correlations and generalizations) is at hand (although, to be fair, when he gave this advice he had "grand theory" in mind—see Merton, 1967, p. 46, and Chapter 3 of this present volume); and this is close to what Glaser and Strauss advocate in their work on "grounded theory" in the social sciences: "Generating a theory from data means that most hypotheses and concepts not only come from the data, but are systematically worked out in relation to data during the course of the research" (Glaser and Strauss, 1967, p. 6).

Q: And I suppose the point you are making is that this is not the historical line of development at all?

R: Indeed—and there is absolutely no reason to suggest that this ought to be adopted as a normative account either, that is, as an account of how scientific work *should* proceed. After all, unless scientists constantly theorize (even in a loose, speculative way) about what they are doing and what they are finding (or not finding), then their work is, at best, mechanical and is the epitome of mindlessness; it is not clear how you can decide what concepts to use when collecting data if you have no theory (however crude or incipient) in mind. (In a sense, concepts and theories *make* the data.) If you think this is harsh, you should see what Dewey and Popper, among others, have to say on this topic! Basically, what actually happened in the case of kinetic theory was that work went ahead on all fronts more or less simultaneously. Scientists were trying to work out what variables to measure, and how to measure them; but they also were trying to find regularities in gas behavior, whilst continually speculating about what deeper or underlying mechanisms might be at work in gases. In other words, in terms of our diagram, work was progressing all over the picture but it was only very late in the history of the field that *this* picture emerged as a static representation of (as it were) the final "logic". (It must be said as well that in this case the precise theory did not emerge until long after the empirical laws had been found; but the point is that the attempt to find a theory did not just start then.)

Q: I guess there is no reason to think that other examples from the natural sciences would suggest anything different. Certainly in at least some cases in the social sciences there are analogous situations—we don't know what to measure (or how to measure the things that might be of interest), we haven't been able to find reliable generalizations or correlations, and we don't know the relevant theoretical story (assuming that there is one to be had).

R: This view of the way in which science moves ought to shock many of your colleagues who set up operational definitions and then collect data and run statistical analyses to find "relationships" in a proudly a-theoretical way (and, of course, they overlook the fact that data are theory-laden anyway, so that they are somewhat deluded); I recall years ago the sociologist C. Wright Mills making the accusation that the social sciences were saturated with "dust bowl empiricism" of this kind (Mills, 1959).

Why don't we drop this and return to more cheerful topics—we have hardly scratched the surface of what the example of kinetic theory has to offer. Again with the caution that this is a somewhat "potted" history (or, as Lakatos might say, it is a "rational reconstruction" of the history; see Lakatos, 1978), let us return to the times when Boyle and Charles and Gay-Lussac and others had made their empirical breakthroughs.

Q: Fine. But what were those breakthroughs?

R: To start with, Boyle found that for any given mass of gas at constant temperature (i.e., for a sample of gas where both the mass and temperature were not allowed to change), the pressure and volume were related in such a way that if the pressure were to be increased, the volume would decrease—in other words, they were inversely proportional to each other, or, in symbolic form, $P = k/V$ or $PV = k$, where k is a constant that depends on the particular gas under consideration and PV is to be read as P multiplied by V. This is regarded as an empirical law, although it only holds true under limited conditions (if it is true at all, rather than just a convenient approximation).

Q: This law appears to be equivalent, as we mentioned earlier, to generalized correlational findings that we discover in the social sciences—I suppose the finding that IQ and success at school are positively related might be an example. I wonder why we don't call this a law?

R: Maybe it is because there are problems with the relationship you cited. First it doesn't hold, even approximately, for a fair number of individuals (that is, not all students with high IQ do well at school); it is, at best, a relation that holds if we take a larger number of individual cases and average the results. Boyle's Law holds, at least approximately, for all gases. Is this a significant difference or not? Second, it is not clear that the relation between IQ and schooling is necessary—it seems that it could change quite easily, for example if the nature of schooling were to change. (One can imagine schools in which high IQ is not necessary for success, as in the recent "accelerated schools" movement in the US which aims to help all students achieve success, especially those who normally would be placed in a low-achieving stream.) But, for a "genuine" law, do we believe that nature could change in such a way that it would cease to hold? Some philosophers (but not all) would argue that there is some sort of necessity about Boyle's Law—it *has* to hold. (Philosophers interested in this issue move off into strange realms, such as whether or not laws would hold in any "possible worlds".)

Q: I imagine that it is kinetic theory that accounts for this feeling of "necessity"; unless I'm mistaken, it shows *why* Boyle's Law has to be what it is.

R: That's certainly one way of looking at the matter—some people would be tempted to say (oversimply, of course) that laws explain phenomena, and theories explain laws! The philosopher Carl Hempel has something to say on the point you just made:

Theories are usually introduced when previous study of a class of phenomena has revealed a system of uniformities that can be expressed in the form of empirical laws. Theories then seek to explain those regularities and, generally, to afford a deeper and more accurate understanding of the phenomena in question. To this end, a theory construes those phenomena as manifestations of entities and processes that lie behind or beneath them, as it were. These are assumed to be governed by characteristic theoretical laws, or theoretic principles ... (Hempel, 1966, p. 70).

Q: Well, this gets us back to the issue of the mechanisms that kinetic theory postulates. But before you proceed with this, you never had an opportunity to remind me what Charles' Law was about.

R: That's easily taken care of. Boyle investigated the relation between volume and pressure where the mass and the temperature were held constant; Charles (and Gay-Lussac) found the relationship between volume, pressure and temperature for a fixed mass of gas. The law states that the product of the pressure and volume at time one, divided by the temperature at that time, is equal to (a constant times) the product of the pressure and volume divided by the temperature at time two. Or, in symbols,

$$\frac{P_1 \, V_1}{T_1} = \frac{(k) \, P_2 \, V_2}{T_2}$$

Q: That's a simple and elegant relationship. Now, how does kinetic theory explain why gases are constituted in such a way that Boyle's and Charles' Laws have to hold?

R: Not only does kinetic theory do that, but it also enables us to see that these laws are genuine laws (if I can be so bold as to use this terminology, which might offend some of my philosophical colleagues).

Q: I'm not clear what the point is here; what is the alternative?

R: Well, assuming for the sake of argument that the relationships found by Boyle and Charles are true of the gases they actually investigated, it might be the case that, instead of being laws that hold true (and in a sense must hold true) for all gases, they are "accidental generalizations". (See Lambert and Brittan, 1970, ch. 3.) They might just happen to hold true at the moment for some gases (or even, I suppose of all gases), but at some later date they might not happen to apply.

Q: Let me give some social science examples to see if I understand this distinction. I suppose the relation between IQ and schooling is one case. Second, we might find that, in all economically developed societies, those people in the highest socioeconomic rank tend to support the conservative political party (and the tendency is a strong one); the issue you raise is whether or not this is a law, and must necessarily (in some sense of this term) be true, or whether it is just a sociotemporal "accident" and that, given certain social developments, we could easily find this not to be the case in some societies in the near future. A third example might be the finding that in all countries, more males than females are enrolled in engineering courses—it would seem to me this is likely just to be an artifact of history, and might well change.

R: That's right. It would be my guess that the middle example is more likely to be a "genuine" law rather than the other two, although probably none of them warrants this label. They are most likely to be "accidental generalizations". I caution you that the point is not simply one about terminology; we use laws to make predictions, to engage in engineering (and in the social sciences, social engineering is more or less the formation and execution of policies) and so on, and we run into greater danger if what we thought were laws turn out only to be "accidentally" true. In other words, we use laws because we are guaranteed (more or less) that they will hold in the future and we can rely upon them, whereas generalizations that just happen to be true today, may very well happen not to be true tomorrow, so any plans we had that relied upon them would be headed for disaster. In short, "accidental generalizations" provide no basis for prediction, whereas laws do.

But let us get back to kinetic theory, and look at how it accounts for the two laws in terms of what Hempel called the "underlying processes". (Actually, to shorten my discussion, I shall just deal with one, namely Boyle's Law.) It is evident that what scientists were after was a theoretical story, that could be stated precisely, and which would have as a consequence the fact that these empirical laws would hold true. The breakthrough came in the form of "the dynamical theory of matter", which one old textbook outlines as follows:

> According to modern ideas, the particles of matter in all states of aggregation are in a violent state of agitation. In gases the molecules move rapidly in all directions. They are, however, so small that they spend most of their time at distances from their nearest neighbours which are large in comparison with their own dimensions; and in most of their flight they are almost free from the influence of other molecules. It seems justifiable to assume that the path of a typical molecule consists of a series of straight portions, changing direction at "collisions" with other molecules (Starling and Woodall, 1955, p. 194).

Now, this is the kernel of the theoretical story that needs to be worked out more carefully: From the story that a gas is a large collection of rapidly moving particles, can we show that Boyle's and Charles' Laws must necessarily be the case? The trick here is to conceive of the pressure that a gas exerts as being caused by the collisions of the molecules with the walls of the container. And it is known that the pressure of a gas rises as the temperature increases, which in terms of the theoretical story must mean that more molecules are colliding with the walls—which in turn suggests that temperature is a measure of how fast the molecules are moving.

Having come this far, it is a short step to making a further breakthrough; molecules in motion can be treated as particles obeying Newton's Laws of Motion. It is possible, therefore, to do some simple mathematics, using Newtonian principles. But let me try to give you the flavor using words rather than math wherever possible: The force exerted by one molecule striking a wall is equivalent to the change in momentum as the molecule hits and "bounces" back. If the molecules of the gas under consideration each have mass m, and if the average velocity in the direction of the wall that was struck was u, then (from Newton) the change in momentum is 2mu for one molecule for one strike. But if the type of gas is not changed, and if temperature is held constant, 2mu will be a constant (for the mass of the individual particles and the average velocity will not change). If n is the number of molecules in one unit of volume, the total force on the wall—which will be the pressure on that unit of wall—would be 2nmu if all the molecules were striking the wall in a given unit of time; but in fact only some fixed proportion of these will be striking the wall at any given moment, producing the pressure on that unit of wall (the proportion is a constant because the average velocities of the particles is not changing because the temperature is being held constant). So the total pressure P on the wall of a cube of unit volume (and this pressure is the same throughout the whole container, assuming the molecules are more or less evenly distributed) will be determined by some fixed proportion of 2nmu. But, for a fixed mass of gas at an unchanging temperature, 2nmu (or a fixed proportion of that) will be a constant (for n, m, and u will not change). In other words, $P = fn(2nmu)$, where fn indicates that some proportion or function of the constant 2nmu is involved.

Now, if we take our crude equation—$P = fn(2nmu)$—and multiply both sides by the total volume of the gas, V, we get the new equation $PV = V \times fn(2nmu)$, or $fn(2Vnmu)$. And eureka!—we are nearing the end, for Vn (the total volume of the gas multiplied by the number of molecules per unit volume) is N, the total number of molecules in the whole fixed sample of gas. So, $PV = fn(2Nmu)$. But—given the conditions that were stipulated, namely, that the mass of gas is fixed and the temperature is not changing—it follows that the right-hand side of the equation is still a constant. Thus, $PV = $ constant, which is Boyle's Law.

Q: That's really impressive; I begin to appreciate why some physicists fall in love with theory.

R: Let me make one final point that will get you really enthusiastic! With the use of kinetic theory, scientists were able to make predictions—ones that could not have been made on the basis of the empirical generalizations alone.

Q: This must certainly have increased their confidence that they were on to something.

R: Unfortunately philosophers are not entirely agreed about *why* scientists ought to have their confidence increased by successful predictions, but in fact they *do*! (There are technical issues in the theory of confirmation, and relating to the link between theories and evidence.) But let me give merely one example of the fruitfulness of kinetic theory: If temperature is seen to be a measure of the velocity of the molecules, then as the temperature increases the molecules will speed up. What will happen as the temperature is lowered?

Q: I suppose it follows that the molecules will slow down. Ah—I see the implication of this; it seems to be a consequence that if the temperature is lowered far enough, the molecular motion will cease. Does this mean that there could be no lower temperature?

R: Correct; you would have reached "absolute zero". Subsequent work confirmed that this lowest temperature is just below $-273°C$. And so our theory has produced a startling new insight.

Q: Let me give a verbal gloss, just to make sure that I followed what happened in this now complex case. (I acknowledge that even so you were simplifying the deductive chains involved, so I won't take the details of your derivation very seriously.)

R: That's good, because I did oversimplify; please chase up the derivation in a basic textbook if you are interested! But I'm glad that this crude account gave you something of the flavor.

Q: What happened here was that scientists had found some regularities—empirical laws—which related variables that were empirically measurable (pressure, volume, temperature). Eventually a "theoretical story" was constructed—it was invented by creative people, I should say, and was not mechanically "generated". At any rate, this story was *not* in terms of P, V or T, but in terms of unobservable mechanisms or processes (involving unobservable particles in very rapid motion), which it was hoped would account for the empirical laws. The story had embedded within it some precise rules or "theoretical laws" as Hempel called them, that allowed specific derivations to be made from the theoretical story—in this case, these theoretical rules were Newton's Laws of Motion.

R: That's not a bad account; but I would add a couple of extra points of some significance. The first is that these days philosophers have problems talking about "unobservables"; there is no clear boundary in nature marking off what is observable from what is indirectly observable and from what is unobservable. And of course the theory/observation distinction has been abandoned. (See the discussion of this in Chapter 4.) Second, it should be noted that because the theoretical story was not told in terms of P, V and T, it needed somehow to be linked or connected to the realm of empirically observable regularities—otherwise it would have remained a nice story but with no relevance to the work of Boyle or Charles. After all, their discoveries were about P, V and T, not about invisible particles in motion! Philosophers have given a variety of names to these links—correspondence rules, bridge principles, or the dictionary (see Hempel, 1966, ch. 6; Nagel, 1961; Campbell, 1973); while I'm on terminology, I could mention that there are also a number of expressions for the rules or "laws" inside the theory—internal principles, theoretical laws, the hypothesis of the theory, or the calculus.

Q: Clearly in the case of kinetic theory the links were provided by equating the pressure (which is observable and measurable) with the force of the molecules striking the walls of the container, and by the insight that temperature (also measurable) could be conceived as indicating the velocity of the molecules. But you had another supplementary point?

R: It is important to note the number of assumptions that had to be made by the theorists. It was assumed that the molecules were evenly distributed in space, that they did not lose energy (and slow down) as a result of striking the walls, and that although they "collided" with each other the velocities and energies were not affected (i.e., it was assumed that the particles were perfectly "elastic"). It was even assumed that molecules could be treated as Newtonian particles. (Some, at least, of these are quite reasonable assumptions, but they are assumptions nevertheless.) In fact, so many assumptions are made about the gas that it is probably not like a *real* gas, but is what physicists have called an *ideal* or *perfect* gas, one that real gases only approximate in their behavior.

Q: That reminds me of the social scientist Max Weber's advocacy of what he called "ideal types"; he felt that we could investigate social phenomena by building models that postulated entities which acted in idealized or "perfect" ways—another victory for the influence of kinetic theory (Weber, 1978, ch. 1)? Also, I suppose, the theories of economists are similar, for they assume that consumers are fully rational, and that competition in the marketplace is completely free—the issue here is whether the real economic life of society even comes close to what the "perfect" theory predicts.

R: These examples strike me as close parallels to the situation we have been discussing in physics. But the sociologist Arthur Stinchcombe reminds us that even if some of the assumptions about the underlying mechanisms or entities in the theory are oversimple, or even wrong, the theory might still work well enough to be very useful:

> "Assumption mongering", showing that the theories of the mechanisms are not true, is therefore seldom a useful strategy in scientific theorizing at an aggregate level. Just as statistical mechanics is still useful even if molecules of gases are not little round elastic balls, so assumptions that all people can calculate at a level two standard deviations above the mean may not be far enough wrong *in relevant ways* to undermine assumptions of rationality in economics (Stinchcombe, 1991, p. 384).

Q: That point is well taken; but, on the other hand, it occurs to me that the fact that there are so many assumptions, and so many "boundary conditions" (such as the conditions that the temperature or the mass of gas must not change), that the theory becomes difficult if not impossible to test. And the same is true, I guess, for the empirical laws. It seems that if negative evidence was found, it would always be possible to claim that one of the important conditions or assumptions had been violated, so that the evidence does not constitute a fair test.

R: That line of thought gets us into the heart of much recent philosophy of science. Nancy Cartwright (who now occupies Popper's former chair) wrote a book called *Why the Laws of Physics Lie* (Cartwright, 1983), where she argued that the deeper or theoretical laws of physics have always been defended in the manner you suggest; there is always understood to be a *ceteris paribus* clause ("other things being equal") associated with scientific theories, and a scientist can always claim that other things are *not* equal! And the work of Lakatos and others (see Lakatos, 1972) can be regarded as attempting to find criteria by which we could judge when such defences of science by deflecting refutation have become suspicious. (For a case study in the social sciences, see Phillips, 1987, ch. 14.)

Q: I'd like us to change direction a little and explore some of the implications of this very rich example for my own work as a social scientist, now that you feel I understand it well enough. And I must say at the outset that I now see why Merton and others were so impressed by kinetic theory.

One thing that immediately comes to mind is that attempts to theorize in the social sciences are often highly deficient from the natural science perspective we have been discussing. Some researchers merely generalize the findings from one setting to all similar settings, and call that a theory. I think that Glaser and Strauss foster this in their highly influential book; they constantly talk of "generating" theory from data, and they give the impression that if data are classified and compared properly, the theory will automatically emerge! (Glaser and Strauss, 1967). Another example would be the work of the sociologists Dornbush and Scott (Dornbush and Scott, 1975), who studied the evaluation of workers in two types of organizations, and then produced a theory consisting of a complex set of propositions simply by generalizing these results to cover all similarly structured organizations. An example of one of their "theoretical propositions" is the following: "To the extent that performers believe that effort affects evaluations, they exert more effort to affect evaluations they consider more important" (Ibid., p. 340).

R: I agree with you that this would not count as a theory in the physical sciences. The theory must embody *different* concepts—make use of different mechanisms—other than the ones that were observed. As Hempel argued, the theory should show why those observed regularities can be expected to hold, and to do this the theory cannot just contain "more of the same" but must "look behind" the phenomena to the underlying mechanisms. Of course, I do not want to imply that the work of these social scientists is not important—to find regularities *is* important. I could remind you that we remember Boyle's name, but not many folk know the names of those who devised the final form of kinetic theory!

Q: I agree, but I presume that Dornbush and Scott and other social scientists are anxious to produce theories not only because it is prestigious, but because it also gives the feeling that we really understand the relevant phenomena. But now I start to have doubts about using kinetic theory as the "standard", as it were; for as we discussed at the outset, there are many things that are called "theory" in the social sciences that bear little resemblance to it. Examples would be "dependency theory" in political science and economics (third world countries, on the periphery of the world system, are held to be dependent on the major powers in various ways); and the theories of Marx and Freud. Now I think of it, I'm not even sure that something so clearly a theory as evolutionary theory fits the physical science model!

R: In general terms I concur with the point you are making; but I want to quibble a bit with one of these examples. I don't have much time for Freud, but it could be argued, I think, that his theory of psychoanalysis actually can be illuminated if it is compared with kinetic theory. For then we are able to see what parts of Freud need to be worked upon if the whole thing is to become a solid theory. More operational definitions of key concepts need to be provided; and the bridge principles and internal principles of the theory itself are very vaguely formulated, hindering the making of derivations and predictions. But if you diagrammed Freudian psychology, you might get something that looked like a preliminary stage on the way to the final diagram we had of kinetic theory; some authorities regard Freudianism as a *proto-science* which is on its way to becoming a well-formed science—and recall that we acknowledged that kinetic theory took a long time to emerge.

But your point really goes deeper than whether or not Freud's and these other theories are on their way to possessing the same type of logical and deductive structure as kinetic theory. The issue is whether or not kinetic theory should be a model for *all* theories. In his recent book *Fact and Method* the philosopher Richard Miller writes that "evolutionary theory turns out to be incapable of the successes that are the job of a theory, on the deductivist acount.... Small wonder, then, that deductivists are driven to deny that evolutionary theory is really a theory" (Miller, 1987, p. 137). But Miller suggests that the correct conclusion is to doubt this "deductivist" account of the nature of theory. His view is that a theory should provide a causal account of the relevant phenomena, but that "many actual theories are not sufficiently well-connected with our knowledge of background conditions to be accepted as tools in the *deductive* style" (Ibid., p. 136). In short, Miller is prepared to accept as a theory an explanatory, causal story even though it might not be as precise as we would like; in fact, he says that few if any theories have lived up to the ideal (Ibid., p. 140).

Q: I find his view attractive, and it certainly seems odd to be forced into a position to deny that evolutionary theory is a theory. But we also have to realize that Miller's somewhat liberal position, especially about the deductive structure of theories, runs counter to what—for several decades—was the prevailing view in the social sciences. One of the classic "methodology" books was Blalock's text *Theory Construction*; here the ideal was espoused of achieving a "completely closed deductive theoretical system in which there would be a minimal set of propositions taken as axioms, from which all other propositions could be deduced by purely mathematical or logical reasoning" (Blalock, 1969, p. 2). It is worth noting in passing that Dornbush and Scott set out their "theory" in the form of axioms and deductions, the axioms being generalized empirical findings—in other words, although their axioms did not resemble those of kinetic theory (where the elements of the theory are not ones that can be formed merely by generalizing the empirical findings), they nevertheless were trying to structure their theory in the same general deductive way that Blalock (presumably influenced by the physical sciences) was advocating.

But we need to move on. Are there any other matters on which philosophers disagree?

R: Of course, for disagreement is the spice of philosophical life. One issue about which there is a great deal of debate concerns the precise logical form in which a theory's "internal principles" or "calculus" should be expressible. (This takes the form of a debate about the syntactic versus the semantic conception of theories, which essentially revolves around the respective merits of logic versus set theory; see Thompson, 1989, for an exposition of this dispute in the context of theories in biology.) There is one other area worthy of mention; I'm surprised you didn't mention it yourself as it raises quite fundamental issues about the explanation of human behavior (or action, as I would prefer to call it).

Q: With that clue, I *can* raise it myself! I suppose you are referring to the debate over whether or not it is entirely mistaken to base theoretical explanations of human rational action on a physical science model. The hermeneuticists, of course, are the school that most powerfully attacks the physical science model here. (See the discussion of hermeneutics in Chapter 1.) The argument is that humans act for reasons; people hold beliefs and intentions that we need to know in order to explain why they acted the way they did. It is a mistake to think that laws can be found here; the proper mode of explanation is more like what is found in literature—or in other branches of the humanities—than it is like the deductive explanation of gas behavior using kinetic theory.

R: This is, indeed, the debate I had in mind. It is not only philosophers who are part of the hermeneutics camp who challenge the appropriateness of the physical science model; the Berkeley "analytical" philosopher John Searle has been quite outspoken here. Perhaps the conclusion of one of his recent papers will give you an inkling of his position:

> If social explanation has logical features different from explanation in the natural sciences, then it must be because social phenomena have factual features that are logically different from the facts of the natural sciences. I believe that such is indeed the case and I have tried to identify two sorts of facts involved: first, that the form of causation is essentially intentional causation and, second that social facts have a logical structure different from natural facts (Searle, 1991, p. 344).

Q: This suggests a closely related point to me—a point that ties this present discussion in with what we were saying earlier about the gas laws and kinetic theory. Scientists like Boyle and Charles find empirical regularities in nature, and some of these eventually get labeled as laws of nature. At some stage the mechanism in nature that is "responsible" for producing these regularities is discovered—and so we get a theory. Kinetic theory describes the mechanism of particles of matter in motion that underlies the regularities now known as Boyle's law and Charles' law. Now, turning to human behavior (and especially to voluntary action), there certainly may be regularities, but it is dubious whether these should be formulated as *laws*—for the point is, humans act because of reasons, values, ideals, social customs and norms, and so forth, and these can change over time. Thus, a regularity that might be found by investigating citizens in the USA in the early 1990s might not hold in 2090, nor might it have held in the 1890s. We might still search for the "mechanism" underlying the regularity that has been found, but it is likely to be some psychological or cultural "mechanism" that could change over time. Thus, there are no laws of human action!

R: You have phrased this point in a very telling way! However, I am not sure that you have completely made your case. It seems to me that it is entirely possible that there might be enduring cross-cultural regularities in the way humans act (it may depend on the level of abstraction to which we are prepared to go—i.e., we might have to delve to deep "structural" levels in order to find such things). But it is also conceivable, I must admit, that we will not find such things. But even generalizations that are specific to the way that individuals act in particular cultures in given eras are not entirely useless—these can be very useful in "social engineering" and in our attempts to understand why people act the ways that they do. In other words, I would not want to say that these "narrower" regularities are merely "accidental generalizations" of the sort we discussed earlier. (Furthermore, we have been talking about laws of human action; but there might well be laws applicable at the "social" or "institutional" level—your objection might not be relevant to these.)

Q: Limited generalizations about human action might not be "accidental generalizations", but it doesn't seem appropriate to call them laws, either!

R: I'm not so sure—after all, the category of "law" is made by humans, and it is not a clearly demarcated category. There are many philosophers who regard "law" as merely an honorific term that is applied to generalizations that are regarded as especially useful in a particular field of inquiry. But again I would stress that if we were able to produce a theory to explain why the particular regularity exists, we would be in a better position to decide if it was "lawlike" enough to be useful for making predictions and for giving explanations. And so we come back to the importance of theory again!

Q: Where does all this leave us? Can anything at all count as a theory?

R: I don't think that's the proper lesson to draw from our discussion.

Theories do important work in the social sciences, no less than in the physical sciences, and some of the same ideals apply; but clearly the view that theories in the social sciences should resemble the structure of theories in the natural sciences (and especially in physics) may be too strong an assumption—and how could we defend it? The fact that we may have to settle for a more liberal view of the nature of theories in the social sciences should not drive us to despair. Speaking for myself, I must admit that the "neutral" description of theory given by Miller is very appealing: "A theory is whatever explains empirical facts (often, regularities or patterns) of relatively observational kinds, through the description of less directly observable phenomena" (Miller, 1987, p. 135). But whatever way we jump on this complex issue, we should use the term "theory" with care, and we should take pains to be clear about what we have in mind.

References

Blalock, Hubert M. (1969). *Theory Construction*. Englewood Cliffs, NJ: Prentice-Hall.

Braithwaite, R. B. (1973). The nature of theoretical concepts and the role of models in an advanced science. In Richard Grandy (Ed.), *Theories and Observation in Science*. Englewood Cliffs, NJ: Prentice-Hall.

Campbell, Norman (1973). Definition of a theory. In Richard Grandy (Ed.), *Theories and Observation in Science*. Englewood Cliffs, NJ: Prentice-Hall.

Caplan, Arthur (1990). Seek and ye might find. In C. Wade Savage (Ed.), *Scientific Theories*. Minnesota Studies in the Philosophy of Science, vol. XIV. Minneapolis, MN: University of Minnesota Press.

Cartwright, Nancy (1983). *How the Laws of Physics Lie*. Oxford: Clarendon Press.

Dornbush, Sandford, and Scott, Richard (1975). *Evaluation and the Exercise of Authority*. San Francisco: Jossey-Bass.

Glaser, Barney and Strauss, Anselm (1967). *The Discovery of Grounded Theory*. NY: Aldine.

Hempel, Carl (1966). *Philosophy of Natural Science*. Englewood Cliffs, NJ: Prentice-Hall.

Kerlinger, Fred (1973). *Foundations of Behavioral Research*, 2nd edition. NY: Holt, Rinehart & Winston.

Lakatos, Imre (1972). Falsification and the methodology of scientific research programs. In I. Lakatos and M. Musgrave (Eds.), *Criticism and the Growth of Knowledge*. Cambridge: Cambridge University Press.

Lakatos, Imre (1978). History of science and its rational reconstructions. In I. Lakatos (Ed.), *The Methodology of Scientific Research Programs*. Cambridge: Cambridge University Press.

Lambert, Karel and Brittan, Gordon (1970). *An Introduction to the Philosophy of Science*. Engelwood Cliffs, NJ: Prentice-Hall.

Matthew, J. A. D. (1991). Cartoons in science. *Physics Education*, **26**, 110-113.

Merton, Robert (1967). *On Theoretical Sociology*. NY: Free Press.

Miller, Richard W. (1987). *Fact and Method*. Princeton, NJ: Princeton University Press.

Mills, C. Wright (1959). *The Sociological Imagination*. NY: Oxford University Press.

Nagel, Ernest (1961). *The Structure of Science*. London: Routledge.

Phillips, D. C. (1987). *Philosophy, Science, and Social Inquiry*. Oxford: Pergamon Press.

Searle, John (1991). Intentionalistic explanations in the social sciences. *Philosophy of the Social Sciences*. **21**, 3, 332-344.

Starling, S. G. and Woodall, A. J. (1955). *Physics*. London: Longmans, Green & Co.

Stinchcombe, Arthur (1991). The conditions of fruitfulnesss of theorizing about mechanisms in social science. *Philosophy of the Social Sciences*, **21**, 3, 367-388.

Suppe, Frederick (Ed.) (1974). *The Structure of Scientific Theories*. Urbana, Ill.: University of Illinois Press.

Thompson, Paul (1989). *The Structure of Biological Theories*. Albany, NY: State University of New York Press.

Weber, Max (1978). *Weber Selections*. In W. G. Runciman (Ed.). Cambridge: Cambridge University Press.

10

Values and Social Inquiry

In the late twentieth century there have been a number of fascinating intellectual developments that are directly pertinent to the work of social scientists. The most notorious, perhaps, has been the rise of interest in relativism—a development fostered in part by the work of Thomas S. Kuhn which, from the time of its first appearance, won a status amongst social scientists that it never quite attained in other domains (not that it was inconsequential elsewhere). Another development—fostered by the apparent demise of what has been popularly labeled as "positivism"— has been the rise in the numbers of those who criticize the doctrine of the value neutrality of the sciences and in particular of the social sciences. Not only has it been pointed out that, in fact, many pieces of science are heavily value-laden, but—more radically—the actual *ideal* of neutrality has come under attack. (See the closely related discussion of the attacks on objectivity in Chapter 5.) In effect these attacks on neutrality and objectivity are part of the questioning of the naturalistic ideal for the social sciences (see Chapter 3).

Whether or not there is a direct logical link between the rise of relativism and the demise of positivism on one hand, and on the other the abandonment of value neutrality, there certainly is a link by way of the rhetorical style that is used—many of the adherents of both positions are cavalier with respect to careful argumentation, and leap to grand conclusions from premises that are not well adapted to serve as such major launching places. The purpose of the present discussion is to subject the arguments against value neutrality to critical scrutiny, even if this means prolonging a debate which, according to Richard Rudner long ago, had reached "The Mystical Moment of Dullness" (Rudner, 1953, p. 231).

The discussion, then, will proceed cautiously by way of a number of steps in which various arguments against neutrality are discussed, and necessary distinctions drawn; the excitement will gradually build from this slow and unpromising beginning.

The Issue at Stake

As a first step it is appropriate to clarify—as far as is possible at this early stage—what is at stake here. (For a somewhat different analysis see Miller, 1987.) But unfortunately there is no simple way to delineate the opposing schools of thought, which each set up the issues differently. With a degree of poetic license, therefore, it can be said that the situation is roughly as follows:

(i) There are some folk (these days members of an endangered species) who hold that, following the lead of the natural sciences (or, more accurately, what they *believe* to be the lead of the natural sciences), the social sciences must expunge any trace of values. Those who hold this view regard it as so holy a quest that they do not always see that it is necessary to be precise about what *aspects* of science it is necessary to expunge values from—from the day-to-day work of researchers, from the theories that are produced, from the empirical data gathering that takes place, or from the criteria by which they judge the merit of justificatory or supporting arguments and evidence? At any rate, it is held by those in this camp that the stakes are high—if we allow any chink through which values can enter, then objectivity will escape through the very same crack. As a consequence, the integrity of the social sciences will be undermined, and subjectivity and/or relativism will dominate—a nasty fate indeed.

(ii) Another group argues that of course values do, and should, play a role in the social sciences (and, indeed, in research in the natural sciences as well), but these are not ethical or political values—which *would* be destructive if allowed to influence the internal workings of science. Those who hold this position, then, are committed to the view that there are different *types* of values and value judgments, some of which have a role to play in the sciences, and some of which do not. This position will be discussed in more detail later, where it will become clearer—it is, after all, the position that the present author favors.

(iii) Others, like Michael Scriven, hold that what is puzzling is how scientists could have come to hold a view of the nature of science—the value-neutral view—"which is so patently unsound" (Scriven, 1974, p. 290). Scriven argues that in a variety of ways values inevitably are involved in the sciences; to cite merely one example, the sciences are riddled with the need to evaluate (e.g., the evaluation of data and research designs and hypotheses), and evaluation requires the making of value judgments. But Scriven takes away from the relativists what he seemingly has just conceded to them, for he also insists that value judgments are not subjective, but can be supported and given rational warrant in a number of ways. (See Scriven, 1972, for another exposition of his views.) Richard

Rudner holds a similar position to Scriven, and for similar reasons (scientists must evaluate, and must accept or reject hypotheses); and he stresses that the nature of objectivity needs to be re-thought—in his view the key to objectivity "lies at least in becoming precise about what value judgments are being and might have been made in a given inquiry ..." (Rudner, 1953, p. 236).

(iv) Finally, there are a number of scholars who agree that values must inevitably play an important role in the sciences and especially in the social sciences, but who give a different set of reasons for this belief— their point is that in the social sciences investigators are dealing with people and institutions, about whom it is not humanly possible (or desirable) to remain neutral; and because the social sciences deal with people, issues of power and influence are ever present. The issue is not so much that values are inevitably present, but rather it becomes: *whose* values shall dominate in the social sciences? Feminist scholars, as we shall see, are likely to argue that the values of one class of persons— namely, white males—have been unduly influential. But they are not alone in attacking value neutrality; Islamic scholars are likely to hold that this position is a "pretext" that "reflects either hypocrisy or self-delusion" (Moten, 1990, p. 169):

> To be sure, Western political science is not value-free. Maintaining a demeanor of rigorous value-neutrality, most Western political scientists affirm the sanctity of Western liberal democracy, with its sole concern for profits and profit-maximization. To put it mildly, "they confuse a vaguely stated conventional democraticism with scientific objectivity" (Ibid., p. 170).

The same author states that while Western political science "confuses or conceals normative considerations, Islam states its values explicitly" (Ibid.). Marxist writers often advance rather similar propositions.

The chief focus of the following discussion will be variants of arguments in the third and fourth of these categories—arguments that in diverse ways oppose value neutrality and support the value-laden nature of social science; but some of what will transpire will also be relevant to the first two, which support (again in different ways) the views that at least some form of neutrality is both desirable and attainable.

An Evaluation of the Arguments

(A) There is an argument against the possibility of neutrality, and for the value-ladenness of social science, that runs as follows: Because social scientists themselves are human, and because humans hold values and often act in accordance with them, then social science—being a product of humans—must embody the values of its human architects. This argument seems an obvious *non-sequitur*; the problem lies in the failure to recognize both that not all of an individual's values are displayed in every activity he or she engages in, and that not every artifact produced by a person reflects all the values that the individual holds. The fact of the matter is that the characteristics an individual displays vary according to the social contexts in which that person is located. Thus, a person might display several characteristics (and might act upon certain values) in one setting, but display quite different characteristics (and act upon different values) in other settings. Indeed, it often happens that a particular setting or social activity might force an individual to *suppress* certain of his or her characteristics or values or tastes. (To cite a trivial example, I recently attended a traditional French wedding, and although I have a strong dislike of—in fact, an aversion to—liver, it seemed appropriate to suppress this negative value and consume vast quantities of paté in order not to commit a breach of hospitality or to provoke an international incident.) It is clear, then, that an argument is needed to establish why it is necessarily the case that the values a person holds must be reflected in the social science activities in which he or she engages—for the pursuit of social science might well be an activity which requires that participants suppress some of their native values and instincts.

It is worth emphasizing that those who advance this first argument with respect to values in social science are, in essence, overlooking the crucial fact that social activities are shaped not just by the characteristics of the people who engage in them, but also by the *rules or conventions* that apply to each particular activity (and which have evolved over perhaps long periods of time). And, as indicated above, sometimes the rules of an activity require that the normal propensities of individuals be kept under tight rein. Thus, a person who in day-to-day life is the most cooperative and kindly of souls might also occasionally play tennis for the purpose of exercise, and may, on the courts, suppress these human instincts and take on an entirely different (and uncharacteristic) demeanor—but one that is entirely in keeping with the point of this competitive sporting activity. In other words, when playing tennis you adopt the rules and attitudes and values that are part and parcel of this game. For present purposes, the general point amounts to this: Under *some* conditions, people do have a propensity to make ethical or political or ideological value judgments, but it is not necessarily the case that they display this propensity under *all* conditions—and engaging in science may be one such exception.

Popper has an interesting variant of this general point: Referring implicitly to what is sometimes called the "context of discovery", he says that we cannot expect the scientist to shed all of his or her values "without destroying him as a human being *and as a scientist*" (Popper, 1976, p. 97); but—especially in the "context of justification"—we can have rules and mechanisms (such as the mechanisms related to the free expression of opinions and the delivery of criticism) that *"achieve the elimination of extra-scientific values from scientific activity"* (emphasis added). In other words, according to Popper science is a social endeavor that proceeds according to certain rules or conventions, one of which is the excision of "extra-scientific" values especially at the stage of testing of hypotheses; it is up to "the committee of the whole", as it were, to enforce the rules.

There is much to be said for Popper's view on this matter. Although (as Popper predicted) individual scientists might sometimes have a difficult time following the convention of value freedom, it is clear that it is almost universally prized as an ideal or as a regulative principle for science—for example, it would be difficult to imagine the scientific community commending a scientist for allowing the interests of a manufacturing company to sway her professional judgment on an issue, and it would be impossible to get strong support for the proposition that a scientist who had falsified data had done a commendable thing (witness the horror displayed in the scientific community when it was discovered that the late Sir Cyril Burt had falsified much of his data on the intelligence of twins; see Hearnshaw, 1979). It would seem that Popper is right: it is communal enforcement of the norms of science that forces scientists to monitor that their own values are not intruding where the rules of the game do not permit this to happen (and which ensures they will be called on it—even posthumously—if a breach of the rules is detected).

(B) There is a much more subtle and powerful argument for value-ladenness that at first sight might seem more difficult to counter: It has been claimed that some value orientations are so embedded in our modes of thought as to be unconsciously held by virtually all scientists. This situation has arisen—so it is argued—because all inquiries have to make use of categories and concepts, principles, rules of evidence and so forth; and these things will of necessity reflect the interests of the most powerful groups in society. Over time these particular ways of conceptualizing the world, and inquiry, will become embedded. Thus, as was seen earlier, Islamic scholars or those in the Marxist tradition may hold that the categories of Western capitalism have permeated the social sciences; and feminist critics of science such as Sandra Harding argue that "the most fundamental categories of scientific thought are male biased" (Harding, 1987, p. 290), a consequence of male power and the resultant domination over modes of inquiry for long periods of time—a phenomenon that had not been noticed until recently.

It is important to note that a two-pronged supporting argument is required from those who espouse such a view (who usually overlook this requirement): First, it needs to be established, by some sort of historical data, that males (or Western capitalists) have in fact been dominant in the requisite way—a fairly easy case to make, it would seem; but, second, it needs to be established—this time by a much more difficult argument— that the "male categories" (or "Western capitalist categories") including such things as the principle objectivity and the quest for truth as a regulative ideal, are in fact *biased*. (No evidence is offered to support *this* charge; see Bunge, 1992, section 11.) And the charge of bias is coherent only if we can imagine some *unbiased* principles. In other words, in order to be able to make the charge of bias, the ideal of a value-neutral social science (or of objective truth) has to be accepted. Harding attempts to escape from this difficulty by means of an interesting stratagem—she wants to replace the male-oriented approach to science with a "feminist successor science", not because the latter is value-free, but because women's "different kinds of interaction with nature and social life ... provide women with distinctive and privileged scientific and epistemo- logical standpoints" (Ibid., p. 295). In short, while there is *no* unbiased social science, women's biases are in some sense *better* than those of men.

At this point an example might be useful. Over the past few years, when I have tried out some of the ideas contained in this present chapter in my classes, often they have been given a cool reception. "You have not made sufficient efforts to understand the points that writers like Harding are making", I have been told. My critics have gone on to say that all scientists of the past were biased—for example, Darwin was biased, and so was Broca. Darwin was biased because he used ideas taken from the reigning politico-economic ideology, and applied these to biology; thus, the struggle for existence and the survival of the fittest, which were implicit parts of his theory of evolution, were taken over (as more than one authority has noted) from the *laissez faire* political and economic thought dominant among middle-class males of his times. On the other hand, Broca, the nineteenth-century French medical researcher, had measured the cranial capacity of skulls of men and women of different races; he believed that brain size was related to intelligence, and that because white men were superior in intelligence they would have larger brains than women and males of other ethnic groups (Gould, 1981, ch. 3; see also House, 1990, for a social scientist who makes use of this example). When Broca came across white males whose brain size was too small, he corrected for such factors as body size and age; but he did not make such corrections for data coming from women, or men of other ethnicities. Now, it seems clear that Broca *was* biased, in a straight- forward sense of this term: He allowed his convictions to interfere with his research procedures, so that he was able to obtain the result that supported his predilections. And as a result, his work was *not only* biased, it was *poor science* (as work that allows values to intrude illegiti- mately is prone to be)—a point that will be pursued later in this chapter. But in what sense was Darwin biased? His work—in common with *all* scientific work—was based upon assumptions, but he supported his ideas with massive and detailed data, and his theory was dissected and used to such great effect by subsequent biologists that it has now become widely acclaimed (by scientists of many races and of both genders) as a pivotal part of modern biology. Unlike Broca's work, Darwin's has even survived Stephen Gould's critical scrutiny! Those who persist in labeling Darwin as "biased" have to provide evidence to support such a charge, and have to make clear what they mean by this term here. The fact that Darwin was a male, or that he was a product of Victorian culture and was stimulated by some of the ideas of his times, does not establish that his work was value-laden in such a way that it was *biased*. In short, there is a confusion here between having presuppositions or the making of assumptions on the one hand, and on the other the presence of value-bias. The first often leads to the second, but it does not *have* to, and those who argue that in any particular case the first has led to the second, have an obligation to support this charge with pertinent evidence.

To return to Harding: Whether or not her position (with respect to male bias in the fundamental categories of science) is sound, the fact is that nowadays (as opposed, perhaps, to the situation in the past) Harding is free to express her views, and to have them published and discussed—so that the scientific and broader academic community is forced to grapple with the issues she raises. If she and her colleagues can substantiate the charges they have brought forward, then an important source of value bias will have been exposed, showing that it is not *necessarily* the case that social science has to be value-laden in this way; and there can be debate about the fruitfulness or validity of other perspectives in science. The Popperian mechanism for ensuring the exposure and elimination of illicit extra-scientific values will have triumphed! (It will, of course, only be a limited triumph if Harding is right and all we can do is trade one value bias for another in science; for Popper to fully triumph, value neutrality will have to triumph. But it seems as if Harding has a hard row to hoe to substantiate her claims.)

(C) There is a third argument about the place of values in social science that runs as follows: Whereas physical scientists study inanimate nature, social scientists study humans and social arrangements, and these are things about which it is impossible to remain neutral—a social scientist must surely notice that either the social arrangements or the people (or both) that he or she is studying are just or unjust, moral or immoral, and so forth. And, of course, this may well be the case—but it still does not follow, as those who hold this position assume, that the social science that is produced *necessarily* must embody these kinds of value judgments.

Even the fact that *some* social science which has been produced over the years has embodied such value judgments cannot be taken as establishing that all social science either *must*, or *should*, follow this path. The early work of anthropologists is a good example of this—the nascent profession was in the beginning dominated by missionaries and colonial officials who allowed their own morality to color their (usually derogatory) reports of the exotic cultures in which they found themselves, but this was not taken, in later years when the discipline reached maturity, as a model which ought to be followed.

There is a stronger variant of this third argument: Investigators have to select terminology with which to describe and explain the social phenomena that they are studying. If they are faced with phenomena that affront their own value systems, they will tend to use negatively-laden terms; and of course they would use positive terms for those phenomena about which they have a more favorable attitude. In this way, values enter the social sciences. And, of course, examples abound: homosexuality may be categorized as a form of deviant behavior; studies of family structure may refer to "father absence" but also—more pejoratively—to "maternal deprivation"; the psychological characteristics or abilities of white males may be taken as the norm, in which case women and ethnic minorities may be seen as below standard and requiring remedial treatment (rather than the boot being on the other foot); and people who attempt suicide may be labeled as psychologically unstable. (A host of documented examples may be found in Campbell, 1989.)

This problem is serious, and minority scholars and women are justifiably angry when they come across examples like these. But two points need to be made. First, it is significant that these scholars *do* get angry; they do not merely shrug their shoulders and adopt the attitude that it is acceptable for values to shape social science in these ways. On the contrary, they wish to *remedy* the situation by pointing to the illicit role of values. Once again, this reaction only makes sense on the assumption that values *can* be excised from social science. (In Popper's terminology, and Kant's, value neutrality is a "regulative ideal".) Second, the fact that such bias *does* occur does not establish that it *must necessarily* or *ought to* occur. As Francis Schrag points out, value-laden descriptions can easily be reformulated to avoid the problem; his example concerns two investigators with quite different value systems studying schoolroom discipline—they both see students throwing spitballs in one class, but they label this behavior differently, and in a nearby school they see "well-behaved" students but they also label this behavior with different terms:

> Suppose you deny that throwing spitballs, talking while the teacher is talking, and so on, constitute discourtesy, and I insist the characterization is apt. We still agree, however, that the students in the one school throw spitballs and the like, and in the other school they do not. If we are interested in the causes of the differential student behavior in the two schools we can, therefore, easily reformulate the question in this way: Why do the students in one school throw spitballs, and so on, while those in the other school do not (Schrag, 1989, p. 174).

It should be noted that not everyone is likely to endorse Schrag's simple procedure. David Papineau, for example, believes that replacing a value term by a "neutral" description is not "a workable suggestion" because the *attitudes* that people have will not change—they will merely carry over and infect the new terminology (Papineau, 1978, pp. 163-167). He is right, of course, about attitudes; but as Popper has pointed out, we should not try to strip scientists of their values—the point is that they should not allow these to poison their work. So forcing a change of terminology, and then communally policing the neutral language to ensure that there is no drift, might well be a sensible—and workable— strategy. At the very least the change in terminology is likely to sensitize members of the relevant research community to the dangers of value-laden terminology.

(D) There is a different line of approach to the issue of the influence of values on science that runs like this: There are infinitely many problems that a scientist can decide to pursue, and from this plenitude he or she manages to select a small number upon which to work. So clearly the scientist has some "decision criteria", and these often—if not always— reflect that scientist's judgment about what is valuable or socially important. Such value decisions are reinforced by governmental or other funding agencies, which have clearcut value priorities—projects that are regarded as trivial or socially frivolous or socially dangerous are not regularly funded (and if, by mistake, they do happen to receive a grant, they are likely to be held up for public ridicule as in the famous Proxmire "Golden Fleece Awards" in the USA).

Ernest Nagel put forward an answer to this line of argument that, as it stands, is not quite incisive enough, but which holds the germ of an important distinction:

> In short, there is no difference between any of the sciences with respect to the fact that the interests of the scientist determine what he (sic) selects for investigation. *But this fact, by itself, represents no obstacle to the successful pursuit of objectivity controlled inquiry in any branch of study* (Nagel, 1961, pp. 486-487).

Nagel is distinguishing, implicitly, between two ways in which values can influence a science: internally and externally. Those who argue that social science is value-laden need to take care to specify which of these claims they have in mind—for the evidence that supports one of them will do nothing to support the other. A science may be externally influenced (as the Nagel extract suggests) without succumbing internally. It is also worth noting that Nagel's distinction is similar to the one that was present in an implicit form in the work of Karl Popper—for the latter's reference to "extra-scientific" values implies that in his view there also are "intra-scientific" values.

The following preliminary clarification can be offered: In most, if not all, human activities, there are decisions to be made and priorities to be sorted out. In tennis, should one serve to the forehand or backhand of an opponent? In philosophy, should one accept Bertrand Russell's or John Dewey's views on the nature of truth? In physics, which of several rival views on the nature of quasars should be tentatively accepted? In all these cases, the decisions of members of the appropriate "community of discourse" are guided by criteria and values that are part and parcel of the relevant field or activity—and if, perchance, an individual makes decisions on such matters using different and extraneous criteria, then other members of the field are likely to be very critical, and/or the decision will turn out to have been a poor one as judged by the standards inherent in the field. (David Papineau makes a similar point here: it is "self-defeating" for scientists to accept views for which the relevant evidence either is lacking or is deficient. See Papineau, 1978, pp. 172-173.) To return for sake of illustration to the philosophical example: The choice between the positions of Russell and Dewey should be made by the philosophical community on philosophical grounds—which case has stronger arguments in its favor, which philosopher best answers the points made by his opponent, which view is most compatible with other well-established philosophical positions. In short, the decision should be made using criteria and values that are internal to the discipline of philosophy, in which case the decision will be philosophically defensible. (For sake of reference, these will be called internal or disciplinary values.) If, however, the decision is made in terms of a philosopher's political values (Russell may have political views that are more conducive than those of Dewey), or in terms of the value that is placed on their ethnic origins (Russell had an aristocratic British background and Dewey came from an American middle class family), or in terms of some ethical criterion (one or other of these luminaries may have acted in a manner which meets with disapproval), then external values are coming into play, and the decision reached might not be philosophically defensible.

And so—to return to the more general discussion—the issue under consideration can be recast more accurately as this: To what extent do, and should, external values play a role in social science? Put in these terms, there is a lot to be said in favor of the traditional value free position: the role of external values should be minimized. It should be stressed that there is no issue here about whether internal values should be influential (there is, of course, an issue about what precisely these internal values are)—for it is entirely appropriate, and indeed it is *necessary*, for the values and criteria inherent in a field or discipline to influence the inner workings of that field. Put more strongly, a field without internal values is not a field at all, while a field that is internally influenced by external values has been seduced.

This discussion should serve to throw light on a recent pronouncement by Michael Scriven, which seems to go off track because of failure to take really seriously the external/internal distinction. Scriven criticizes those

> who are essentially arguing for the position that value judgments within science are *improper* or *illegitimate*. Because this formulation is a value claim itself, one that is said to be rationally defensible in terms of the usual scientific standards of evidence and inference, it thereby becomes self-refuting (Scriven, 1991, p. 31n).

But *is* this a value claim, in the normal sense of the term? Consider a simple but direct analogy, where the issues become unmistakeably clear: If I were to say that in tennis it is not allowable to strike one's opponent over the head with a racquet, have I made a value judgment? I think not; what I am doing is to report that, according to the (formal and informal) rules of tennis, i.e., the internal criteria, values and so on), physical abuse of one's opponent is not allowed. And, in reporting what the rules state, I am not taking a stand on whether these rules are good or bad. Furthermore, when I play tennis, and abide by the internal rules of the game by not smiting my opponent over the cranium, I have not made a value judgment either— I simply have been *playing* the game. (For, if I were to flaunt the internal rules of any game or activity, I would thereby be demonstrating that I was not pursuing that activity—to play a particular game *is* to play by the rules!) So, to return to Scriven, he is wrong when he claims that it is self-refuting to report that, according to the (internal) rules of science, it is improper to allow (external) value judgments to play a decisive (internal) role. Indeed, rather than this statement being a value judgment, as Scriven holds, it seems more like a factual report of a real state of affairs—for this *is* one of the internal rules of science.

This is not the whole story, however, for it is clear that external values do play *some* sort of role. Every science is pursued within a social context—and this context might be supportive, directive, or punitive. Thus, the physical sciences are these days pursued within an environment where they are heavily dependent upon governmental financing, and it is a fact of life that some projects (such as those relating to defense or those having direct industrial applications) are greatly favored. In other words, values espoused by agencies of government—extra-scientific values—may have a direct influence upon what problems certain physicists will pursue. And, of course, scientists themselves, being complex people, have complex motivations which lead them to personally favor some kind of problems rather than others—again showing that extra-scientific values may "externally" shape the track that a science follows. But great care has to be taken not to overestimate the significance of this fact. A vital point needs to be insisted upon here: It must be recognized that the sort of evidence that is required to substantiate a claim that in any particular case external values are having an external influence, is quite different from the evidence required to substantiate a claim that such external values are having an internal influence. From the fact that, in a particular case, governmental values are influencing (via funding decisions) the nature of the problems that scientists are pursuing, it *cannot* be concluded that governmental values are influencing the internal criteria and values of that particular branch of science. While external influences upon science are a distasteful but probably an inevitable fact of life, external influences upon the internal workings are very distasteful but certainly not inevitable.

Indeed, it can be stated that a branch of science that is externally influenced by values, may not (and indeed, will often not) be internally affected. For the point is that if extra-scientific values are allowed to influence the internal dynamic, the resulting science will in all probability be *poor* science—for the rules and procedures of the science will have been overridden by these external values (a point that was made earlier). And so, researchers who wish to do *good* work will be eager to expose and expunge such illicit values, and they will have as allies in this endeavor the Popperian mechanisms of criticism and freedom of expression of opposing viewpoints that were mentioned earlier. (For, good science is science that is judged as worthy on *internal* criteria.) Thus, a group of physical scientists whose research program has been externally shaped by government funding priorities, nonetheless will try, while pursuing this program, to adhere to the internal working rules and conventions of science—and if the group doesn't, then other scientists will be quick to expose any scientific flaws. (This is one reason why good research universities, like my own institution, refuse to undertake governmentally-sponsored research that is also secret; for secret research is relatively immune from the scrutiny of the wider scientific community.)

The "Lysenko Affair", as it is commonly known, is a nice example here (Zirkle, 1959; Lecourt, 1977). In the USSR, when Stalin was in power, Western-style genetics fell into disfavor for ideological reasons—it was regarded as a bourgeois field that was incompatible with the principles of Marxism-Leninism. The government externally influenced this area of science, both by funding decisions and by the rather severe mechanism of purging Western-style geneticists! Academician Lysenko became influential, and developed theories of inheritance that also were *internally* influenced by the government-favored ideology (he adopted a form of Lamarckian heredity, which, although long abandoned in mainstream biology, seemed to him to be easily related to the principles of Marxism). When put into practice (for example, in Soviet agricultural policy) his theories led to disaster, and in the end *he* —together with his pseudo-science—was purged, and genetics was reinstated.

(E) The acknowledgment that there are internal values in science, and that these must by necessity play a central role, might seem to concede the whole topic in dispute: Science is not value free, and could never be so, because there are essential internal values; insofar as scientists value truth, objectivity, simplicity, testability, precision, consistency, unbiasedness, mathematical elegance, and so on, their work is not value free.

The philosopher Hilary Putnam endorses the general position that there are such internal values, in his influential discussion "Fact and Value" (Putnam, 1981); and he stresses that these are *genuine ethical values* (or rest upon such values). But he also acknowledges that his view is somewhat out of fashion. He supports the view that "the practices of scientific inquiry upon which we rely to decide what is and what is not a fact, presuppose values" (p. 128). He then goes on to explain why this view is out of fashion:

> The reason this is a somewhat discredited move is that there is an obvious rejoinder to it. The rejoinder to the view that science presupposes values is a protective concession. The defenders of the fact-value dichotomy concede that science does presuppose some values, for example, science presupposes that we want *truth*, but argue that these values are not *ethical* values (p. 128).

But is Putnam correct in claiming that values like these are, indeed, *ethical* values? The point that Putnam's "opponents" make—and to which the present author is sympathetic—can be amplified in the following manner. As stressed earlier, most (if not all) human social activities—ranging from the doing of philosophy, the pursuit of science, the writing of poetry, the playing of tennis, the coaching of a football team, or engaging in competitive ice-skating—are "governed" by rules, norms, conventions, criteria, and theories. If they were not, of course, any untutored person could participate successfully in these activities. The term "governed" is placed in inverted commas to highlight the obvious fact that the governance is to some degree loose; the rules or conventions are sometimes broken by an expert practitioner in that field but when they are contravened it is either done accidentally (as when an ice-skater makes a new move because she has slipped) or more usually for some definite reason—which is only to say that the rule-breaker can justify the new practice by reference to some other rules or criteria or theories within the relevant domain. Thus, a poet like e.e. cummings can decide to flaunt the normal rules of spelling and punctuation, and a football coach can decide to adopt a novel offensive formation—as when the "T" formation was first introduced into American football; but in both cases they are able to justify their new practices in terms of the theories of their field, and the goals of the activities in which they are engaged.

Now, these rules and theories and so on—which clearly are what we have been calling the internal aspects of a field—are what allow the practitioners of that field to make judgments of value within the field. In other words these are the elements that are appealed to in order to justify and to inform the intra-scientific value judgments that are made. "That was a good freestyle exhibition by Torville and Dean", an ice-skating judge may decide, and award the competitors a perfect score; "this is a good poem and it will be published", a journal editor may decide; and "this scientific paper is so flawed that we should reject it outright, and it is so bad the authors ought not be invited to rework it and then re-submit it for publication", a scientific referee may write. All these judgments are value judgments, to be sure, but—contrary to Putnam's view—they are *not* ethical value judgments: They are judgments that are made within domains of activity or discourse, and they are judgments that stand or fall according to how well they can be justified in terms of the technical considerations internal to the relevant fields.

The moral is simple and worth stating clearly: The fact that there are internal or intra-scientific values, does *not* establish that extra-scientific values do, or ought to, play a role in the internal dynamics of science.

The preceding discussion should not be read as arguing that a field's internal theories, criteria, conventions, rules and so forth, are sacrosanct. As mentioned above, they are sometimes flaunted by experts in the field (but for a reason), and it is evident that they gradually evolve or change over time. The rules of tennis, baseball and football have not been static; views of scientific method have undergone change over the ages; even the criteria of good music have not remained static. (I recall coming across a book more than a century old that depicts composers arranged in a pyramid, with the best at the top; Mozart was somewhere down near the base, and at the very pinnacle was—Palestrina! Judgments made today would somewhat demote the latter, and would no doubt slightly promote the former.)

Recent developments in philosophy of science are quite relevant here. The "new historicist" work of Kuhn, Lakatos, Feyerabend and others has led to a change in some of the internal criteria of science (or, a cynic might say, has merely led philosophers to a more adequate understanding of the criteria that scientists have always used but which "ivory tower" philosophers have not appreciated); but at any rate—to cite merely one example—it is no longer the case that the use of *ad hoc* hypotheses to defend a scientific theory against criticism is judged to be an entirely bad thing. In short, an important value judgment has changed. And of course the work of feminist critics of science, such as Sandra Harding, might conceivably result in other important revisions.

There is one loose end to be dealt with here. Why did Putnam hold that the internal values of science *were* genuine ethical values of the kind that have been contentious in the dispute over the presence of values in the social sciences? His reasoning appears to have followed these lines: It is revealing to ask how these internal values are themselves justified. The answer I have given is that they depend upon the corpus of theories, rules, procedures, criteria, and goals of the field. Putnam, however, suggests that this answer does not go deep enough—we have not reached "the bottom line" (Putnam, 1981, p. 130). If we push, he suggests, we eventually come face to face with the issue of why the whole corpus of scientific rules and theories and so forth are valued. At the base we will come across our general criteria of "rational acceptability", and these in turn are part-and-parcel of "our idea of human cognitive flourishing" (Ibid., p. 134). Thus,

> What I am saying is that we must have criteria of rational acceptability to even have an empirical world, that these reveal part of our notion of an optimal speculative intelligence. In short, I am saying that the "real world" depends upon our values (and again, vice versa) (Ibid., pp. 134-135).

Putnam might well have used an example of a system like voodoo (although he doesn't); here the natural realm is populated with entities quite different from those seen from the scientific point of view. And arguably the difference results from the different standards or ideals of rationality that are accepted within the two systems of voodoo and modern science.

This argument is not convincing. Certainly a person might not *pursue* a scientific career if his or her values run counter to those values that are embedded within the practice of science—a charismatic mystic or a voodoo priestess would not, presumably, choose to become an experimental physicist or a cognitive psychologist. And I may choose not to play American football because my personal values make it difficult for me to accept the physical violence that is part of this activity—but this is a point about my personal motivations, and it is not an argument about the foundations of the rules of football. On the other hand, it must be emphasized that the game of football *is* a game, and one can decide to play it (and thereby decide to abide by its internal rules, criteria and values) without being committed to anything more. It is logically possible for the toughest of football tacklers to be a political pacifist. Thus it is simply a *non sequitur* to argue that, because I play football, I am committed to a lifestyle of violence off the field. Similarly, I might be a person with strong religious or metaphysical leanings and yet decide that it would be interesting (or simply a panacea against boredom, much like chess) to view the world according to the principles of the "science game"—to pursue this as far as it could be pursued, without thereby committing myself in advance to accepting or believing all that this game turns up. Clearly, most mortals would find this a hard thing to do—most people who play games end up being converts; but this is a psychological point about people and it is not a logical point. The notion of, as it were, a pragmatic acceptance of the values of science, without implying a commitment to broader views of rationality, is not incoherent; and it shows that the former commitment does not *depend upon* the latter. And, to offer some empirical evidence here, there are many cases of competent scientists who, on the weekends, abandon the values internal to science, and the broader value of rationality that Putnam says must undergird it, and who adopt quite different values and principles of rationality as found in, for example, many religions. This example shows that it is possible to engage in social science without having at a deeper level some sort of overriding value commitment to a particular ideal of rationality.

(F) We are now in a position to consider a final argument for the value-laden nature of the social sciences. This particular argument hinges upon the supposition that the distinction between facts and values is no longer viable. (This distinction is traceable back to the philosopher David Hume in the eighteenth century.) As long ago as 1962, the British philosopher J. L. Austin wrote negatively of the "fact/value fetish" (Austin, cited in Flew, 1964)—although, as Anthony Flew points out, Austin never lived to substantiate this judgment. Flew suggests that it is not clear when and how this distinction was ever decisively refuted, but he reports that:

> The word nevertheless seems to have gone round that the idea that there is a radical difference between *ought* and *is* is old hat, something which though still perhaps cherished by out-group backwoodsmen has long since been seen through and discarded by all with-it mainstream philosophers (Flew, 1964, p. 135).

Writing more recently, Brenda (Cohen) Almond also agrees that the substantial body of literature on this topic has not undermined the distinction between on one side "the world of empirical facts", and on the other "the world of moral judgement" (Cohen/Almond, 1982, pp. 62-63); she sees the arguments as focusing upon a somewhat different issue—the relationship between these two realms, and in particular upon the issue of whether statements of one of these kinds can be *deduced* from statements of the other kind.

The point of all this is as follows: If those who accept that the fact/value distinction does not hold water can substantiate their position, then it would automatically follow (so, at least, the train of thought runs) that values *do* enter the sciences, for facts and values are not clearly demarcated and it is apparent that so-called facts do enter into deliberations in the sciences. And whence go facts, there also go values.

There are two simple replies. First, as Flew and Almond point out, it is far from clear that the distinction does not hold up. The onus is upon the opponents of the distinction to back up their claim with arguments of substance. (For a guide to this literature, as at least it stood some years ago, see Hudson, 1969.) Second, even if the distinction is abandoned—which I do not believe it has to be—the rest of the argument does not follow through. Even if it should turn out that no clear-cut distinction can be drawn between facts and values, it does not follow that anything and everything is admissable into social science. Certain considerations— whether facts or values or whatever—can still be ruled inadmissable on the grounds of irrelevance. After all, because it is a fact that it is a fine day outside, it does not follow that this is a matter that ought to be of influence in a particular piece of social science, say some work on the caste-like nature of ethnic groups within the USA. This meteorological fact can be dismissed from consideration on the ground that it is not relevant to the matter at hand. Similarly, because a scientist holds a particular religious or value position, it does not follow that this must be admitted as relevant to his or her work simply because the fact/value distinction has been abandoned!

Conclusions

We have now reached the exciting *piece de resistance* more-or-less promised at the outset: It is the revelation that in complex topics, such as the present one concerning the role played by values in the social sciences, there *are* no simple and exciting conclusions to be reached! Truth is often more complex, and less exciting, than fiction.

The substantive conclusion that has been reached is many-pronged. (i) Those who are pursuing a science have a commitment to abide by the internal rules, theories, goals, and so on, of their field. This, in essence, is no different from the commitment undertaken by auditors, mathematicians, or football players. As scientists they can depart from these disciplinary principles, but only for reasons that can be publicly justified to their colleagues in a context of open communication. The commitment to the internal rules and principles does not have to be justified in terms of some further allegiance to deeper metaphysical or ethical principles or values; it just may come from these scientists regarding their work as an interesting enterprise with rules and conventions that seem well adjusted to achieve the goals that have evolved for it. (ii) These disciplinary rules, conventions and the like, provide the framework within which the scientists can make intra-scientific value judgments; but the framework also enables them to detect the improper intrusion of extra-scientific values. (iii) Science in which extra-scientific values are internally influential, is generally (if not always) poor science; this means that it can be criticized on some technical internal basis. (iv) Value neutrality of science, in the sense of freedom from internal interference by extra-scientific values, is widely prized; and it is presupposed as a regulative ideal even by those who argue that examples of bias and lack of value neutrality can rather easily be found. (v) The fact that some scientists do succumb, and allow extra-scientific values or biases to intrude into their work, is not an argument either that the ideal of internal freedom from extra-scientific values is flawed or that it is widely challenged (for those who do succumb almost always are embarrassed when they are caught). (vi) The social sciences, like the natural and medical sciences, are influenced externally by values, as when research programs are started or terminated because of governmental funding decisions. (vii) Neither physical scientists, nor social scientists, have to engage in some superhuman (and misguided) effort to lose the values and interests that, as human beings, they necessarily possess. As Popper argues, the objectivity of science does not come from scientists shedding their values, but rather it flows from the freedom of their colleagues to issue a challenge when it is judged that these values are intruding improperly (improperly, that is, according to the internal values and criteria and theories of the particular branch of science).

References

Bunge, Mario (1992). A critical examination of the new sociology of science: Part 2. *Philosophy of the Social Sciences*, **22**, 1, 46-76.

Campbell, Patricia (1989). *The Hidden Discriminator: Sex and Race Bias in Educational Research*. Newton, MA: WEEA Publishing Center.

Cohen, Brenda (1982). Return to the cave. Reprinted in Brenda Almond (Ed.), *Moral Concerns*. Atlantic Highlands, NJ: Humanities Press International, 1987.

Flew, Anthony (1964). On not deriving "ought" from "is". Reprinted in W. D. Hudson (Ed.), *The Is/Ought Question*. London: Macmillan.

Gould, Stephen J (1981). *The Mismeasure of Man*. NY: W. W. Norton.

Harding, Sandra (1987). The instability of the analytical categories of feminist theory. In Sandra Harding and Jean O'Barr (Eds.), *Sex and Scientific Inquiry*. Chicago: University of Chicago Press.

Hearnshaw, L. S. (1979). *Cyril Burt: Psychologist*. Ithaca, NY: Cornell University Press.

House, Ernest (1990). Methodology and justice. In K. Sirotnik (Ed.), *Evaluation and Social Justice* (New Directions in Program Evaluation, 45). San Francisco: Jossey-Bass.

Hudson, W. D. (1969). *The Is/Ought Question*. London: Macmillan.

Lecourt, Dominique (1977). *Proletarian Science? The Case of Lysenko*. London: NLB.

Miller, Richard (1987). *Fact and Method*. Princeton, NJ: Princeton University Press.

Moten, A. Rashid (1990). Islamization of knowledge: methodology of research in political science. *American Journal of Islamic Social Science*, **7**, 106-113.

Nagel, Ernest (1961). *The Structure of Science*. London: Routledge.

Papineau, David (1978). *For Science in the Social Sciences*. London: Macmillan.

Popper, Karl (1976). The logic of the social sciences. In Theodor Adorno *et al.* (Eds.), *The Positivist Dispute in German Sociology*. NY: Harper & Row.

Putnam, Hilary (1981). *Reason, Truth and History*. Cambridge: Cambridge University Press.

Rudner, Richard (1953). The scientist *qua* scientist makes value judgments. Reprinted in E. D. Klemke, Robert Hollinger and A. David Kline (Eds.), *Introductory Readings in the Philosophy of Science*. Buffalo, NY: Prometheus Books, 1980.

Schrag, Francis (1989). Values in educational inquiry. *American Journal of Education*, **97**, 2, 171-183.

Scriven, Michael (1972). Objectivity and subjectivity in educational research. In Lawrence Thomas (Ed.), *Philosophical Redirection of Educational Research*, (Seventy-first Yearbook of the NSSE). Chicago: University of Chicago Press.

Scriven, Michael (1974). The exact role of value judgments in science. In E. D. Klemke, Robert Hollinger and A. David Kline (Eds.), *Introductory Readings in the Philosophy of Science*. Buffalo, NY: Prometheus Books, 1980.

Scriven, Michael (1991). *Evaluation Thesaurus*. Beverly Hills, CA: Sage.
Zirkle, Conway (1959). *Evolution, Marxian Biology, and the Social Scene*. Philadelphia: University of Pennsylvania Press.

Index